Anonymous

Manual of Devotion and Hymns for the House of Refuge, City of New York

Anonymous

Manual of Devotion and Hymns for the House of Refuge, City of New York

ISBN/EAN: 9783337083595

Printed in Europe, USA, Canada, Australia, Japan

Cover: Foto ©Thomas Meinert / pixelio.de

More available books at **www.hansebooks.com**

A MANUAL OF DEVOTION AND HYMNS FOR THE HOUSE OF REFUGE, CITY OF NEW YORK.

New York:
PUBLISHED FOR THE HOUSE OF REFUGE
BY CARLTON & LANAHAN.
1869.

Offices of Devotion for the Chapel of the House of Refuge.

¶ *The Minister shall begin the services by reading one or more of the following sentences of Scripture, all standing.*

THE Lord is in his holy temple; let all the earth keep silence before him. *Hab.* ii. 20.

From the rising of the sun even unto the going down of the same, my name shall be great among the Gentiles: and in every place incense shall be offered unto my name, and a pure offering: for my name shall be great among the heathen, saith the Lord of hosts. *Mal.* i. 11.

Let the words of my mouth, and the meditation of my heart, be alway acceptable in thy sight, O Lord, my strength and my Redeemer. *Psal.* xix. 14, 15.

When the wicked man turneth away from his wickedness that he hath committed, and doeth that which is lawful and right, he shall save his soul alive. *Ezek.* xviii. 27.

I acknowledge my transgressions; and my sin is ever before me. *Psal.* li. 3.

Hide thy face from my sins; and blot out all mine iniquities. *Psal.* li. 9.

The sacrifices of God are a broken spirit; a broken and a contrite heart, O God, thou wilt not despise. *Psal.* li. 17.

Rend your heart and not your garments, and turn unto the Lord your God; for he is gracious and merciful, slow to anger, and of great kindness, and repenteth him of the evil. *Joel* ii. 13.

To the Lord our God belong mercies and forgivenesses, though we have rebelled against him; neither have we obeyed the voice of the Lord our God, to walk in his laws which he set before us. *Dan.* ix. 9, 10.

O Lord, correct me, but with judgment; not in thine anger, lest thou bring me to nothing. Jer. x. 24. *Psal.* vi. 1.

Repent ye; for the kingdom of heaven is at hand. *St. Matt.* iii. 2.

I will arise, and go to my father, and will say unto him, Father, I have sinned against heaven, and before thee, and am no more worthy to be called thy son. *St. Luke* xv. 18, 19.

Enter not into judgment with thy servant, O Lord; for in thy sight shall no man living be justified. *Psal.* cxliii. 2.

If we say that we have no sin, we deceive ourselves, and the truth is not in us; but if we confess our sins, God is faithful and just to forgive us our sins, and to cleanse us from all unrighteousness. 1 *John* i. 8, 9.

¶ *Then the Minister shall say,*

DEARLY beloved, the Scripture moveth us, in sundry places, to acknowledge and confess our manifold sins and wickedness; and that we should not dissemble nor cloak them before the face of Almighty God our heavenly Father; but confess them with an humble, lowly, penitent, and obedient heart; to the end that we may obtain forgiveness of the same, by his infinite goodness and mercy. And although we ought, at all times, humbly to acknowledge our sins before God; yet ought we chiefly so to do, when we assemble and meet together to render thanks for the great benefits that we have received at his hands, to set forth his most worthy praise, to hear his most holy word, and to ask those things which are requisite and necessary, as well for the body as the soul. Wherefore I pray and beseech you, as many as are here present, to accompany me with a pure heart, and humble voice, unto the throne of the heavenly grace, saying—

¶ *A general Confession.*

¶ *To be repeated after the Minister.*

ALMIGHTY and most merciful Father; We have erred and strayed from thy ways like lost sheep. We have followed too much the devices and desires of our own hearts. We have offended against thy holy laws. We have left undone those things which we ought to have done; and we have done those things which we ought not to have done; and there is no health in us. But thou, O Lord, have mercy upon us, miserable offenders. Spare thou those, O God, who confess their faults. Restore thou those who are penitent; according to thy promises declared unto mankind in Christ Jesus our Lord. And grant, O most merciful Father, for his sake, that we may hereafter live a godly, righteous, and sober life, to the glory of thy holy name. Amen.

¶ *Then shall be said the Lord's Prayer.*

¶ *The Children uniting with the Minister.*

OUR Father, who art in Heaven, hallowed be thy Name: thy kingdom come, thy will be done on earth, as it is in Heaven. Give us this day our daily bread. And forgive us our trespasses, as we forgive those who trespass against us. And lead us not into temptation; but deliver us from evil; for thine is the Kingdom, and the power, and the glory, for ever and ever. Amen.

¶ *After which there shall then be sung a Hymn, to be selected and read by the Minister. The children will rise and stand while singing; or one of the following Anthems may be sung instead thereof:*

O COME, let us sing unto the Lord; let us heartily rejoice in the strength of our salvation.

Let us come before his presence with thanksgiving; and show ourselves glad in him with psalms.

For the Lord is a great God; and a great King above all gods.

In his hand are all the corners of the earth; and the strength of the hills is his also.

The sea is his, and he made it; and his hands prepared the dry land.

O come, let us worship, and fall down, and kneel before the Lord our Maker.

For he is the Lord our God; and we are the people of his pasture, and the sheep of his hand.

O worship the Lord in the beauty of holiness; let the whole earth stand in awe of him.

For he cometh, for he cometh to judge the earth; and with righteousness to judge the world, and the people with his truth.

Gloria in excelsis.

GLORY be to God on high, and on earth peace, good will towards men. We praise thee, we bless thee, we worship thee, we glorify thee, we give thanks to thee for thy great glory, O Lord God, heavenly King, God the Father Almighty.

O Lord, the only begotten Son, Jesus Christ; O Lord God, Lamb of God, Son of the Father, that takest away the sins of the world, have mercy upon us. Thou that takest away the sins of the world, have mercy upon us. Thou that takest away the sins of the world, receive our prayer. Thou that sittest at the right hand of God the Father, have mercy upon us.

For thou only art holy; thou only art the Lord; thou only, O Christ, with the Holy Ghost, art most high in the glory of God the Father. Amen.

¶ *A portion of Scripture shall then be read by the Minister, as he may select, children seated; to be followed by the Ten Commandments, all standing.*

Minister.

GOD spake these words, and said; I am the Lord thy God: Thou shalt have no other gods before me.

Children. Lord, have mercy upon us, and incline our hearts to keep this law.

Minister. Thou shalt not make unto thee any graven image, or any likeness of any thing that is in heaven above, or that is in the earth beneath, or that is in the water under the earth: thou shalt not bow down thyself to them, nor serve them: for I the Lord thy God am a jealous God, visiting the iniquities of the fathers upon the children unto the third and fourth generation of them that hate me; and showing mercy unto thousands of them that love me, and keep my commandments.

Children. Lord. have mercy upon us, and incline our hearts to keep this law.

Minister. Thou shalt not take the name of the Lord thy God in vain; for the Lord will not hold him guiltless that taketh his name in vain.

Children. Lord, have mercy upon us, and incline our hearts to keep this law.

Minister. Remember the Sabbath day to keep it holy. Six days shalt thou labour, and do all thy work: but the seventh day is the Sabbath of the Lord thy God: in it thou shalt not do any work, thou, nor thy son, nor thy daughter, thy man-servant, nor thy maid-servant, nor thy cattle, nor thy stranger that is within thy gates: for in six days the Lord made heaven and earth, the sea, and all that in them is, and rested the seventh day wherefore the Lord blessed the Sabbath day, and hallowed it.

Children. Lord, have mercy upon us, and incline our hearts to keep this law.

Minister. Honour thy father and thy mother, that thy days may be long upon the land which the Lord thy God giveth thee.

Children. Lord, have mercy upon us, and incline our hearts to keep this law.

Minister. Thou shalt not kill.

Children. Lord, have mercy upon us, and incline our hearts to keep this law.

Minister. Thou shalt not commit adultery.

Children. Lord, have mercy upon us, and incline our hearts to keep this law.

Minister. Thou shalt not steal.

Children. Lord, have mercy upon us, and incline our hearts to keep this law.

Minister. Thou shalt not bear false witness against thy neighbour.

Children. Lord, have mercy upon us, and incline our hearts to keep this law.

Minister. Thou shalt not covet thy neighbour's house, thou shalt not covet thy neighbour's wife, nor his man-servant, nor his maid-servant, nor his ox, nor his ass, nor any thing that is thy neighbour's.

Children. Lord, have mercy upon us, and write all these thy laws in our hearts, we beseech thee.

¶ *Then the Minister may say,*

Hear also what our Lord Jesus Christ saith.

THOU shalt love the Lord thy God with all thy heart, and with all thy soul, and with all thy mind. This is the first and great commandment.

And the secona is like unto it; thou shalt love thy neighbour as thyself. On these two commandments hang all the law and the prophets.

¶ *Then shall be sung one of the following Chants, all standing:*

WE praise thee, O God; we acknowledge thee t be the Lord.

All the earth doth worship thee, the Father ev erlasting.

To thee all Angels cry aloud; the Heavens and all the Powers therein.

To thee, Cherubim and Seraphim continually do cry,

Holy, Holy, Holy, Lord God of Sabaoth;

Heaven and Earth are full of the Majesty of thy glory.

The glorious company of the Apostles praise thee.

The goodly fellowship of the Prophets praise thee.

The noble army of Martyrs praise thee.

The holy Church, throughout all the world, doth acknowledge thee;

The Father, of an infinite Majesty;

Thine adorable, true, and only Son;

Also the Holy Ghost, the Comforter.

Thou art the King of Glory, O Christ.

Thou art the everlasting Son of the Father.

When thou tookest upon thee to deliver man, thou didst humble thyself to be born of a virgin.

When thou hadst overcome the sharpness of death, thou didst open the kingdom of heaven to all believers.

Thou sittest at the right hand of God, in the glory of the father.

We believe that thou shalt come to be our Judge.

We therefore pray thee, help thy servants, whom thou hast redeemed with thy precious blood.

Make them to be numbered with thy saints, in glory everlasting.

O Lord, save thy people, and bless thine heritage.

Govern them, and lift them up for ever.

Day by day we magnify thee;

And we worship thy name ever, world without end.

Vouchsafe, O Lord, to keep us this day without sin.

O Lord, have mercy upon us, have mercy upon us.

O Lord, let thy mercy be upon us, as our trust is in thee.

O Lord, in thee have I trusted; let me never be confounded.

O ALL ye Works of the Lord, bless ye the Lord; praise him, and magnify him for ever.

O ye Angels of the Lord, bless ye the Lord; praise him, and magnify him for ever.

O ye Heavens, bless ye the Lord; praise him, and magnify him for ever.

O ye Waters that be above the firmament, bless ye the Lord: praise him, and magnify him for ever.

O all ye Powers of the Lord, bless ye the Lord; praise him, and magnify him for ever.

O ye Sun and Moon, bless ye the Lord; praise him, and magnify him for ever.

O ye Stars of Heaven, bless ye the Lord; praise him, and magnify him for ever.

O ye Showers and Dew, bless ye the Lord; praise him, and magnify him for ever.

O ye Winds of God, bless ye the Lord; praise him, and magnify him for ever.

O ye Fire and Heat, bless ye the Lord; praise him, and magnify him for ever.

O ye Winter and Summer, bless ye the Lord; praise him, and magnify him for ever.

O ye Dews and Frosts, bless ye the Lord; praise him, and magnify him for ever.

O ye Frost and Cold, bless ye the Lord; praise him, and magnify him for ever.

O ye Ice, and Snow, bless ye the Lord: praise him, and magnify him for ever.

O ye Nights and Days, bless ye the Lord; praise him, and magnify him for ever.

O ye Light and Darkness, bless ye the Lord; praise him, and magnify him for ever.

O ye Lightnings and Clouds, bless ye the Lord; praise him, and magnify him for ever.

O let the Earth bless the Lord; yea, let it praise him, and magnify him for ever.

O ye Mountains and Hills, bless ye the Lord; praise him, and magnify him for ever.

O all ye green Things upon the earth, bless ye the Lord; praise him, and magnify him for ever.

O ye Wells, bless ye the Lord; praise him, and magnify him for ever.

O ye Seas and Floods, bless ye the Lord; praise him, and magnify him for ever.

O ye Whales, and all that move in the waters, bless ye the Lord; praise him, and magnify him for ever.

O all ye Fowls of the Air, bless ye the Lord; praise him, and magnify him for ever.

O all ye Beasts and Cattle, bless ye the Lord; praise him, and magnify him for ever.

O ye Children of Men, bless ye the Lord; praise him, and magnify him for ever.

O let Israel bless the Lord; praise him, and magnify him for ever.

O ye Priests of the Lord, bless ye the Lord; praise him, and magnify him for ever.

O ye Servants of the Lord, bless ye the Lord; praise him and magnify him for ever

O ye Spirits and Souls of the Righteous, bless ye the Lord; praise him, and magnify him for ever.

O ye holy and humble Men of heart, bless ye the Lord; praise him, and magnify him for ever.

O BE joyful in the Lord, all ye lands; serve the Lord with gladness, and come before his presence with a song.

Be ye sure that the Lord he is God; it is he that hath made us, and not we ourselves; we are his people, and the sheep of his pasture.

O go your way into his gates with thanksgiving, and into his courts with praise; be thankful unto him, and speak good of his name.

For the Lord is gracious, his mercy is everlasting; and his truth endureth from generation to generation.

BLESSED be the Lord God of Israel; for he hath visited and redeemed his people;

And hath raised up a mighty salvation for us, in the house of his servant David;

As he spake by the mouth of his holy Prophets, which have been since the world began;

That we should be saved from our enemies, and from the hand of all that hate us.

¶ *Or this.*

O SING unto the Lord a new song: for he hath done marvellous things.

With his own right hand, and with his holy arm, hath he gotten himself the victory.

The Lord declared his salvation; his righteousness hath he openly showed in the sight of the heathen.

He hath remembered his mercy and truth toward

the house of Israel; and all the ends of the world have seen the salvation of our God.

Show yourselves joyful unto the Lord, all ye ands; sing, rejoice, and give thanks.

Praise the Lord upon the harp; sing to the harp with a psalm of thanksgiving.

With trumpets also and shawms, O show yourselves joyful before the Lord, the King.

Let the sea make a noise, and all that therein is the round world, and they that dwell therein.

Let the floods clap their hands, and let the hills be joyful together before the Lord; for he cometh to judge the earth.

With righteousness shall he judge the world, and the people with equity.

¶ *Or this.*

IT is a good thing to give thanks unto the Lord, and to sing praises unto thy name, O Most Highest;

To tell of thy loving kindness early in the morning, and of thy truth in the night season;

Upon an instrument of ten strings, and upon the lute; upon a loud instrument, and upon the harp.

For thou, Lord, hast made me glad through thy works; and I will rejoice in giving praise for the operations of thy hands.

¶ *Or this.*

GOD be merciful unto us, and bless us, and show us the light of his countenance, and be merciful unto us;

That thy way may be known upon earth, thy saving health among all nations.

Let the people praise thee, O God; yea, let all the people praise thee.

O let the nations rejoice and be glad; for thou

shalt judge the folk righteously, and govern the nations upon earth.

Let the people praise thee, O God; yea, let all the people praise thee.

Then shall the earth bring forth her increase; and God, even our own God, shall give us his blessing.

God shall bless us; and all the ends of the world shall fear him.

¶ *Or this.*

PRAISE the Lord, O my soul; and all that is within me, praise his holy name.

Praise the Lord, O my soul, and forget not all his benefits;

Who forgiveth all thy sin, and healeth all thine infirmities;

Who saveth thy life from destruction, and crowneth thee with mercy and loving kindness.

O praise the Lord, ye Angels of his, ye that excel in strength; ye that fulfil his commandment, and hearken unto the voice of his word.

O praise the Lord, all ye his hosts; ye servants of his that do his pleasure.

O speak good of the Lord, all ye works of his, in all places of his dominion: Praise thou the Lord, O my soul.

¶ *The Minister shall then read, alternately, with the Children, one of the following Selections of Psalms—the Congregation seated.*

SELECTIONS OF PSALMS,

To be read by the Minister, and Children.

SELECTION I.

From Psalm 19.

THE heavens declare the glory of God; and the firmament showeth his handywork.

Day unto day uttereth speech, and night unto night sheweth knowledge.

There is no speech nor language, where their voice is not heard.

Their line is gone out through all the earth, and their words to the end of the world. In them hath he set a tabernacle for the sun,

Which is as a bridegroom coming out of his chamber, and rejoiceth as a strong man to run a race.

His going forth is from the end of the heaven, and his circuit unto the ends of it: and there is nothing hid from the heat thereof.

The law of the Lord is perfect, converting the soul: the testimony of the Lord is sure, making wise the simple.

The statutes of the Lord are right, rejoicing the heart: the commandment of the Lord is pure, enlightening the eyes.

The fear of the Lord is clean, enduring for ever: the judgments of the Lord are true and righteous altogether.

More to be desired are they than gold, yea, than much fine gold: sweeter also than honey and the honeycomb.

Moreover by them is thy servant warned: and in keeping of them there is great reward.

Who can understand his errors? cleanse thou me from secret faults.

Keep back thy servant also from presumptuous sins; let them not have dominion over me: then shall I be upright, and I shall be innocent from the great transgression.

Let the words of my mouth, and the meditation of my heart, be acceptable in thy sight, O Lord, my strength, and my redeemer.

Psalm 24.

THE earth is the Lord's, and the fulness thereof; the world, and they that dwell therein.

For he hath founded it upon the seas, and established it upon the floods.

Who shall ascend into the hill of the Lord? or who shall stand in his holy place?

He that hath clean hands, and a pure heart; who hath not lifted up his soul unto vanity, nor sworn deceitfully.

He shall receive the blessing from the Lord, and righteousness from the God of his salvation.

This is the generation of them that seek him, that seek thy face, O Jacob. Selah.

Lift up your heads, O ye gates; and be ye lifted up, ye everlasting doors; and the King of glory shall come in.

Who is this King of glory? The Lord strong and mighty, the Lord mighty in battle.

Lift up your heads, O ye gates; even lift them up, ye everlasting doors; and the King of glory shall come in.

Who is this King of glory? The Lord of hosts, he is the King of glory. Selah.

Psalm 103.

BLESS the Lord, O my soul: and all that is within me, bless his holy name.

Bless the Lord, O my soul, and forget not all his benefits:

Who forgiveth all thine iniquities; who healeth all thy diseases;

Who redeemeth thy life from destruction; who crowneth thee with lovingkindness and tender mercies;

Who satisfieth thy mouth with good things; so that thy youth is renewed like the eagle's.

The Lord executeth righteousness and judgment for all that are oppressed.

He made known his ways unto Moses, his acts unto the children of Israel.

The Lord is merciful and gracious, slow to anger, and plenteous in mercy.

He will not always chide: neither will he keep his anger for ever.

He hath not dealt with us after our sins; nor rewarded us according to our iniquities.

For as the heaven is high above the earth, so great is his mercy toward them that fear him.

As far as the east is from the west, so far hath he removed our transgressions from us.

Like as a father pitieth his children, so the Lord pitieth them that fear him.

For he knoweth our frame; he remembereth that we are dust.

As for man, his days are as grass: as a flower of the field, so he flourisheth.

For the wind passeth over it, and it is gone; and the place thereof shall know it no more.

But the mercy of the Lord is from everlasting to everlasting upon them that fear him, and his righteousness unto children's children;

To such as keep his covenant, and to those that remember his commandments to do them.

The Lord hath prepared his throne in the heavens; and his kingdom ruleth over all.

Bless the Lord, ye his angels, that excel in strength, that do his commandments, hearkening unto the voice of his word.

Bless ye the Lord, all ye his hosts; ye ministers of his, that do his pleasure.

Bless the Lord, all his works in all places of his dominion: bless the Lord, O my soul.

SELECTION II.

From Psalm 139

O LORD, thou hast searched me, and known me.

Thou knowest my down-sitting and mine uprising; thou understandest my thought afar off.

Thou compassest my path and my lying down, and art acquainted with all my ways.

For there is not a word in my tongue, but, lo, O Lord, thou knowest it altogether.

Thou hast beset me behind and before, and laid thine hand upon me.

Such knowledge is too wonderful for me; it is high, I cannot attain unto it.

Whither shall I go from thy Spirit? or whither shall I flee from thy presence?

If I ascend up into heaven, thou art there: if I make my bed in hell, behold, thou art there.

If I take the wings of the morning, and dwell in the uttermost parts of the sea;

Even there shall thy hand lead me, and thy right hand shall hold me.

If I say, Surely the darkness shall cover me; even the night shall be light about me.

Yea, the darkness hideth not from thee; but the night shineth as the day: the darkness and the light are both alike to thee.

For thou hast possessed my reins; thou hast covered me in my mother's womb.

I will praise thee; for I am fearfully and wonderfully made: marvellous are thy works; and that my soul knoweth right well.

My substance was not hid from thee, when I was made in secret, and curiously wrought in the lowest parts of the earth.

Thine eyes did see my substance, yet being unperfect; and in thy book all my members were written, which in continuance were fashioned, when as yet there was none of them.

How precious also are thy thoughts unto me, O God! how great is the sum of them!

If I should count them, they are more in number than the sand: when I am awake, I am still with thee.

Search me, O God, and know my heart: try me, and know my thoughts:

And see if there be any wicked way in me, and lead me in the way everlasting.

Psalm 145.

I WILL extol thee, my God, O King; and I will bless thy name for ever and ever.

Every day will I bless thee; and I will praise thy name for ever and ever.

Great is the Lord, and greatly to be praised: and his greatness is unsearchable.

One generation shall praise thy works to another, and shall declare thy mighty acts.

I will speak of the glorious honour of thy majesty, and of thy wondrous works.

And men shall speak of the might of thy terrible acts: and I will declare thy greatness.

They shall abundantly utter the memory of thy great goodness, and shall sing of thy righteousness.

The Lord is gracious, and full of compassion; slow to anger, and of great mercy.

The Lord is good to all: and his tender mercies are over all his works.

All thy works shall praise thee, O Lord; and thy saints shall bless thee.

They shall speak of the glory of thy kingdom, and talk of thy power;

To make known to the sons of men his mighty acts, and the glorious majesty of his kingdom.

Thy kingdom is an everlasting kingdom, and thy dominion endureth throughout all generations.

The Lord upholdeth all that fall, and raiseth up all those that be bowed down.

The eyes of all wait upon thee; and thou givest them their meat in due season.

Thou openest thine hand, and satisfiest the desire of every living thing.

The Lord is righteous in all his ways, and holy in all his works.

The Lord is nigh unto all them that call upon him, to all that call upon him in truth.

He will fulfil the desire of them that fear him: he also will hear their cry, and will save them.

The Lord preserveth all them that love him: but all the wicked will he destroy.

My mouth shall speak the praise of the Lord: and let all flesh bless his holy name for ever and ever.

SELECTION III.

From Psalm 51.

HAVE mercy upon me, O God, according to thy lovingkindness: according unto the multitude of thy tender mercies blot out my transgressions.

Wash me thoroughly from mine iniquity, and cleanse me from my sin.

For I acknowledge my transgressions: and my sin is ever before me.

Against thee, thee only, have I sinned, and done this evil in thy sight: that thou mightest be justified when thou speakest, and be clear when thou judgest.

Behold, I was shapen in iniquity; and in sin did my mother conceive me.

Behold, thou desirest truth in the inward parts: and in the hidden part thou shalt make me to know wisdom.

Purge me with hyssop, and I shall be clean: wash me, and I shall be whiter than snow.

Make me to hear joy and gladness; that the bones which thou hast broken may rejoice.

Hide thy face from my sins, and blot out all mine iniquities.

Create in me a clean heart, O God; and renew a right spirit within me.

Cast me not away from thy presence; and take not thy Holy Spirit from me.

Restore unto me the joy of thy salvation; and uphold me with thy free Spirit.

Then will I teach transgressors thy ways; and sinners shall be converted unto thee.

Deliver me from blood-guiltiness, O God, thou God of my salvation: and my tongue shall sing aloud of thy righteousness.

O Lord, open thou my lips; and my mouth shall show forth thy praise.

For thou desirest not sacrifice; else would I give it: thou delightest not in burnt offering.

The sacrifices of God are a broken spirit; a broken and a contrite heart, O God, thou wilt not despise.

Psalm 42.

AS the hart panteth after the water brooks, so panteth my soul after thee, O God.

My soul thirsteth for God, for the living God: when shall I come and appear before God?

My tears have been my meat day and night, while they continually say unto me, Where is thy God?

When I remember these things, I pour out my

soul in me: for I had gone with the multitude, I went with them to the house of God, with the voice of joy and praise, with a multitude that kept holyday.

Why art thou cast down, O my soul? and why art thou disquieted in me? hope thou in God; for I shall yet praise him for the help of his countenance.

O my God, my soul is cast down within me: therefore will I remember thee from the land of Jordan, and of the Hermonites, from the hill Mizar.

Deep calleth unto deep at the noise of thy waterspouts: all thy waves and thy billows are gone over me.

Yet the Lord will command his lovingkindness in the daytime, and in the night his song shall be with me, and my prayer unto the God of my life.

I will say unto God my rock, Why hast thou forgotten me? why go I mourning because of the oppression of the enemy?

As with a sword in my bones, mine enemies reproach me; while they say daily unto me, Where is thy God?

Why art thou cast down, O my soul? and why art thou disquieted within me? hope thou in God: for I shall yet praise him, who is the health of my countenance, and my God.

SELECTION IV.

Psalm 37.

FRET not thyself because of evil doers, neither be thou envious against the workers of iniquity.

For they shall soon be cut down like the grass, and wither as the green herb.

Trust in the Lord, and do good: so shalt thou dwell in the land, and verily thou shalt be fed.

Delight thyself also in the Lord; and he shall give thee the desires of thine heart.

Commit thy way unto the Lord; trust also in him; and he shall bring it to pass.

And he shall bring forth thy righteousness as the light, and thy judgment as the noonday.

Rest in the Lord, and wait patiently for him fret not thyself because of him who prospereth in his way, because of the man who bringeth wicked devices to pass.

Cease from anger, and forsake wrath: fret not thyself in any wise to do evil.

For evil doers shall be cut off: but those that wait upon the Lord, they shall inherit the earth.

For yet a little while, and the wicked shall not be: yea, thou shalt diligently consider his place, and it shall not be.

But the meek shall inherit the earth; and shall delight themselves in the abundance of peace.

The wicked plotteth against the just, and gnasheth upon him with his teeth.

The Lord shall laugh at him: for he seeth that his day is coming.

The wicked have drawn out the sword, and have bent their bow, to cast down the poor and needy, and to slay such as be of upright conversation.

Their sword shall enter into their own heart, and their bows shall be broken.

A little that a righteous man hath is better than the riches of many wicked.

For the arms of the wicked shall be broken; but the Lord upholdeth the righteous.

The Lord knoweth the days of the upright: and their inheritance shall be for ever.

They shall not be ashamed in the evil time: and in the days of famine they shall be satisfied.

But the wicked shall perish, and the enemies

of the Lord shall be as the fat of lambs: they shall consume; into smoke shall they consume away.

The wicked borroweth, and payeth not again: but the righteous showeth mercy, and giveth.

For such as be blessed of him shall inherit the earth; and they that be cursed of him shall be cut off.

The steps of a good man are ordered by the Lord: and he delighteth in his way.

Though he fall, he shall not be utterly cast down: for the Lord upholdeth him with his hand.

I have been young, and now am old; yet have I not seen the righteous forsaken, nor his seed begging bread.

He is ever merciful, and lendeth; and his seed is blessed.

Depart from evil, and do good; and dwell for evermore.

For the Lord loveth judgment, and forsaketh not his saints; they are preserved for ever: but the seed of the wicked shall be cut off.

The righteous shall inherit the land, and dwell therein for ever.

The mouth of the righteous speaketh wisdom, and his tongue talketh of judgment.

The law of his God is in his heart; none of his steps shall slide.

The wicked watcheth the righteous, and seeketh to slay him.

The Lord will not leave him in his hand, nor condemn him when he is judged.

Wait on the Lord, and keep his way, and he shall exalt thee to inherit the land: when the wicked are cut off, thou shalt see it.

I have seen the wicked in great power, and spreading himself like a green bay tree.

Yet he passed away, and, lo, he was not: yea, I sought him, but he could not be found.

Mark the perfect man, and behold the upright: for the end of that man is peace.

But the transgressors shall be destroyed together: the end of the wicked shall be cut off.

But the salvation of the righteous is of the Lord: he is their strength in the time of trouble.

And the Lord shall help them, and deliver them: he shall deliver them from the wicked, and save them, because they trust in him.

SELECTION V.

Psalm 1.

BLESSED is the man that walketh not in the counsel of the ungodly, nor standeth in the way of sinners, nor sitteth in the seat of the scornful.

But his delight is in the law of the Lord; and in his law doth he meditate day and night.

And he shall be like a tree planted by the rivers of water, that bringeth forth his fruit in his season; his leaf also shall not wither; and whatsoever he doeth shall prosper.

The ungodly are not so: but are like the chaff which the wind driveth away.

Therefore the ungodly shall not stand in the judgment, nor sinners in the congregation of the righteous.

For the Lord knoweth the way of the righteous: but the way of the ungodly shall perish.

Psalm 15.

LORD, who shall abide in thy tabernacle? who shall dwell in thy holy hill?

He that walketh uprightly, and worketh righteousness, and speaketh the truth in his heart.

He that backbiteth not with his tongue, nor doeth evil to his neighbour, nor taketh up a reproach against his neighbour.

In whose eyes a vile person is contemned; but he honoureth them that fear the Lord. He that sweareth to his own hurt, and changeth not.

He that putteth not his money to usury, nor taketh reward against the innocent. He that doeth these things shall never be moved.

Psalm 91.

HE that dwelleth in the secret place of the Most High shall abide under the shadow of the Almighty.

I will say of the Lord, He is my refuge and my fortress: my God; in him will I trust.

Surely he shall deliver thee from the snare of the fowler, and from the noisome pestilence.

He shall cover thee with his feathers, and under his wings shalt thou trust: his truth shall be thy shield and buckler.

Thou shalt not be afraid for the terror by night; nor for the arrow that flieth by day;

Nor for the pestilence that walketh in darkness; nor for the destruction that wasteth at noonday.

A thousand shall fall at thy side, and ten thousand at thy right hand; but it shall not come nigh thee.

Only with thine eyes shalt thou behold and see the reward of the wicked.

Because thou hast made the Lord, which is my refuge, even the Most High, thy habitation;

There shall no evil befall thee, neither shall any plague come nigh thy dwelling.

For he shall give his angels charge over thee, to keep thee in all thy ways.

They shall bear thee up in their hands, lest thou dash thy foot against a stone.

Thou shalt tread upon the lion and adder: the young lion and the dragon shalt thou trample under feet.

Because he hath set his love upon me, therefore will I deliver him: I will set him on high, because he hath known my name.

He shall call upon me, and I will answer him: I will be with him in trouble; I will deliver him, and honour him.

With long life will I satisfy him, and show him my salvation.

SELECTION VI.

Psalm 32.

BLESSED is he whose trangression is forgiven, whose sin is covered.

Blessed is the man unto whom the Lord imputeth not iniquity, and in whose spirit there is no guile.

I acknowledge my sin unto thee, and mine iniquity have I not hid. I said, I will confess my transgressions unto the Lord; and thou forgavest the iniquity of my sin. Selah.

For this shall every one that is godly pray unto thee in a time when thou mayest be found: surely in the floods of great waters they shall not come nigh unto him.

Thou art my hiding place; thou shalt preserve me from trouble; thou shalt compass me about with songs of deliverance. Selah.

I will instruct thee and teach thee in the way which thou shalt go: I will guide thee with mine eye.

Many sorrows shall be to the wicked: but he

that trusteth in the Lord, mercy shall compass him about.

Be glad in the Lord, and rejoice, ye righteous: and shout for joy, all ye that are upright in heart.

Psalm 130.

OUT of the depths have I cried unto thee, O Lord.

Lord, hear my voice: let thine ears be attentive to the voice of my supplications.

If thou, Lord, shouldest mark iniquities, O Lord, who shall stand?

But there is forgiveness with thee, that thou mayest be feared.

I wait for the Lord, my soul doth wait, and in his word do I hope.

My soul waiteth for the Lord more than they that watch for the morning: I say, more than they that watch for the morning.

Let Israel hope in the Lord: for with the Lord there is mercy, and with him is plenteous redemption.

And he shall redeem Israel from all his iniquities.

Psalm 121.

I WILL lift up mine eyes unto the hills, from whence cometh my help.

My help cometh from the Lord, which made heaven and earth.

He will not suffer thy foot to be moved: he that keepeth thee will not slumber.

Behold, he that keepeth Israel shall neither slumber nor sleep.

The Lord is thy keeper: the Lord is thy shade upon thy right hand.

The sun shall not smite thee by day, nor the moon by night.

The Lord shall preserve thee from all evil: he shall preserve thy soul.

The Lord shall preserve thy going out and thy coming in from this time forth, and even for evermore.

SELECTION VII.

Psalm 23.

THE Lord is my shepherd; I shall not want.

He maketh me to lie down in green pastures: he leadeth me beside the still waters.

He restoreth my soul: he leadeth me in the paths of righteousness for his name's sake.

Yea, though I walk through the valley of the shadow of death, I will fear no evil: for thou art with me; thy rod and thy staff they comfort me.

Thou preparest a table before me in the presence of mine enemies: thou anointest my head with oil; my cup runneth over.

Surely goodness and mercy shall follow me all the days of my life: and I will dwell in the house of the Lord for ever.

Psalm 34.

I WILL bless the Lord at all times: his praise shall continually be in my mouth.

My soul shall make her boast in the Lord: the humble shall hear thereof, and be glad.

O magnify the Lord with me, and let us exalt his name together.

I sought the Lord, and he heard me, and delivered me from all my fears.

They looked unto him, and were lightened: and their faces were not ashamed.

This poor man cried, and the Lord heard him, and saved him out of all his troubles.

The angel of the Lord encampeth round about them that fear him, and delivereth them.

O taste and see that the Lord is good: blessed is the man that trusteth in him.

O fear the Lord, ye his saints: for there is no want to them that fear him.

The young lions do lack, and suffer hunger: but they that seek the Lord shall not want any good thing.

Come, ye children, hearken unto me: I will teach you the fear of the Lord.

What man is he that desireth life, and loveth many days, that he may see good?

Keep thy tongue from evil, and thy lips from speaking guile.

Depart from evil, and do good; seek peace, and pursue it.

The eyes of the Lord are upon the righteous, and his ears are open unto their cry.

The fear of the Lord is against them that do evil, to cut off the remembrance of them from the earth.

The righteous cry, and the Lord heareth, and delivereth them out of all their troubles.

The Lord is nigh unto them that are of a broken heart; and saveth such as be of a contrite spirit.

Many are the afflictions of the righteous: but the Lord delivereth him out of them all.

He keepeth all his bones: not one of them is broken.

Evil shall slay the wicked: and they that hate the righteous shall be desolate.

The Lord redeemeth the soul of his servants: and none of them that trust in him shall be desolate.

Psalm 65.

PRAISE waiteth for thee, O God in Zion: and unto thee shall the vow be performed.

O thou that hearest prayer, unto thee shall all flesh come.

Iniquities prevail against me: as for our transgressions, thou shalt purge them away.

Blessed is the man whom thou choosest, and causest to approach unto thee, that he may dwell in thy courts: we shall be satisfied with the goodness of thy house, even of thy holy temple.

By terrible things in righteousness wilt thou answer us, O God of our salvation; who art the confidence of all the ends of the earth, and of them that are afar off upon the sea:

Which by his strength setteth fast the mountains; being girded with power:

Which stilleth the noise of the seas, the noise of their waves, and the tumult of the people.

They also that dwell in the uttermost parts are afraid at thy tokens: thou makest the outgoings of the morning and evening to rejoice.

Thou visitest the earth, and waterest it: thou greatly enrichest it with the river of God, which is full of water: thou preparest them corn, when thou hast so provided for it.

Thou waterest the ridges thereof abundantly: thou settlest the furrows thereof: thou makest it soft with showers: thou blessest the springing thereof.

Thou crownest the year with thy goodness; and thy paths drop fatness.

They drop upon the pastures of the wilderness: and the little hills rejoice on every side.

The pastures are clothed with flocks; the valleys also are covered over with corn; they shout for joy, they also sing.

SELECTION VIII.

Psalm 84.

HOW amiable are thy tabernacles, O Lord of hosts!

My soul longeth, yea, even fainteth for the courts of the Lord: my heart and my flesh crieth out for the living God.

Yea, the sparrow hath found a house, and the swallow a nest for herself, where she may lay her young, even thine altars, O Lord of hosts, my King, and my God.

Blessed are they that dwell in thy house: they will be still praising thee. Selah.

Blessed is the man whose strength is in thee; in whose heart are the ways of them.

Who passing through the valley of Baca make it a well; the rain also filleth the pools.

They go from strength to strength, every one of them in Zion appeareth before God.

O Lord God of hosts, hear my prayer: give ear, O God of Jacob. Selah.

Behold, O God our shield, and look upon the face of thine anointed.

For a day in thy courts is better than a thousand. I had rather be a doorkeeper in the house of my God, than to dwell in the tents of wickedness.

For the Lord God is a sun and shield: the Lord will give grace and glory: no good thing will he withhold from them that walk uprightly.

O Lord of hosts, blessed is the man that trusteth in thee.

Psalm 85.

LORD, thou hast been favourable unto thy land: thou hast brought back the captivity of Jacob.

Thou hast forgiven the iniquity of thy people; thou hast covered all their sin. Selah.

Thou hast taken away all thy wrath: thou hast turned thyself from the fierceness of thine anger.

Turn us, O God of our salvation, and cause thine anger toward us to cease.

Wilt thou be angry with us for ever? wilt thou draw out thine anger to all generations?

Wilt thou not revive us again: that thy people may rejoice in thee?

Show us thy mercy, O Lord, and grant us thy salvation.

I will hear what God the Lord will speak: for he will speak peace unto his people, and to his saints: but let them not turn again to folly.

Surely his salvation is nigh them that fear him: that glory may dwell in our land.

Mercy and truth are met together; righteousness and peace have kissed each other.

Truth shall spring out of the earth; and righteousness shall look down from heaven.

Yea, the Lord shall give that which is good; and our land shall yield her increase.

Righteousness shall go before him; and shall set us in the way of his steps.

Psalm 93.

THE Lord reigneth, he is clothed with majesty; the Lord is clothed with strength, wherewith he hath girded himself: the world also is established, that it cannot be moved.

Thy throne is established of old: thou art from everlasting.

The floods have lifted up, O Lord, the floods have lifted up their voice; the floods lift up their waves.

The Lord on high is mightier than the noise of many waters, yea, than the mighty waves of the sea.

Thy testimonies are very sure: holiness becometh thine house, O Lord, for ever.

Psalm 97.

THE Lord reigneth; let the earth rejoice; let the multitudes of the isles be glad thereof.

Clouds and darkness are round about him: righteousness and judgment are the habitation of his throne.

A fire goeth before him, and burneth up his enemies round about.

His lightnings enlightened the world: the earth saw, and trembled.

The hills melted like wax at the presence of the Lord, at the presence of the Lord of the whole earth.

The heavens declare his righteousness, and all the people see his glory.

Confounded be all they that serve graven images, that boast themselves of idols: worship him, all ye gods.

Zion heard, and was glad; and the daughters of Judah rejoiced because of thy judgments, O Lord.

For thou, Lord, art high above all the earth: thou art exalted far above all gods.

Ye that love the Lord, hate evil: he preserveth the souls of the saints: he delivereth them out of the hand of the wicked.

Light is sown for the righteous, and gladness for the upright in heart.

Rejoice in the Lord, ye righteous; and give thanks at the remembrance of his holiness.

SELECTION IX.

Psalm 8.

O LORD our Lord, how excellent is thy name in all the earth! who hast set thy glory above the heavens.

Out of the mouth of babes and sucklings hast thou ordained strength because of thine enemies, that thou mightest still the enemy and the avenger.

When I consider thy heavens, the work of thy fingers, the moon and the stars, which thou hast ordained;

What is man, that thou art mindful of him? and the son of man, that thou visitest him?

For thou hast made him a little lower than the angels, and hast crowned him with glory and honour.

Thou madest him to have dominion over the works of thy hands; thou hast put all things under his feet:

All sheep and oxen, yea, and the beasts of the field:

The fowl of the air, and the fish of the sea, and whatsoever passeth through the paths of the seas.

O Lord our Lord, how excellent is thy name in all the earth!

From Psalm 33.

REJOICE in the Lord, O ye righteous: for praise is comely for the upright.

Praise the Lord with harp: sing unto him with the psaltery and an instrument of ten strings.

Sing unto him a new song; play skilfully with a loud noise.

For the word of the Lord is right; and all his works are done in truth.

He loveth righteousness and judgment: the earth is full of the goodness of the Lord.

By the word of the Lord were the heavens made; and all the host of them by the breath of his mouth.

He gathereth the waters of the sea together as a heap: he layeth up the depth in storehouses.

Let all the earth fear the Lord: let all the inhabitants of the world stand in awe of him.

For he spake, and it was done; he commanded, and it stood fast.

Psalm 147.

PRAISE ye the Lord: for it is good to sing praises unto our God; for it is pleasant; and praise is comely.

The Lord doth build up Jerusalem: he gathereth together the outcasts of Israel.

He healeth the broken in heart, and bindeth up their wounds.

He telleth the number of the stars; he calleth them all by their names.

Great is our Lord, and of great power: his understanding is infinite.

The Lord lifted up the meek: he casteth the wicked down to the ground.

Sing unto the Lord with thanksgiving; sing praise upon the harp unto our God:

Who covereth the heaven with clouds, who prepareth rain for the earth, who maketh grass to grow upon the mountains.

He giveth to the beast his food, and to the young ravens which cry.

He delighteth not in the strength of the horse: he taketh not pleasure in the legs of a man.

The Lord taketh pleasure in them that fear him, in those that hope in his mercy.

Praise the Lord, O Jerusalem; praise thy God, O Zion.

For he hath strengthened the bars of thy gates; he hath blessed thy children within thee.

He maketh peace in thy borders, and filleth thee with the finest of the wheat.

He sèndeth forth his commandment upon earth: his word runneth very swiftly.

He giveth snow like wool: he scattereth the hoar frost like ashes.

He casteth forth his ice like morsels: who can stand before his cold?

He sendeth out his word, and melteth them: he causeth his wind to blow, and the waters flow.

He showeth his word unto Jacob, his statutes and his judgments unto Israel.

He hath not dealt so with any nation: and as for his judgments, they have not known them. Praise ye the Lord.

From Psalm 57.

BE thou exalted, O God, above the heavens; let thy glory be above all the earth.

They have prepared a net for my steps; my soul is bowed down: they have digged a pit before me, into the midst whereof they have fallen themselves. Selah.

My heart is fixed, O God, my heart is fixed: I will sing and give praise.

Awake up, my glory; awake, psaltery and harp: I myself will awake early.

I will praise thee, O Lord, among the people: I will sing unto thee among the nations.

For thy mercy is great unto the heavens, and thy truth unto the clouds.

Be thou exalted, O God, above the heavens: let thy glory be above all the earth.

SELECTION X.

From Psalm 96.

O SING unto the Lord a new song: sing unto the Lord, all the earth.

Sing unto the Lord, bless his name; show forth his salvation from day to day.

Declare his glory among the heathen, his wonders among all people.

For the Lord is great, and greatly to be praised: he is to be feared above all gods.

Psalm 148.

PRAISE ye the Lord. Praise ye the Lord from the heavens: praise him in the heights.

Praise ye him, all his angels: praise ye him, all his hosts.

Praise ye him, sun and moon: praise him, all ye stars of light.

Praise him, ye heavens of heavens, and ye waters that be above the heavens.

Let them praise the name of the Lord: for he commanded, and they were created.

He hath also stablished them for ever and ever: he hath made a decree which shall not pass.

Praise the Lord from the earth, ye dragons, and all deeps:

Fire, and hail; snow, and vapour; stormy wind fulfilling his word:

Mountains, and all hills; fruitful trees, and all cedars:

Beasts, and all cattle; creeping things, and flying fowl:

Kings of the earth, and all people; princes, and all judges of the earth:

Both young men, and maidens; old men, and children:

Let them praise the name of the Lord: for his name alone is excellent; his glory is above the earth and heaven.

He also exalteth the horn of his people, the praise of all his saints; even of the children of Israel, a people near unto him. Praise ye the Lord.

From Psalm 149.

PRAISE ye the Lord. Sing unto the Lord a new song, and his praise in the congregation of saints.

Let Israel rejoice in him that made him: let the children of Zion be joyful in their King.

Let them praise his name in the dance: let them sing praises unto him with the timbrel and harp.

For the Lord taketh pleasure in his people: he will beautify the meek with salvation.

Psalm 150.

PRAISE ye the Lord. Praise God in his sanctuary: praise him in the firmament of his power.

Praise him for his mighty acts: praise him according to his excellent greatness.

Praise him with the sound of the trumpet: praise him with the psaltery and harp.

Praise him with the timbrel and dance: praise him with stringed instruments and organs.

Praise him upon the loud cymbals: praise him upon the high sounding cymbals.

Let every thing that hath breath praise the Lord. Praise ye the Lord.

SELECTION XI.

Psalm 116.

I LOVE the Lord, because he hath heard my voice and my supplications.

Because he hath inclined his ear unto me, therefore will I call upon his name as long as I live.

The sorrows of death compassed me, and the pains of hell gat hold upon me: I found trouble and sorrow.

Then called I upon the name of the Lord: O Lord, I beseech thee, deliver my soul.

Gracious is the Lord, and righteous; yea, our God is merciful.

The Lord preserveth the simple: I was brought low, and he helped me.

Return unto thy rest, O my soul: for the Lord hath dealt bountifully with thee.

For thou hast delivered my soul from death, mine eyes from tears, and my feet from falling.

I will walk before the Lord in the land of the living.

I believed, therefore have I spoken: I was greatly afflicted:

I said in my haste, All men are liars.

What shall I render unto the Lord for all his benefits toward me?

I will take the cup of salvation, and call upon the name of the Lord.

I will pay my vows unto the Lord now in the presence of all his people.

Precious in the sight of the Lord is the death of his saints.

O Lord, truly I am thy servant; I am thy servant, and the son of thine handmaid: thou hast loosed my bonds.

I will offer to thee the sacrifice of thanksgiving, and will call upon the name of the Lord.

I will pay my vows unto the Lord now in the presence of his people,

In the courts of the Lord's house, in the midst of thee, O Jerusalem. Praise ye the Lord.

Psalm 122.

I WAS glad when they said unto me, Let us go into the house of the Lord.

Our feet shall stand within thy gates, O Jerusalem.

Jerusalem is builded as a city that is compact together:

Whither the tribes go up, the tribes of the Lord, unto the testimony of Israel, to give thanks unto the name of the Lord.

For there are set thrones of judgment, the thrones of the house of David.

Pray for the peace of Jerusalem: they shall prosper that love thee.

Peace be within thy walls, and prosperity within thy palaces.

For my brethren and companions' sake, I will now say, Peace be within thee.

Because of the house of the Lord our God I will seek thy good.

Psalm 46.

GOD is our refuge and strength, a very present help in trouble.

Therefore will not we fear, though the earth be removed, and though the mountains be carried into the midst of the sea;

Though the waters thereof roar and be troubled, though the mountains shake with the swelling thereof. Selah.

There is a river, the streams whereof shall make glad the city of God, the holy place of the tabernacles of the Most High.

God is in the midst of her; she shall not be moved: God shall help her, and that right early.

The heathen raged, the kingdoms were moved: he uttered his voice, the earth melted.

The Lord of hosts is with us; the God of Jacob is our refuge. Selah.

Come, behold the works of the Lord, what desolations he hath made in the earth.

He maketh wars to cease unto the end of the earth; he breaketh the bow, and cutteth the spear in sunder; he burneth the chariot in the fire.

Be still, and know that I am God: I will be exalted among the heathen, I will be exalted in the earth.

The Lord of hosts is with us; the God of Jacob is our refuge. Selah.

SELECTION XII.

From Psalm 119.

WHEREWITHAL shall a young man cleanse his way? by taking heed thereto according to thy word.

With my whole heart have I sought thee: O let me not wander from thy commandments.

Thy word have I hid in mine heart, that I might not sin against thee.

Blessed art thou, O Lord: teach me thy statutes.

With my lips have I declared all the judgments of thy mouth.

I have rejoiced in the way of thy testimonies, as much as in all riches.

I will meditate in thy precepts, and have respect unto thy ways.

I will delight myself in thy statutes: I will not forget thy word.

Deal bountifully with thy servant, that I may live, and keep thy word.

Open thou mine eyes, that I may behold wondrous things out of thy law.

I am a stranger in the earth: hide not thy commandments from me.

My soul breaketh for the longing that it hath unto thy judgments at all times.

Thou hast rebuked the proud that are cursed, which do err from thy commandments.

Remove from me reproach and contempt; for I have kept thy testimonies.

Princes also did sit and speak against me: but thy servant did meditate in thy statutes.

Thy testimonies also are my delight, and my counsellors.

My soul cleaveth unto the dust: quicken thou me according to thy word.

I have declared my ways, and thou heardest me: teach me thy statutes.

Make me to understand the way of thy precepts: so shall I talk of thy wondrous works.

My soul melteth for heaviness: strengthen thou me according unto thy word.

Remove from me the way of lying; and grant me thy law graciously.

I have chosen the way of truth: thy judgments have I laid before me.

I have stuck unto thy testimonies: O Lord, put me not to shame.

I will run the way of thy commandments, when thou shalt enlarge my heart.

Teach me, O Lord, the way of thy statutes; and I shall keep it unto the end.

Give me understanding, and I shall keep th law; yea, I shall observe it with my whole heart.

Make me to go in the path of thy command ments; for therein do I delight.

Incline mine heart unto thy testimonies, and not to covetousness.

Turn away mine eyes from beholding vanity; and quicken thou me in thy way.

Stablish thy word unto thy servant, who is devoted to thy fear.

Turn away my reproach which I fear; for thy judgments are good.

Behold, I have longed after thy precepts: quicken me in thy righteousness.

Thy word is a lamp unto my feet, and a light unto my path.

I have sworn, and I will perform it, that I will keep thy righteous judgments.

I am afflicted very much: quicken me, O Lord, according unto thy word.

Accept, I beseech thee, the freewill offerings of my mouth, O Lord, and teach me thy judgments.

My soul is continually in my hand: yet do I not forget thy law.

The wicked have laid a snare for me: yet I erred not from thy precepts.

Thy testimonies have I taken as a heritage for ever: for they are the rejoicing of my heart.

I have inclined mine heart to perform thy statutes always, even unto the end.

CHRISTMAS DAY.

From Psalm 45.

MY heart is inditing a good matter: I speak of the things which I have made touching the King: my tongue is the pen of a ready writer.

Thou art fairer than the children of men: grace is poured into thy lips: therefore God hath blessed thee for ever.

Gird thy sword upon thy thigh, O most Mighty, with thy glory and thy majesty.

And in thy majesty ride prosperously, because of truth and meekness and righteousness; and thy right hand shall teach thee terrible things.

Thine arrows are sharp in the heart of the King's enemies; whereby the people fall under thee.

Thy throne, O God, is for ever and ever: the sceptre of thy kingdom is a right sceptre.

Thou lovest righteousness, and hatest wickedness: therefore God, thy God, hath anointed thee with the oil of gladness above thy fellows.

From Psalm 89.

I WILL sing of the mercies of the Lord for ever: with my mouth will I make known thy faithfulness to all generations.

For I have said, Mercy shall be built up for ever: thy faithfulness shalt thou establish in the very heavens.

I have made a covenant with my chosen, I have sworn unto David my servant,

Thy seed will I establish for ever, and build up thy throne to all generations. Selah.

And the heavens shall praise thy wonders, O Lord: thy faithfulness also in the congregation of the saints.

For who in the heaven can be compared unto the Lord? who among the sons of the mighty can be likened unto the Lord?

Blessed is the people that know the joyful sound: they shall walk, O Lord, in the light of thy countenance.

In thy name shall they rejoice all the day: and in thy righteousness shall they be exalted.

For thou art the glory of their strength: and in thy favour our horn shall be exalted.

For the Lord is our defence; and the Holy One of Israel is our King.

I have found David my servant; with my holy oil have I anointed him:

With whom my hand shall be established: mine arm also shall strengthen him.

The enemy shall not exact upon him; nor the son of wickedness afflict him.

And I will beat down his foes before his face, and plague them that hate him.

But my faithfulness and my mercy shall be with him: and in my name shall his horn be exalted.

I will set his hand also in the sea, and his right hand in the rivers.

He shall cry unto me, Thou art my Father, my God, and the Rock of my salvation.

Also I will make him my firstborn, higher than the kings of the earth.

My mercy will I keep for him for evermore, and my covenant shall stand fast with him.

His seed also will I make to endure for ever, and his throne as the days of heaven.

From Psalm 110.

THE Lord said unto my Lord, Sit thou at my right hand, until I make thine enemies thy footstool.

The Lord shall send the rod of thy strength out of Zion: rule thou in the midst of thine enemies.

Thy people shall be willing in the day of thy power, in the beauties of holiness from the womb of the morning: thou hast the dew of thy youth.

The Lord hath sworn, and will not repent, Thou art a priest for ever after the order of Melchizedek.

From Isa. 9, Micah 5, and Isa. 11.

FOR unto us a child is born, unto us a son is given: and the government shall be upon his shoulder: and his name shall be called Wonderful,

Counsellor, The mighty God, The Everlasting Father, The Prince of Peace.

Of the increase of his government and peace there shall be no end, upon the throne of David. and upon his kingdom, to order it, and to establish it with judgment and with justice from henceforth even for ever. The zeal of the Lord of hosts will perform this.

But thou, Beth-lehem Ephratah, though thou be little among the thousands of Judah, yet out of thee shall he come forth unto me that is to be the ruler in Israel; whose goings forth have been from of old, from everlasting.

Therefore will he give them up, until the time that she which travaileth hath brought forth: then the remnant of his brethren shall return unto the children of Israel.

And he shall stand and feed in the strength of the Lord, in the majesty of the name of the Lord his God; and they shall abide: for now shall he be great unto the ends of the earth.

And there shall come forth a rod out of the stem of Jesse, and a branch shall grow out of his roots:

And the Spirit of the Lord shall rest upon him the spirit of wisdom and understanding, the spirit of counsel and might, the spirit of knowledge and of the fear of the Lord;

And shall make him of quick understanding in the fear of the Lord: and he shall not judge after the sight of his eyes, neither reprove after the hearing of his ears:

But with righteousness shall he judge the poor, and reprove with equity for the meek of the earth: and he shall smite the earth with the rod of his mouth, and with the breath of his lips shall he slay the wicked.

And righteousness shall be the girdle of his loins, and faithfulness the girdle of his reins.

The wolf also shall dwell with the lamb, and the leopard shall lie down with the kid; and the calf and the young lion and the fatling together; and a little child shall lead them.

And the cow and the bear shall feed; their young ones shall lie down together: and the lion shall eat straw like the ox.

And the sucking child shall play on the hole of the asp, and the weaned child shall put his hand on the cockatrice' den.

They shall not hurt nor destroy in all my holy mountain: for the earth shall be full of the knowledge of the Lord, as the waters cover the sea.

And in that day there shall be a root of Jesse, which shall stand for an ensign of the people; to it shall the Gentiles seek: and his rest shall be glorious.

¶ *After which, the Minister shall lead in prayer, either extempore, or using the following form; the Congregation standing:*

ALMIGHTY God, our Heavenly Father, the only living and true God, we praise and adore thee as our God, the God of our fathers, who art from everlasting to everlasting, the same yesterday, today, and for ever. We come into thy presence, on this holy Sabbath morning, to worship thee in accordance with thy word, and in humble dependence upon thy mercy and never-failing goodness. Most merciful God, we draw near unto thee, in the name of thy Son Jesus Christ, trusting in thy promise to hear us for his sake, and asking thy favour only through the merit that is in his blood. We humbly confess our sins, which are many and great, and look to thee for pardon through his atonement and intercession. We have sinned against the clearest light, the tenderest love, and the most faithful warnings of God: and now, O Lord, what shall we say? We cannot answer thee for one of a thousand of our iniquities, and can only deplore our entire unworthiness, trusting in thy boundless mercy, granted unto us through thy Son, our Saviour, Jesus Christ Amen.

In his name we present our prayers and supplications Deliver us from all our transgressions; wash us thoroughly from our iniquity, and cleanse us from our sin. Create in us a clean heart, O God, and renew a right spirit within us. Work in us the work of faith with power, disposing us to a godly sorrow for our sins, and shedding abroad in our hearts thy love given unto us by the Holy Ghost. Keep us from all pride, and clothe us with humility, filling us with all charity and brotherly love, that we may keep the unity of the spirit in the bond of peace. May our consciences be always tender, and may we abstain from even the appearance of evil.

Grant that we may increase in all goodness, that we may grow in grace and in the knowledge of our Lord and Saviour Jesus Christ. O Lord, who art the confidence of all the ends of the earth, preserve us from temptation; support us under afflictions; comfort us in sorrows; make us useful in life, and prepare us for death; and when we have done serving thee here below, admit us, we beseech thee, to that state of rest and blessedness which thou hast reserved for thy people in the heavenly world: through Jesus Christ our Lord. Amen.

O Lord our God, we desire to lift up our hearts to thee, in a grateful acknowledgment of all thy mercies and benefits to us. We bless thee for thy preserving care; for our lives, our health, our food and raiment; for our friends, our comforts, and all our temporal enjoyments. Above all, we praise thee. O most merciful Father, for spiritual blessings in heavenly places in Christ Jesus. We thank thee for the promise of a Saviour; that in due time he came to bear our sins upon the tree; that he hath ascended to heaven, and that he ever liveth to make intercession for us.

We thank thee, O Lord God of grace, for the Holy Spirit; for thy Word; for the Gospel ministry and the institution of all thine ordinances; for the Sabbath and all its blessed privileges, and for sanctuary blessings. We thank thee for the knowledge here imparted unto us of the way of salvation and the means of redemption; and for the opportunities granted to us to improve our hearts and minds, to reform our evil habits, to gain useful knowledge, and to fit ourselves to live good and useful lives, through Jesus Christ, to whom, with thee and the Holy Spirit, be all honour and glory, world without end. Amen.

We look unto thee, O thou Most High, for thy favour unto all the children of men. Extend, we beseech thee, thy mercy to a guilty world, and let all the ends of the earth see the salvation of our God. Pour out thy Spirit upon all thy Churches, revive thy work in the midst of the years; cause pure and undefiled religion universally to prevail.

Give, O Lord, we entreat thee, prosperity to the inhabitants of this country in all their lawful pursuits. Let our land yield her increase, and our trees their fruit. Abundantly bless our provision, and satisfy our poor with bread. O Lord, bless the President of the United States and all in authority over us; counsel our counsellors, and teach our senators wisdom. Make our officers peace, and our exactors righteousness: through Jesus Christ our Saviour. Amen.

We humbly pray and beseech thee, O Lord, to look in an especial manner upon this institution, and to favour it with the outpouring of thy gracious Spirit, and the evidences of thine abounding love. Grant thy favour to all its officers, endue them plenteously with thy Spirit, and enable them all to work with zeal and efficiency in their several spheres of duty, supported by thy strength, and led by thine almighty hand. Most gracious God, we beseech thee to extend compassion to the sons and daughters of affliction. Heal the sick, ease the pained, support the distressed, succour the tempted, comfort mourners, restore to their right mind those who are deprived of their reason; be the God of the widow, the Father of the fatherless, and the orphan's stay. Bless all our dear friends and relations from whom we are now separated. Keep them from all evil, danger, and sickness. May thy Spirit go forth and ever be with those of our former associates who have left this institution; and whether placed with their friends or in other homes, and amid other scenes and relations, grant that they may strive to do their duty faithfully, that they shall live honestly, soberly, and righteously in this present world, walking humbly with thee their God, and earnestly seeking for that better kingdom in reserve for thy faithful followers.

And now, O Lord our God, we commit ourselves unto thee; we hope in thy mercies, and we wait for thy salvation. We ask and offer all our requests in the name of our once crucified but now exalted Redeemer, the Lord Jesus Christ: to whom, with the Father and the Spirit of all grace, be ascribed glory, honour, dominion, and praise, for ever and ever. Amen.

¶ *Or this,*

O LORD, our merciful Redeemer, who didst take up little children in thy arms and bless them; look down graciously on us, and bless us also. We confess that we are miserable sinners; we have erred and strayed from thee like lost sheep. But, O Lord, have mercy on us, turn us and so shall we be turned; and wash away all our guilt in the blood of Jesus Christ, our only Mediator and Advocate. Amen.

Father of mercies, who out of the mouths of babes and sucklings hast ordained praise, fill our hearts, we beseech thee, with love, and our lips with thanksgiving. To thy goodness we owe every blessing we enjoy: thou art succouring us by day and by night, and giving us food, and health, and raiment; we bless thee for these thy mercies toward us, but above all, we bless thee for the redeeming love of Christ, for all the means of grace, and for the hope of glory. Accept these our praises through thy beloved Son, to whom, with thee and the Holy Ghost, be all honour and glory, world without end. Amen.

Almighty and everlasting God, forasmuch as without thee we are not able to please thee, grant us the aid of thy heavenly grace in the important duties in which we are now to be engaged. Look graciously and favourably, O merciful Father, upon this institution. Let thy good Spirit assist those that have the charge of it to form in the minds of the children the principles of religion and virtue; to teach them to remember thee, their Creator, in the days of their youth, and to train them up in thy fear and service. May these young persons from the heart believe in thee, the Lord their God; and worship and serve thee their Creator, Redeemer, and Sanctifier. Give them quickness to comprehend, and memory to retain, the instructions which they may here receive. *Make them dutiful and obedient, humble and reverent. Deliver them from sloth, idleness, and evil company; from all danger both of soul or body, and help them daily as they grow in stature, like their Divine Lord, to grow also in wisdom, and in favour with God and man. Grant this, we beseech thee, through Jesus Christ our Mediator and Redeemer. Amen.

O God, the Creator and Preserver of all mankind, we beseech thee for all sorts and conditions of men. Bless the President of the United States and all other magistrates. Let thy blessing descend also upon all ministers of the Gospel, and may thy kingdom be established in the hearts of all people. Look down in mercy on our relations and friends, and teach them to value thy favour above life itself. Finally, we beseech thee to bless us, even us also; help us to improve the hours we spend in this place; make us obedient to our teachers, and affectionate to our companions.

Especially bless us on this holy day; may thy presence be with us in the house of prayer, enabling us to worship thee in a spiritual manner, and preventing us from being forgetful hearers of thy Word.

Open our understandings to understand the Holy Scriptures. Endue our souls with every holy disposition, and preserve us from the corruptions and evils which are in the world; we ask every blessing for the sake of Jesus Christ, our Saviour. Amen.

May the God of peace make us perfect in every good work to do his will, working in us that which is well pleasing in his sight, through Jesus Christ our Lord, to whom be glory for ever and ever. Amen.

¶ *The Minister shall then select a hymn, the children to be seated while it is read, and to stand during the singing.*
Then the sermon; after which a short prayer, the children standing during prayer.
Another hymn to be sung with the Doxology, and the services to conclude with the Benediction.

¶ *Prayer at close.*

ALMIGHTY God, our heavenly Father, we humbly beseech thee to look in mercy upon us. Grant that thy blessing may accompany the instruction which these children have now received, and that it may, by thy grace, be so grafted in their hearts as to bring forth in them the fruit of good living, to the honour and praise of thy name, and the salvation of their own souls. Teach them, almighty God, to believe in thee, and to love thee with all their heart, to worship thee, and to give thee thanks, to honour thy holy name and word, and to serve thee truly all the days of their lives. Pardon our manifold transgressions. Defend us by night and by day. Build us up in thy most holy faith. Preserve us from the wickedness that is in the world, and make us to be thy humble and faithful disciples, through Jesus Christ our Lord. Amen.

O Almighty God, whom truly to know is everlasting life, grant us perfectly to know thy Son Jesus Christ to be the way, the truth, and the life; that following in his steps we may steadfastly walk in the way that leadeth to eternal life, through thy Son Jesus Christ our Lord. Amen.

The Lord bless us, and keep us: the Lord make his face to shine upon us, and be gracious unto us: the Lord lift up his countenance upon us and give us peace both now and evermore. Amen.

Sabbath-School Service.

¶ *The presiding teacher, or officer, shall begin the service by reading these sentences:*

REMEMBER now thy Creator in the days of thy youth. Eccles. xii, 1.

Thou shalt worship the Lord thy God, and him only shalt thou serve. Matt. iv, 10.

For God so loved the world that he gave his only begotten Son, that whosoever believeth in him should not perish, but have everlasting life. John iii, 16.

I will arise and go to my Father, and will say unto him, Father, I have sinned against heaven and before thee, and am no more worthy to be called thy son. Luke xv, 18, 19.

¶ *Then shall the leader say:*

DEARLY beloved children, you have assembled and met together to receive instruction, in order that you may acquire that religious knowledge which will make you wise unto salvation. You ought to come with humble and serious hearts, in the fear of God, and in humble dependence on his grace. Remember that his all-seeing eye is upon you, and that all your thoughts and actions are known to him. It is, therefore, your duty to look up to him for the assistance of his Holy Spirit, that you may worship him with reverence, truly confess your sins to him, and implore his pardon, through our Lord Jesus Christ.

¶ *Then shall be said the Lord's prayer, the children uniting with the teacher.*

OUR Father, who art in heaven, hallowed be thy Name: thy kingdom come, thy will be done on earth, as it is in heaven. Give us this day our daily bread. And forgive us our trespasses, as we forgive those who trespass against us. And lead us not into temptation; but deliver us from evil; for thine is the kingdom, and the power, and the glory, for ever and ever. Amen.

¶ *Then shall the leader give out a hymn, and read a selection from the Scriptures; after which the leader and children shall repeat the following Scriptures and responses:*

Leader. Come, ye children, hearken unto me. I will teach you the fear of the Lord.

Children. The fear of the Lord is the beginning of wisdom.

L. Wherewithal shall a young man cleanse his way?

C. By taking heed thereto according to thy word.

L. Search the Scriptures, for in them ye think ye have eternal life, and they are they which testify of me.

C. Open thou mine eyes, that I may see wondrous things out of thy law.

L. O Lord, thou hast searched me and known me

C. Thou knowest my down-sitting and mine uprising; thou understandest my thoughts afar off.

L. Thou compassest my path, and my lying down, and art acquainted with all my ways.

C. For there is not a word in my tongue, but lo, O Lord, thou knowest it altogether.

L. Blessed is the man that feareth the Lord; that delighteth greatly in his commandments.

C. Blessed are they that keep his testimonies; and seek him with their whole heart.

L. Mark the perfect man, and behold the upright, for the end of that man is peace.

C. As for the transgressors, they shall perish together; and the end of the ungodly is, they shall be rooted out at the last.

L. Blessed are the undefiled in the way, who walk in the law of the Lord.

C. Blessed are they that keep his testimonies, and that seek him with the whole heart.

L. They also do no iniquity: they walk in his ways.

C. Thou hast commanded us to keep thy precepts diligently.

L. O that my ways were directed to keep thy statutes!

C. Then shall I not be ashamed, when I have respect unto all thy commandments.

L. I will praise thee with uprightness of heart, when I shall have learned thy righteous judgments.

C. I will keep thy statutes: O forsake me not utterly.

L. Glory be to the Father, and to the Son, and to the Holy Ghost;

C. As it was in the beginning, is now, and ever shall be, world without end. Amen.

¶ *Then shall the leader offer an extempore prayer, or unite with the children in the following:*

ALMIGHTY God, whose blessed Son humbly sat among the children in the Temple, seeking instruction from the Jewish doctors, mercifully grant that we, taking him as our example, may reverently listen to those whom thou hast appointed to teach us, and may have grace to improve our talents to thy honour and glory, through thy Son Jesus Christ our Lord. Amen.

O GOD, the Fountain of all wisdom and the source of true knowledge, give us grace above all things to know thee, the only true God, and Jesus Christ whom thou hast sent; and in all our learning, grant that we may learn to fear and love thy holy name, Father, Son, and Holy Ghost. Amen.

Leader. Help us, Almighty God, to increase in the knowledge of thee and thy word. Show us the way in which we should walk, and grant that we may never depart from thy holy law.

Children. Keep us, O God, by thy mighty power.

L. Bless to us, O Lord, what good instructions may be given us, and help us carefully to remember and seriously to practice them, that we may continually grow in knowledge, wisdom, and goodness.

C. Teach us, O Lord, to be wise unto salvation.

L. Remember not, Lord, our offences, neither take thou vengeance of our sins; spare us, good Lord, spare thy children whom thou hast redeemed with thy most precious blood.

C. Spare us, good Lord.

L. From unbelief and coldness of heart, from idleness and evil company, from falsehood and deceit, from sinful words, and wicked thoughts and actions,

C. Good Lord, deliver us.

L. Almighty and everlasting God, from whom cometh every good and perfect gift, send down upon us the healthful spirit of thy grace. Bless, we humbly beseech thee, the means which are used to bring up these children in thy fear and service. May they from the heart believe in thee, the Lord their God, and worship and serve thee, God the Father, who hath made them and all the world; God the Son, who hath redeemed them and all mankind; God the Holy Ghost, who sanctifieth them and all the people of God. Grant them the continual aids of thy grace, that they may renounce the devil and all his works, the pomps and vanities of this wicked world, and all the sinful lusts of the flesh, and may keep thy holy will and commandments all the days of their life. Lord of all power and might, who art the author and giver of all good things, graft in their hearts the love of thy name; increase in them true religion; nourish them with all goodness; and of thy great mercy keep them in the same, that so they may in the end obtain everlasting life, through Jesus Christ our Lord. Amen.

¶ *Then a hymn shall be sung. If visitors are present they may be called upon for remarks. The appointed lessons will then be heard, and the exercises be closed by singing the Doxology, or pronouncing the Benediction.*

Manual for Daily Service.

MORNING PRAYER.

LEADER. What shall I render unto the Lord for all his benefits toward me?

Children. I will take the cup of salvation, and call upon the name of the Lord.

Leader. I will offer to thee the sacrifice of thanksgiving, and will call upon the name of the Lord.

Children. I will pay my vows unto the Lord now in the presence of all his people.

Leader. O give thanks unto the Lord: for he is good: because his mercy endureth for ever.

Children. Let them now that fear the Lord say, that his mercy endureth for ever.

Leader. Thou art my God, and I will praise thee: thou art my God, I will exalt thee.

Children. O give thanks unto the Lord, for he is good: for his mercy endureth for ever.

Leader. O Lord, thou hast searched me and known me.

Children. Thou knowest my down-sitting and mine up-rising; thou understandest my thoughts afar off.

Leader. For there is not a word in my tongue, but lo, O Lord, thou knowest it altogether.

Children. Whither shall I go from thy Spirit; or whither shall I flee from thy presence?

Leader. If I ascend up into heaven, thou art there: if I make my bed in hell, behold thou art there.

Children. If I take the wings of the morning, and dwell in the uttermost parts of the sea;

Leader. Even there shall thy hand lead me, and thy right hand shall hold me.

Children. If I say, Surely the darkness shall cover me; even the night shall be light about me.

Leader. Yea, darkness hideth not from thee; but the night shineth as the day: and the darkness and the light are both alike to thee.

Children. How precious also are thy thoughts unto me, O God: how great is the sum of them!

Leader. If I count them, they are more in number than the sand: when I awake, I am still with thee.

Children. Search me, O God, and know my heart; try me and know my thoughts:

Leader. And see if there be any wicked way in me, and lead me in the way everlasting.

Let us Pray.

ALMIGHTY and eternal God, our Creator and Preserver, and never-failing Benefactor! we desire to begin this day with the acknowledgment of thy power and goodness, and of our obligation to love and serve thee; and we beseech thee to grant us grace to pass the whole of it in thy fear, and in obedience to thy commandments. Thou hast appointed to each of us our work in life: O Lord. enable us all diligently to perform every duty falling to our lot. Let us not waste our time in idleness, nor be unfaithful to any trust committed to us, or to any confidence reposed in us. Let us not put on the mere appearance of goodness; nor endeavour in any respect to deceive those around us; but let us remember that thine eye is upon us, and let us have the testimony of our consciences, that in simplicity and godly sincerity we have our conversation in the world. Let truth be ever on our lips; let us be examples of integrity and uprightness. Help us to perform a kind and Christian part toward all with whom we associate, forgiving those that injure us, rendering good for evil, and doing all the service in our power to all that we may in any measure offer aid: through Jesus Christ our Lord. Amen.

Most merciful and gracious God! we thank thee for all thine unnumbered mercies; for thy preserving care during the past night, and throughout our lives. We thank thee for our renewed health and strength, for our food and raiment, and friends, and every earthly blessing. We thank thee for a Christian birth; for all our opportunities to improve our minds, and to prepare ourselves for an honourable and useful life; we thank thee for the Gospel of thy Son; for the Holy Bible, for the influences of thy Spirit, for the privilege of prayer, and for the mediation of our Lord Jesus Christ, who ever liveth to intercede for us at thy right hand: to whom, with thee and the Holy Spirit, be all honour and glory, world without end. Amen.

We confess, O merciful Father, that we are very

unworthy to come into thy presence; for our lives have been unholy, and our sins are many and great. O God, be merciful to us, sinners. Through him who loved us, and gave himself to die for us, grant unto us true repentance. Help us to feel how exceedingly sinful sin is, committed against such love and such light. May we be enabled to trust in him alone for forgiveness, and may we have peace with God through our Lord Jesus Christ. Help us to overcome our easily besetting sins. Cleanse thou the thoughts of our hearts. Help us to grow in grace, and in the knowledge of our Lord Jesus Christ. May we every day become more holy in thy sight; and when it shall please thee to call us from this mortal state, may we resign our souls into thy hands with confidence and hope; and may we finally find mercy and obtain a joyful resurrection to eternal life, through Jesus Christ our Lord. Amen.

We commend to thy Fatherly Goodness all our relatives and friends; the Managers and Officers of this Institution. Bless the President of the United States, and all in authority. Extend thy goodness to our whole land. Pity the sorrows and relieve the necessities of all mankind. We now commit ourselves to thee for this day; help us to live according to these our prayers; and thus may we be prepared for thy heavenly kingdom: we ask it for our Saviour's sake. Amen.

EVENING PRAYER.

LEADER. I will lift up my eyes unto the hills, from whence cometh my help.

Children. My help cometh from the Lord, which made heaven and earth.

Leader. He will not suffer thy foot to be moved; he that keepeth thee will not slumber.

Children. Behold, he that keepeth Israel shall neither slumber nor sleep.

Leader. The Lord is thy keeper: the Lord is thy shade upon thy right hand.

Children. The sun shall not smite thee by day, nor the moon by night.

Leader. The Lord shall preserve thee from all evil: he shall preserve thy soul.

Children. The Lord shall preserve thy going out and thy coming in, from this time forth, and ever for evermore.

Leader. O Lord, deal not with us according to our sins,

Children. Neither reward us according to our iniquities.

Leader. O Lord, let thy mercy be showed upon us,

Children. As we do put our trust in thee.

Let us Pray.

O LORD God Almighty, Father of mercies, from whom we derive the temporal comforts which we enjoy, and to whom we owe the blessed and glorious hope of everlasting life, we desire to render unto thee this our evening sacrifice of prayer and praise. We acknowledge thy goodness to us during the past day; and we beseech thee to continue to us thy gracious protection during the darkness and silence of the coming night. Thou art ever present with us, though we see thee not. Thou art our protection in all danger, our support in trouble, our guide in difficulty, our consolation in sickness, and our only refuge in the hour of death.

We would lament the sins which we have this day committed. Thou seest, O Lord, all our hearts; thou knowest every false way in which we have allowed ourselves to walk. Pardon, we beseech thee, for Jesus Christ's sake, every wrong thought, and word, and act, that thy pure and searching eyes have seen in us. Grant unto us, we pray thee, sincere repentance, and a humble trust for forgiveness, in the merits of thy Son Jesus Christ our Lord and Saviour. Amen.

We desire, our heavenly Father, to thank thee for all the mercies which we have enjoyed to-day; for our health and strength, our food and raiment; for our opportunities for labour and for study; and for all our innocent pleasures. We thank thee for thy kind protection over us; for the friends that thou hast disposed to feel an interest in our behalf; and above all, for the religious privileges with which we are favoured; for thy precious Word; for the means of grace, and for the hope of heaven, through the death and intercession of our Lord Jesus Christ. Amen.

Into thy hands, most merciful Father, we commit the keeping of our bodies and our souls. Defend us from all danger and mischief, and from the fear of them, that we may enjoy such refreshing sleep as may fit us for the duties of the coming day. Make us ever mindful of the time when we shall lie down in the dust; and grant us grace always to live in such a state that we may never be afraid to die: so that, living and dying, we may be thine, through the merits and satisfaction of thy Son, Christ Jesus, in whose name we offer these our imperfect prayers. Amen.

The grace of our Lord Jesus Christ, and the love of God, and the fellowship of the Holy Spirit, be with us all evermore. Amen.

Miscellaneous Occasions.

PRAYER FOR PARDON.

LEADER. I have heard of thee by the hearing of the ear: but now mine eye seeth thee:

Children. Wherefore I abhor myself, and repent in dust and ashes.

Leader. My heart panteth, my strength faileth me; as for the light of mine eyes, it also is gone.

Children. I will declare mine iniquity; I will be sorry for my sin.

Leader. I acknowledge my transgressions; and my sin is ever before me:

Children. Against thee, thee only, have I sinned, and done this evil in thy sight.

Leader. The sacrifices of God are a broken spirit: a broken and a contrite heart, O God, thou wilt not despise.

Children. I will arise and go to my father, and will say unto him, Father, I have sinned against heaven, and before thee, and am no more worthy to be called thy son: make me as one of thy hired servants.

Leader. The publican, standing afar off, would not lift up so much as his eyes unto heaven, but smote upon his breast, saying, God be merciful to me a sinner.

Children. The Lord is nigh unto them that are of a broken heart; and saveth such as be of a contrite spirit.

Leader. Let the wicked forsake his way, and the unrighteous man his thoughts: and let him return unto the Lord, and he will have mercy upon him; and to our God, for he will abundantly pardon.

Children. Blessed is he whose transgression is forgiven, whose sin is covered.

Let us Pray.

ALMIGHTY and most merciful Father! we have erred and strayed from thy ways like lost sheep. We have followed too much the devices and desires of our own hearts. We have offended against thy holy laws. We have left undone those things which we ought to have done; and we have done those things which we ought not to have done: and there is no health in us. But thou, O Lord, have mercy upon us, miserable offenders; spare thou those, O God, who confess their faults. Restore thou those who are penitent; according to thy promises declared unto mankind, in Christ Jesus our Lord. And grant, O most merciful Father, for his sake, that we may hereafter live a godly, righteous, and sober life, to the glory of thy holy name. Amen.

We would humbly confess, most merciful Father, our many and great sins. We have wasted our time; we have forgotten thee; we have broken thy law; we have shown evil tempers—pride, and envy, and anger, and ingratitude. We have spoken idle and wicked words. We have been guilty of disobedient and ungodly conduct. Above all, we have not listened to the voice of our Saviour who died for us; but have turned away from his tender invitations, and hardened our hearts against all his sufferings in our behalf. Make us truly sorry for these our sins. Help us to feel the exceeding sinfulness of them. Work within us sincere repentance, and help us to forsake every evil way, through Jesus Christ our Lord. Amen.

Help us, O merciful Father, to rely in no measure, for our forgiveness, upon ourselves, upon our sorrows, upon our promises of a better life, or even upon our prayers; but solely upon the death for us of our Lord Jesus Christ. May we, poor sinners and utterly unworthy, be assisted to trust in that blood which cleanseth from all unrighteousness, and to believe in him who ever liveth to intercede for us at thy right hand, and who is able to save unto the uttermost all that come unto God through him. O merciful Saviour, save us, according to the riches of thy grace, that, being justified by faith, we may have peace with God through our Lord Jesus Christ. Amen.

We pray thee, O Son of God, say to our hearts, Thy sins be forgiven thee; go in peace and sin no more. Through Christ strengthening us, may we be enabled to live a new life. Bestow upon us a new heart—take away the heart of stone and give us a heart of flesh. Help us to devote ourselves to thy service: may it be more than our meat or drink to do thy will. May we show the fruits of repentance in a humble and godly life; and through thy merits, who art our only Saviour, may we hereafter hear thee say, Come, ye blessed of my Father, inherit the kingdom prepared for you from the foundation of the world. And all the praise of our salvation shall be ascribed to the Father, and to the Son, and to the Holy Ghost. Amen.

FUNERAL SERVICE.

LEADER. Lord, make me to know mine end, and the measure of my days, that I may know how frail I am.

Children. For I know that thou wilt bring me to death, and to the house appointed for all living.

Leader. What is your life? It is even a vapour, that appeareth for a little time, and then vanisheth away.

Children. There is but a step between me and death.

Leader. No man hath power over the spirit to retain the spirit, neither hath he power in the day of death.

Children. There is no discharge in that war; neither shall wickedness deliver those that are given to it.

Leader. They that trust in wealth, and boast themselves in the multitude of their riches; none of them can by any means redeem his brother, nor give to God a ransom for him; that he should still live.

Children. It is appointed unto man once to die, but after this the judgment.

Leader. We must all appear before the judgment seat of Christ, that every man may receive the things done in the body, according to that he hath done, whether it be good or bad.

Children. The hour is coming, in which all that are in the graves shall hear his voice, and shall come forth; they that have done good, unto the resurrection of life, and they that have done evil, unto the resurrection of damnation.

Leader. Whatsoever thy hand findeth to do, do it with thy might:

Children. For there is no work, nor device, nor knowledge, nor wisdom, in the grave, whither thou goest.

Leader. Behold, I come quickly; and my reward is with me, to give every man according as his work shall be.

Children. So teach us to number our days, that we may apply our hearts unto wisdom.

Leader. Blessed are the dead that die in the Lord: yea saith the Spirit, that they may rest from their labours, and their works do follow them.

Children. Let me die the death of the righteous, and let my last end be like his.

Leader. Though I walk through the valley of the shadow of death, I will fear no evil, for thou art with me; thy rod and thy staff they comfort me.

Children. Then shall be brought to pass the saying that is written, O Death, where is thy sting? O Grave, where is thy victory? The sting of death is sin; the strength of sin is the law: but thanks be to God, who giveth us the victory through our Lord Jesus Christ.

Let us Pray.

ALMIGHTY and eternal God! Before the mountains were brought forth, or ever thou hadst formed the earth and the world, from everlasting to everlasting thou art God: the same yesterday, to-day, and for ever. The earth and the heavens are the work of thy hands: they shall perish, but thou shalt endure; all of them shall wax old like a garment: as a vesture shalt thou change them, and they shall be changed; but thou art the same, and thy years shall have no end. In this solemn hour we would bow humbly before thee, and acknowledge thy presence and thy power. In thee we live, and move, and have our being: thou bringest low and liftest up; thou bringest down to the grave and bringest up. We know that affliction cometh not forth of the dust, neither doth trouble spring out of the ground. There is not a sparrow falleth to the earth without the Father, and the hairs of our head are all numbered. Thou art too wise to err, and too good to do aught in anger. Thou dost not afflict willingly, nor grieve the children of men. Grant, O Lord, that we may make a right improvement of this solemn event which has removed one of our number into the unseen world; and while our hearts are softened into tenderness, do thou impress upon them the lessons which we ought to learn, and which thou dost intend to teach us by it. Help us to feel the shortness and uncertainty of life, and the certainty and solemnity of the hour of death. May we hear thy voice speaking to us through these cold lips, and saying, Be ye also ready; for in an hour that ye think not, the Son of man cometh. We confess that we are too prone to drive from our minds the thought of death, and to put off preparation for it. May we lay it to heart, as we look upon these silent remains, that this event is certainly before us, and that there is only a step between us and the grave; that at any moment, even without the warning of sickness, we may be called to enter upon all the realities of the eternal life. Help us to consider that we can die but once, and that dying unprepared, we for ever lose the opportunity to seek the aid of our Redeemer. May we remember that sin is the sting of death, and that safety after death can only be secured by the forgiveness of our sins and the renewal of our hearts;

that death is welcome only to those that sleep in Jesus. Help us to live in such a constant readiness for this event, that death may find us with our work done, and well done; and grant, most merciful Father, that when the dead shall come forth from the slumbers of the grave, we may arise unto the resurrection of life, and hear our Saviour say, Well done, good and faithful servants; enter ye into the joy of your Lord: for his sake, who tasted death for every man, our Lord and Saviour Jesus Christ. Amen.

We thank thee, Almighty God, that the Gospel of thy Son hath brought life and immortality to light; and that whosoever believeth in him, though he were dead, yet shall he live again. We adore thee for the gift of a Saviour, who came to seek and to save the lost; and who has gone to prepare in heaven, mansions for those that love and trust in him. We thank thee that his blood can wash and purify our hearts, preparing us to dwell with all the sanctified above; that his grace takes away the fear and the sting of death, and all the gloom from the grave. We bless thee that thou hast revealed to us the glories of the heavenly world, and taught us how we may obtain them; that we may look forward to an hour when all tears shall be wiped away, and there shall be no temptation to sin; when the wicked shall cease from troubling, and the weary shall be at rest; and when all sorrow and sighing shall be done away; that there will be no night there, and they will need no candle, neither light of the sun, for the Lord God giveth them light, and they shall reign for ever. Thanks be to God who giveth us this victory, through our Lord Jesus Christ. Amen.

Almighty God, grant that we may not fail to obey the solemn instructions of this hour. May we not put aside the strivings of thy Spirit, nor presume upon our present health and mercies. Help us, in this hour of deep and solemn feeling, humbly to confess our sins, and sincerely to seek the divine forgiveness, and a preparation for the hour when we also shall be borne to our long home.

Sanctify this event to all the friends of the departed; sustain them under this and all thy afflictive providences; fit us all for thy holy will on the earth; and when the hour of our departure comes, trusting in our Saviour, sustained by a lively hope of the resurrection from the dead, and comforted by the Holy Spirit, may we peacefully fall asleep in Jesus. And all the praise of our salvation shall be ascribed to the Father, and to the Son, and to the Holy Ghost, now and for ever. Amen.

HYMNS.

INDEX OF SUBJECTS.

HYMNS.

THE SABBATH.

1 S. M.

The eternal Sabbath.

HAIL to the Sabbath day!
The day divinely given,
When men to God their homage pay,
And earth draws near to heaven.

2 Lord, in this sacred hour,
Within thy courts we bend,
And bless thy love, and own thy power
Our Father and our Friend.

3 But thou art not alone
In courts by mortals trod;
Nor only is the day thine own
When man draws near to God:

4 Thy temple is the arch
Of yon unmeasured sky;
Thy Sabbath, the stupendous march
Of vast eternity.

5 Lord, may that holier day
Dawn on thy servants' sight;
And purer worship may we pay
In heaven's unclouded light.

2

7s & 6s.

Sabbath Morning Hymn.

THE rosy light is dawning
  Upon the mountain's brow;
It is the Sabbath morning,
  Arise and pay thy vow.
Lift up thy voice to heaven
  In sacred praise and prayer,
While unto thee is given
  The light of life to share.

2 The landscape, lately shrouded
  By evening's paler ray,
Smiles beauteous and unclouded
  Before the eye of day.
So let our souls, benighted
  Too long in folly's shade,
Lord, by thy smiles be lighted
  To joys that never fade.

3 O see those waters streaming
  In crystal purity,
While earth, with verdure teeming,
  Gives rapture to the eye.
Let rivers of salvation
  In larger currents flow,
Till every tribe and nation
  Their healing virtues know.

3

6 *lines* 7s.

The Sabbath in the sanctuary.

SAFELY through another week
  God has brought us on our way;
Let us now a blessing seek,
  Waiting in his courts to-day—
Day of all the week the best,
Emblem of eternal rest.

2 While we seek supplies of grace
  Through the dear Redeemer's name,
Show thy reconciling face,
  Take away our sin and shame;
From our worldly cares set free,
May we rest, this day, in thee.

3 Here we come thy name to praise:
  Let us feel thy presence near;
May thy glory meet our eyes
  While we in thy house appear;
Here afford us, Lord, a taste
Of our everlasting feast.

4 May the gospel's joyful sound
  Conquer sinners, comfort saints,
Make the fruits of grace abound,
  Bring relief from all complaints.
Thus let all our Sabbaths prove
Till we join the Church above.

4 — 7s & 6s.

Sabbath in the light of God.

PLEASANT is the Sabbath bell
  In the light, in the light;
Seeming much of joy to tell
  In the light of God.
But a music sweeter far,
  In the light, in the light,
Breathes where angel spirits are,
  In the light of God.

CHORUS.

Let us walk in the light,
Walk in the light:
Let us walk in the light,
In the light of God.

2 Shall we ever rise to dwell
Where immortal praises swell?
And can children ever go
Where eternal Sabbaths glow?
CHORUS.—Let us walk, etc.

3 Yes, that bliss our own may be,
All the good shall Jesus see;
For the good a rest remains,
Where the glorious Saviour reigns.
CHORUS.—Let us walk, etc.

5 4 6s & 2 8s.

Welcome Morn.

WELCOME, delightful morn!
Thou day of sacred rest:
I hail thy kind return;
Lord, make these moments blest.
From low delights and trifling toys
I soar to reach immortal joys.

2 Now may the King descend,
And fill his throne of grace;
Thy scepter, Lord, extend,
While saints address thy face;
Let sinners feel thy quick'ning word,
And learn to know and fear the Lord.

3 Descend, celestial Dove,
With all thy quick'ning powers;
Reveal a Saviour's love,
And bless these sacred hours:
Then shall my soul new life obtain,
Nor Sabbaths be enjoyed in vain.

6 S. M.

The Sabbath welcomed.

WELCOME, sweet day of rest,
That saw the Lord arise;
Welcome to this reviving breast,
And these rejoicing eyes.

2 The King himself comes near,
And feasts his saints to-day;
Here may we sit and see him here,
And love, and praise, and pray.

3 One day, amid the place
Where Christ, my Lord, has been,
Is sweeter than ten thousand days
Of pleasure and of sin.

4 My willing soul would stay
In such a frame as this,
Till called to rise and soar away
To everlasting bliss.

7 L. M.

The earthly and heavenly Sabbath.

THINE earthly Sabbaths, Lord, we love;
But there's a nobler rest above.
To that our longing souls aspire,
With cheerful hope and strong desire.

2 No more fatigue, no more distress,
Nor sin, nor death, shall reach the place;
No groans shall mingle with the songs
Which dwell upon immortal tongues;

3 No rude alarms of angry foes;
No cares to break the long repose;
No midnight shade, no clouded sun,
But sacred, high, eternal noon.

4 O long expected day, begin!
Dawn on these realms of pain and sin;
With joy we'll tread th' appointed road,
And sleep in death, to rest with God.

8 7s & 4s.

We love the Sabbath day.—TUNE, *Happy Land.*

WE love the Sabbath day
Best of the week;
Here now we meet to pray,
And Jesus seek.

O precious day of rest,
Day which God our Saviour blest,
Day which we love the best,
Best of the week!

2 We love the sacred place—
Dear Sabbath rest;
Here Jesus sheds his grace
On every guest.
O may our hearts ascend
To our dearest heavenly Friend,
Who loves us to the end,
Forever blessed!

3 We love the precious truth,
God sent from heaven;
O may it guide our youth
While life is given.
Bright may it shine below,
Brighter as we further go,
Till light eternal glow,
Brightest in heaven.

4 There, filled with joy and peace,
We'll sweetly sing;
Our songs shall never cease
Praising our King.
While endless ages move
We shall feast upon his love,
And seraphs far above
Join in our song.

9 — 8s & 7s.

Sabbath bells are ringing.

SABBATH bells are ringing, ringing,
Like soft voices, in the air,
Of the angels, winging, winging,
To the sacred house of prayer.

'Tis the day of holy rest,
When the world with all its care,
Shall not rule the anxious breast
God reigns triumphant there.
CHORUS.—Sabbath bells, etc.

2 Children's voices, pealing, pealing,
Are the echoes of their souls;
When they worship, kneeling, kneeling,
In their pleasant Sabbath schools.
There the child, in humble trust,
Lisps the blessed Saviour's name;
There the teacher, bowed in dust,
The cross his only claim.
CHORUS.—Sabbath bells, etc.

3 Light from heaven beaming, beaming,
Breaks in glory on the soul;
Hope in beauty, gleaming, gleaming,
Cheers the children's Sunday-school.
Light and hope, and faith and love,
Peace and joy are their reward;
Heavenly blessings from above,
For children of the Lord.
CHORUS.—Sabbath bells, etc.

10 — 8s & 7s.

My Sabbath Song.

STRAINS of music often greet me
As I join the busy throng,
But there's nothing half so pleasant
As the holy Sabbath song.

CHORUS.

No fear of ill, no fear of wrong,
While I can sing my Sabbath song;
My Sabbath song, my Sabbath song,
I love to sing my Sabbath song.

2 'Tis a song of love and mercy,
Speaking peace to all mankind;
Telling sinners, poor and needy,
Where the Saviour they may find.
CHORUS.—No fear of ill, etc.

3 Angels sweetly sing in glory
Songs of praise to God, their King;
But the song of blest redemption,
Man, redeemed, alone can sing.
CHORUS.—No fear of ill, etc.

4 While I live, O may I ever
Love the holy Sabbath song;
And when death shall call me homeward,
Join it with the blood-bought throng.
CHORUS.—No fear of ill, etc.

11 L. M.

Holy Sabbath.

ANOTHER six days' work is done,
Another Sabbath is begun:
Return, my soul, enjoy the rest,
Improve the day that God hath blest.

2 Come, bless the Lord, whose love assigns
So sweet a rest to wearied minds,
Draws us away from earth to heaven,
And gives this day the food of seven.

3 O may our prayers and praises rise
As grateful incense to the skies,
And draw from heaven that sweet repose
Which none but he who feels it knows.

4 In holy duties may the day
In holy pleasures pass away;
How sweet a Sabbath thus to spend
In hope of one that ne'er shall end!

12 8 lines 6s.

We love to meet.

JESUS, we love to meet
On this thy holy day.
We worship round thy seat
On this thy holy day.
Thou tender, heavenly Friend,
To thee our prayers ascend;
O'er our young spirits bend
On this thy holy day.

2 We dare not trifle now
On this thy holy day.
In silent awe we bow
On this thy holy day.
Check every wandering thought,
And let us all be taught
To serve thee as we ought,
On this thy holy day.

3 We listen to thy word
On this thy holy day.
Bless all that we have heard
On this thy holy day.
Go with us when we part,
And to each youthful heart
Thy saving grace impart,
On this thy holy day.

13 8 lines 8s.

Sweet Sabbath.

HOW sweet is the Sabbath to me,
The day when the Saviour arose!
'Tis heaven his beauties to see
And in his soft arms to repose:
He knows I am weak and defiled,
My life is but empty and vain;
But if he will make me his child,
I'll never forsake him again.

2 This day he invites me to come:
  How kindly he bids me draw near!
He offers me heaven for home,
  And wipes off the penitent tear:
He offers to pardon my sin,
  And keep me from every snare;
To sprinkle and cleanse me within,
  And show me his tenderest care.

3 I cannot, I must not refuse;
  His goodness has conquered my heart:
The Lord for my portion I choose,
  And bid all my folly depart.
How sweet is the Sabbath to me,
  The day my Redeemer arose!
'Tis heaven his beauties to see,
  And in his soft arms to repose.

14 — 7s & 6s.

Sabbath Morning.

THINE holy day's returning,
  Our hearts exult to see,
And with devotion burning,
  Ascend, our God, to thee.
To-day with purest pleasure,
  Our thoughts from earth withdraw;
We search for sacred treasure,
  We learn thy holy law.

2 We join to sing thy praises,
  God of the Sabbath day!
Each voice in gladness raises
  Its loudest, sweetest lay.
Thy richest mercies sharing,
  O fill us with thy love!
By grace our souls preparing
  For nobler praise above.

THE BIBLE.

15 C. M.

Excellency and sufficiency.

FATHER of mercies, in thy word
 What endless glory shines;
Forever be thy Name adored
 For these celestial lines.

2 Here the fair tree of knowledge grows,
 And yields a free repast;
Sublimer sweets than nature knows
 Invite the longing taste.

3 Here the Redeemer's welcome voice
 Spreads heavenly peace around;
And life, and everlasting joys,
 Attend the blissful sound.

4 O may these heavenly pages be
 Our ever dear delight;
And still new beauties may we see,
 And still increasing light.

5 Divine Instructor, gracious Lord,
 Be thou forever near;
Teach us to love thy sacred word,
 And view the Saviour there.

16 8s & 7s.

Holy Bible.

HOLY Bible, well I love thee;
 Thou didst shine upon my way,
Like the glorious sun above me,
 Turning darkness into day.

Just as the sun rolls back the night,
 Breaking forth with morning ray,
So does the Bible's spreading light
 Chase the shades of sin away.

2 Holy Bible, mines of treasure
 In thy precious folds I see;
Earthly good would know no measure
 If this world were ruled by thee.
Just as the sun, from morn till noon,
 Stately climbs the eastern sky,
So over all the earth shall soon
 Beam the Day-spring from on high.

3 Holy Bible, do thou cheer me
 When I lay me down to die;
Christ has promised to be near me:
 Can I fear when he is nigh?
Just as the sun descends at eve,
 Soon with fresher beams to rise,
So shall the dying saint receive
 Life eternal in the skies.

17 — 4 *lines* 11s.

Precious Bible.

THE Bible! the Bible! more precious than gold
 The hopes and the glories its pages unfold:
It speaks of a Saviour, and tells of his love;
It shows us the way to the mansions above.

2 The Bible! the Bible! blest volume of truth,
How sweetly it smiles on the season of youth!
It bids us seek early the pearl of great price,
Ere the heart is enslaved in the bondage of vice.

3 The Bible! the Bible! we hail it with joy;
Its truths and its glories our tongues shall employ;
We'll sing of its triumphs, we'll tell of its worth,
And send its glad tidings afar o'er the earth.

4. The Bible! the Bible! the valleys shall ring,
And hill-tops re-echo the notes that we sing;
Our banners, inscribed with its precepts and rules,
Shall long wave in triumph, the joy of our schools.

18 C. M.

The Bible the light of the world.

WHAT glory gilds the sacred page!
Majestic, like the sun,
It gives a light to every age;
It gives, but borrows none.

2 The power that gave it still supplies
The gracious light and heat:
Its truths upon the nations rise;
They rise, but never set.

3 Let everlasting thanks be thine
For such a bright display,
As makes a world of darkness shine
With beams of heavenly day.

4 My soul rejoices to pursue
The steps of him I love,
Till glory breaks upon my view
In brighter worlds above.

19 C. M.

The revealing Spirit.

FATHER of all, in whom alone
We live, and move, and breathe;
One bright celestial ray dart down,
And cheer thy sons beneath.

2 While in thy word we search for thee,
(We search with trembling awe,)
Open our eyes, and let us see
The wonders of thy law.

3 Now let our darkness comprehend
The light that shines so clear;
Now the revealing Spirit send,
And give us ears to hear.

4 Before us make thy goodness pass,
Which here by faith we know;
Let us in Jesus see thy face,
And die to all below.

20 C. M.

Teach me thy word.

JESUS, my Saviour and my Lord,
To thee I lift mine eyes:
Teach and instruct me by thy word,
And make me truly wise.

2 Make me to know and understand
Thy whole revealed will;
Fain would I learn to comprehend
Thy love more clearly still.

3 Help me to read the Bible o'er
With ever new delight:
Help me to love its Author more;
To seek thee day and night.

4 O let it purify my heart,
And guide me all my days;
Its wonders, Lord, to me impart,
And thou shalt have the praise.

21 S. M.

Power of God's word.

BEHOLD, the morning sun
Begins his glorious way;
His beams through all the nations run,
And life and light convey.

2 But where the Gospel comes,
  It spreads diviner light:
It calls dead sinners from their tombs,
  And gives the blind their sight.

3 How perfect is thy word!
  And all thy judgments just!
Forever sure thy promise, Lord,
  And we securely trust.

4 My gracious God, how plain
  Are thy directions given!
O may I never read in vain,
  But find the path to heaven.

22 C. M.

The riches of God's word.

LET worldly men, from shore to shore,
  Their chosen good pursue;
Thy word, O Lord, we value more
  Than treasures of Peru.

2 Here mines of knowledge, love, and joy,
  Are opened to our sight:
The purest gold without alloy,
  And gems divinely bright.

3 The counsels of redeeming grace
  These sacred leaves unfold;
And here the Saviour's lovely face
  Our raptured eyes behold.

4 Here light, descending from above,
  Directs our doubtful feet;
Here promises of heavenly love
  Our ardent wishes meet.

5 Our numerous griefs are here redressed,
  And all our wants supplied:
Naught we can ask to make us blest
  Is in this book denied.

23 L. M.

Bible reveals God.

THE heavens declare thy glory, Lord,
  In every star thy wisdom shines;
But when our eyes behold thy word
  We read thy name in fairer lines.

2 The rolling sun, the changing light,
  And nights and days thy power confess;
But the blest volume thou hast writ
  Reveals thy justice and thy grace.

3 Sun, moon, and stars convey thy praise
  Round the whole earth, and never stand
So when thy truth began its race,
  It touched and glanced on every .and.

4 Nor will thy spreading Gospel rest,
  Till through the world thy truth has run.
Till Christ has all the nations blest
  That see the light or feel the sun.

24 C. M.

The Bible the defense of truth.

HOW shall the young secure their hearts,
  And guard their lives from sin?
Thy word the choicest rules imparts
  To keep the conscience clean.

2 'Tis like the sun, a heavenly light,
  That guides us all the day;
And through the dangers of the night,
  A lamp to lead our way.

3 Thy precepts make me truly wise;
  I hate the sinner's road;
I hate my own vain thoughts that rise,
  But love thy law, my God!

4 Thy word is everlasting truth;
  How pure is every page!
That holy book shall guide our youth
  And well support our age.

PRAISE AND PRAYER TO GOD.

25 C. M.

God seen in his works.

THERE'S not a star whose twinkling light
 Illumes the distant earth,
And cheers the solemn gloom of night,
 But goodness gave it birth.

2 There's not a cloud whose dews distill
 Upon the parching clod,
And clothe with verdure vale and hill,
 That is not sent by God.

3 There's not a place in earth's vast round,
 In ocean deep, or air,
Where skill and wisdom are not found;
 For God is everywhere.

4 Around, beneath, below, above,
 Wherever space extends.
There Heaven displays its boundless love,
 And power with gooduess blends.

26 6s & 4s.

Help us to praise.

COME, thou Almighty King,
 Help us thy name to sing,
  Help us to praise!
Father, all glorious,
O'er all victorious,
Come and reign over us,
  Ancient of days.

2 Jesus, our Lord, arise,
Scatter our enemies;
  Now make them fall!

Let thine almighty aid
Our sure defense be made,
Our souls on thee be stayed:
Lord, hear our call!

3 Come, thou incarnate Word,
Gird on thy mighty sword;
Our prayer attend!
Come, and thy people bless;
Come, give thy word success;
Spirit of holiness,
On us descend!

27 — 4 6s & 2 8s.

Prayer for grace.

AGAIN we meet, O Lord,
Again we fill this place,
To hear thy holy word
And ask thy promised grace;
To thank thee for the gifts we share,
The children of thy love and care.

2 Grant us the list'ning ear,
The understanding heart,
The mind and will sincere,
To choose the better part,
To take the learner's lowly seat,
And gather wisdom at thy feet.

3 Through this, and every day,
Teach us thy path to tread;
Nor let our feet astray
By Satan's wiles be led;
But keep us in the narrow road,
The way to glory and to God.

28 — C. M.

Glory, mercy, grace.

FATHER, how wide thy glory shines,
How high thy wonders rise!
Known through the earth by thousand signs,
By thousands through the skies.

2 Those mighty orbs proclaim thy power;
Their motions speak thy skill:
And on the wings of every hour
We read thy patience still.

3 Part of thy Name divinely stands,
On all thy creatures writ;
They show the labor of thy hands,
Or impress of thy feet:

4 But when we view thy strange design
To save rebellious worms,
Where vengeance and compassion join
In their divinest forms:

5 Here the whole Deity is known,
Nor dares a creature guess
Which of the glories brighter shone,
The justice or the grace.

6 Now the full glories of the Lamb
Adorn the heavenly plains;
Bright seraphs learn Immanuel's name,
And try their choicest strains.

7 O may I bear some humble part
In that immortal song!
Wonder and joy shall tune my heart,
And love command my tongue.

29 C. M.

Prayer for God's blessing.

NOW condescend, Almighty King,
To bless this happy throng;
And kindly listen while we sing
Our grateful morning song.

2 We come to own the power divine
That watches o'er our days:
For this our cheerful voices join
In hymns of grateful praise.

3 We come to learn thy holy word,
And ask thy tender care;
Before thy throne, Almighty Lord,
We bend in humble prayer.

4 May we in safety pass this day,
From sin and danger free;
And ever walk in that sure way
That leads to heaven and thee.

30 L. M.

Grateful adoration.

BEFORE Jehovah's awful throne,
Ye nations, bow with sacred joy;
Know that the Lord is God alone,
He can create, and he destroy.

2 His sovereign power, without our aid,
Made us of clay, and formed us men;
And when like wandering sheep we strayed,
He brought us to his fold again.

3 We'll crowd thy gates with thankful songs,
High as the heavens our voices raise;
And earth, with her ten thousand tongues,
Shall fill thy courts with sounding praise.

4 Wide as the world is thy command;
Vast as eternity thy love;
Firm as a rock thy truth shall stand,
When rolling years shall cease to move.

31 4 *lines* 7s.

Earnest of eternal rest.

GRACIOUS Spirit, Love divine!
Let thy light within me shine;
All my guilty fears remove;
Fill me with thy heavenly love.

2 Speak thy pard'ning grace to me;
Set the burdened sinner free;
Lead me to the Lamb of God;
Wash me in his precious blood.

3 Life and peace to me impart;
Seal salvation on my heart,
Breathe thyself into my breast,
Earnest of immortal rest.

4 Let me never from thee stray;
Keep me in the narrow way;
Fill my soul with joy divine;
Keep me, Lord, forever thine.

32 C. M.

The Lamb worshiped.

COME, let us join our cheerful songs
With angels round the throne:
Ten thousand thousand are their tongues,
But all their joys are one.

2 Worthy the Lamb that died, they cry,
To be exalted thus:
Worthy the Lamb, our hearts reply,
For he was slain for us.

3 Jesus is worthy to receive
Honor and power divine;
And blessings more than we can give,
Be, Lord, forever thine.

4 The whole creation join in one,
To bless the sacred Name
Of Him that sits upon the throne,
And to adore the Lamb.

33 L. M.

Infinite in wisdom.

PRAISE ye the Lord! 'tis good to raise
Your hearts and voices in his praise:
His nature and his works invite
To make this duty our delight.

2 He formed the stars, those heavenly flames;
He counts their numbers, calls their names:
His wisdom's vast, and knows no bound,
A deep where all our thoughts are drowned.

3 Sing to the Lord! exalt him high,
Who spreads the clouds along the sky;
There he prepares the fruitful rain,
Nor lets the drops descend in vain.

4 He makes the grass the hills adorn;
He clothes the smiling fields with corn;
The beasts with food his hands supply,
And the young ravens when they cry.

5 What is the creature's skill or force?
The sprightly man, or warlike horse?
The piercing wit, the active limb?
All are too mean delights for him.

6 But saints are lovely in his sight;
He views his children with delight:
He sees their hope, he knows their fear,
He looks, and loves his image there.

34 L. M.

Grace.

NOW to the Lord a noble song!
Awake, my soul! awake, my tongue!
Hosanna to the eternal Name!
And all his boundless love proclaim.

2 See where it shines in Jesus' face,
The brightest image of his grace;
God, in the person of his son,
Has all his mightiest works outdone.

3 Grace! 'tis a sweet, a charming theme
My thoughts rejoice at Jesus' name;
Ye angels, dwell upon the sound;
Ye heavens, reflect it to the ground.

4 O, may I reach that happy place
Where he unvails his lovely face,
Where all his beauties you behold,
And sing his name to harps of gold.

35 C. M.

Spirit's quickening power.

COME, Holy Spirit, heavenly Dove,
With all thy quick'ning powers,
Kindle a flame of sacred love
In these cold hearts of ours.

2 Look how we grovel here below,
Fond of these earthly toys;
Our souls, how heavily they go,
To reach eternal joys.

3 In vain we tune our formal songs,
In vain we strive to rise;
Hosannas languish on our tongues,
And our devotion dies.

4 Father, and shall we ever live
At this poor dying rate;
Our love so faint, so cold to thee,
And thine to us so great?

5 Come, Holy Spirit, heavenly Dove,
With all thy quick'ning powers;
Come, shed abroad a Saviour's love,
And that shall kindle ours.

36 L. M.

From everlasting to everlasting.

ERE mountains reared their forms sublime,
Or heaven and earth in order stood,
Before the birth of ancient time,
From everlasting thou art God.

2 A thousand ages, in their flight,
With thee are as a fleeting day;
Past, present, future, to thy sight
At once their various scenes display.

3 But our brief life's a shadowy dream,
A passing thought, that soon is o'er,
That fades with morning's earliest beam,
And fills the musing mind no more.

4 To us, O Lord, the wisdom give,
Each passing moment so to spend,
That we at length with thee may livo
Where life and bliss shall never end.

37 L. M.

The creation invited to praise God.

FROM all that dwell below the skies,
Let the Creator's praise arise;
Let the Redeemer's name be sung
Through every land, by every tongue.

2 Eternal are thy mercies, Lord;
Eternal truth attends thy word:
Thy praise shall sound from shore to shore,
Till suns shall rise and set no more.

3 Your lofty themes, ye mortals, bring;
In songs of praise divinely sing;
The great salvation loud proclaim,
And shout for joy the Saviour's name.

4 In every land begin the song;
To every land the strains belong:
In cheerful sounds all voices raise,
And fill the world with loudest praise.

38 S. M.

The universal King.

COME, sound his praise abroad,
And hymns of glory sing;
Jehovah is the sov'reign God,
The universal King.

2 He formed the deeps unknown;
He gave the seas their bound;
The watery worlds are all his own,
And all the solid ground.

3 Come, worship at his throne,
Come, bow before the Lord;
We are his works, and not our own;
He formed us by his word.

4 To-day attend his voice,
Nor dare provoke his rod;
Come, like the people of his choice,
And own your gracious God.

39

4 6s & 2 8s.

Greatness and condescension.

THE Lord Jehovah reigns,
His throne is built on high;
The garments he assumes
Are light and majesty:
His glories shine with beams so bright,
No mortal eye can bear the sight.

2 The thunders of his hand
Keep the wide world in awe;
His wrath and justice stand
To guard his holy law;
And where his love resolves to bless,
His truth confirms and seals the grace.

3 Through all his mighty works
Amazing wisdom shines;
Confounds the powers of hell,
And all their dark designs;
Strong is his arm, and shall fulfill
His great decrees and sov'reign will.

4 And will this sov'reign King
Of glory condescend;—
And will he write his name,
My Father and my Friend?
I love his Name, I love his word:
Join all my powers to praise the Lord.

40

4 *lines* 7s.

God's glorious perfections celebrated.

GLORY be to God on high,
God, whose glory fills the sky;
Peace on earth to man forgiven,
Man, the well-beloved of Heaven.

2 Sov'reign Father, heavenly King,
Thee we now presume to sing;
Glad thine attributes confess,
Glorious all, and numberless.

3 Hail, by all thy works adored!
Hail, the everlasting Lord!
Thee with thankful hearts we prove,
God of power, and God of love.

4 Christ our Lord and God we own,
Christ, the Father's only Son;
Lamb of God for sinners slain,
Saviour of offending man.

5 Jesus, in thy name we pray,
Take, O take our sins away;
Bow thine ear, in mercy bow,
Hear, the world's atonement, Thou!

41 C. M.

Teach us to pray.

THE Lord attends when children pray,
  A whisper he can hear;
He knows not only what we say,
  But what we wish or fear.

2 He sees us when we are alone,
  Though no one else can see;
And all our thoughts to him are known,
  Wherever we may be.

3 'Tis not enough to bend the knee,
  And words of prayer to say:
The heart must with the lips agree,
  Or else we do not pray.

4 Teach us, O Lord, to pray aright,
  Thy grace to us impart,
That we in prayer may take delight,
  And serve thee with the heart.

5 Then, heavenly Father! at thy throne
Thy praise we will proclaim;
And daily our requests make known,
In our Redeemer's name.

42 6s & 5s

God is good.

MORN amid the mountains,
Lovely solitude!
Gushing streams and fountains
Murmur, "God is good."
Murmur, murmur, murmur, "God is good"

2 Now the glad sun, breaking,
Pours a golden flood;
Deepest vales, awaking,
Echo, "God is good."
Echo, echo, echo, "God is good."

3 Hymns of praise are ringing
Through the leafy wood;
Songsters, sweetly singing,
Warble, "God is good."
Warble, warble, warble, "God is good."

4 Wake, and join the chorus,
Child, with soul endued;
God, whose smile is o'er us,
Evermore is good.
Ever, ever, evermore is good.

43 5s, 7s, & 8s.

O come, let us sing!

O COME, let us sing!
Our youthful hearts now swelling,
To God above, a God of love,
O come, let us sing!
Our joyful spirits, glad and free,
With high emotions rise to thee
In heavenly melody—
O come, let us sing!

2 O swell, swell the song,
His praises oft repeating:
His Son he gave our souls to save—
O swell, swell the song.
The humble heart's devotion bring
Whence gushing streams of love do spring,
And make the welkin ring
With sweet-swelling song.

3 We'll chant, chant his praise,
Our lofty strains now blending:
A tribute bring to Christ our King,
And chant, chant his praise!
Our Saviour, Prince, was crucified,
"'Tis finished!" then he meekly cried,
And bowed his head and died,
Then chant, chant his praise!

4 All full chorus join,
To Jesus condescending
To bless our race with heavenly grace,
All full chorus join!
To God, whose mercy on us smiled,
And Holy Spirit, reconciled
By Christ, the meek and mild,
All full chorus join!

44

4 *lines* 7s.

God cares for me.

POOR and needy though I be,
God, my Maker, cares for me;
Gives me clothing, shelter, food,
Gives me all I have of good.

2 He will listen when I pray,
He is with me night and day;
When I sleep and when I wake,
Keeps me safe for Jesus' sake.

3 He who reigns above the sky
Once became as poor as I;
He whose blood for me was shed
Had not where to lay his head.

4 Though I labor here a while,
He will bless me with his smile;
And when this short life is past,
I shall rest with him at last.

45

4 *lines* 7s.

God sees me.

WHEN I sleep, and when I wake,
When my daily walks I take,
Though my eyes no God can see,
Still he ever looks at me.

2 When I speak a wicked word,
By my Saviour it is heard;
Though I seek from God to flee,
Still from heaven he looks at me.

3 When I break this holy day,
And indulge in sinful play,
Could I still so thoughtless be,
If I felt he looks at me?

4 When with wicked ones I play,
When my heart forgets to pray,
Though I may forgetful be,
Still my Saviour looks at me.

5 When my angry passions rise,
God can hear my sinful cries;
When rebellious I would be,
Still he ever looks at me.

6 Every disobedient word,
False or cross, in heaven is heard;
Though no human eye can see,
God my Saviour looks at me.

46 L. M.

God sees me everywhere.

AMONG the deepest shades of night,
Can there be one who sees my way?
Yes, God is as a shining light
That turns the darkness into day.

2 When every eye around me sleeps,
May I not sin without control?
No, for a constant watch he keeps
On every thought of every soul.

3 If I could find some cave unknown,
Where human feet have never trod,
Yet there I should not be alone:
On every side there would be God.

4 He smiles in heaven, he frowns in hell,
He fills the earth, the air, the sea;
I must within his presence dwell,
I cannot from his anger flee.

5 Yet I may flee; he shows me where;
To Jesus Christ he bids me fly;
And while I seek for pardon there,
There's only mercy in his eye.

47 S. M.

The sacrifice of praise.

WITH joy we lift our eyes
To those bright realms above,
That glorious temple in the skies,
Where dwells eternal Love.

2 Before thy throne we bow,
O thou almighty King;
Here we present the solemn vow,
And hymns of praise we sing.

3 While in thy house we kneel,
With trust and holy fear,
Thy mercy and thy truth reveal,
And lend a gracious ear.

4 Lord, teach our hearts to pray,
And tune our lips to sing;
Nor from thy presence cast away
The sacrifice we bring.

48 C. M.

Heaven and earth are full of His glory.

ETERNAL Wisdom! thee we praise,
Thee the creation sings;
With thy loved name, rocks, hills, and seas,
And heaven's high palace, rings.

2 Thy hand, how wide it spreads the sky,
How glorious to behold!
Tinged with a blue of heavenly dye,
And starred with sparkling gold.

3 There thou hast bid the globes of light
Their endless circuits run:
There the pale planet rules the night:
The day obeys the sun.

4 Thy glories blaze all nature round,
And strike the wondering sight,
Through skies, and seas, and solid ground,
With terror and delight.

5 Infinite strength, and equal skill,
Shine through thy works abroad;
Our souls with vast amazement fill,
And speak the builder God!

49 S. M.

Praise the Saviour's name.

TO praise the Saviour's name,
Let little children try;
While saints and angels do the same
In the bright world on high.

2 His love in heaven is sung,
His name is there adored;
And children here, however young,
May learn to praise the Lord.

3 The wonders of that love
No earthly tongue can tell,
Which brought the Saviour from above,
To save our souls from hell.

4 For us he wept and bled,
And suffered all his pain;
For us was numbered with the dead,
And rose to life again.

5 And still for us he prays,
And makes our souls his care;
He loves to hear our feeble praise
And listen to our prayer.

6 Lord Jesus! grant that we
May know thy saving grace,
On earth thy humble followers be,
In heaven behold thy face.

50 S. M.

Bless the Lord, O my soul.

O BLESS the Lord, my soul,
His grace to thee proclaim;
And all that is within me, join
To bless his holy name.

2 O bless the Lord, my soul,
His mercies bear in mind;
Forget not all his benefits,
Who is to thee so kind.

3 He pardons all thy sins,
Prolongs thy feeble breath;
He healeth thine infirmities,
And ransoms thee from death.

4 He feeds thee with his love,
Upholds thee with his truth;
And, like the eagles, he renews
The vigor of thy youth.

5 Then bless the Lord, my soul,
His grace, his love, proclaim;
Let all that is within me join
To bless his holy name.

51 L. M.

Bless, O my soul, the living God.

BLESS, O my soul, the living God,
Call home thy thoughts that rove abroad;
Let all the powers within me join
In work and worship so divine.

2 Bless, O my soul, the God of grace:
His favors claim thy highest praise;
Why should the wonders he hath wrought
Be lost in silence and forgot?

3 'Tis he, my soul, that sent his Son
To die for crimes which thou hast done:
He owns the ransom, and forgives
The hourly follies of our lives.

4 Let the whole earth his power confess,
Let the whole earth adore his grace:
The Gentile with the Jew shall join
In work and worship so divine.

52 L. M.

God all around me.

LORD, thou hast searched and seen me through;
Thine eye commands with piercing view
My rising and my resting hours,
My heart and flesh, with all their powers.

2 My thoughts, before they are my own,
Are to my God distinctly known;
He knows the words I mean to speak,
Ere from my opening lips they break.

3 Within thy circling power I stand:
On every side I find thy hand;
Awake, asleep, at home, abroad,
I am surrounded still with God.

4 How awful is thy searching eye!
Thy knowledge, O how deep, how high!
My soul, with all the powers I boast,
Is in the boundless prospect lost.

5 O may these thoughts possess my breast
Where'er I rove, where'er I rest;
Nor let my evil passions dare
Consent to sin, for God is there.

53 S. M.

Our Father in heaven.

OUR heavenly Father, hear
The prayer we offer now!
Thy name be hallowed far and near,
To thee all nations bow.

2 Thy kingdom come; thy will
On earth be done in love,
As saints and seraphim fulfill
Thy perfect law above.

3 Our daily bread supply,
While by thy word we live;
The guilt of our iniquity
Forgive, as we forgive.

4 From dark temptation's power
Our feeble hearts defend;
Deliver in the evil hour,
And guide us to the end.

5 Thine, then, forever be
Glory and power divine;
The scepter, throne, and majesty
Of heaven and earth are thine.

54 L. M.

God everywhere worshiped.

O THOU, to whom, in ancient time,
The Psalmist's sacred harp was strung,
Whom kings adored in song sublime
And prophets praised with glowing tongue!

2 Not now on Zion's height alone,
The favored worshiper may dwell;
Nor where, at sultry noon, thy Son
Sat, weary, by the patriarch's well.

3 From every place below the skies,
The grateful song, the fervent prayer,
The incense of the heart, may rise
To heaven, and find acceptance there.

4 O Thou to whom, in ancient time,
The holy prophets' harp was strung!
To thee at last, in every clime,
Shall temples rise, and praise be sung.

55 L. M.

Christ's kingdom universal.

JESUS shall reign where'er the sun
Does his successive journeys run:
His kingdom stretch from shore to shore,
Till moons shall wax and wane no more.

2 For him shall endless prayer be made,
And endless praises crown his head;
His name, like sweet perfume, shall rise
With every morning sacrifice.

3 People and realms of every tongue
Dwell on his love with sweetest song;
And infant voices shall proclaim
Their early blessings on his name.

4 Blessings abound where'er he reigns;
The joyful prisoner bursts his chains;
The weary find eternal rest,
And all the sons of want are blest.

5 Let every creature rise and bring
Peculiar honors to our King;
Angels descend with songs again,
And earth repeat the loud Amen.

56 L. M.

Enjoyment in the service.

FAR from my thoughts, vain world, be gone,
  Let my religious hours alone;
Fain would my eyes my Saviour see;
I wait a visit, Lord, from thee.

2 O warm my heart with holy fire,
And kindle there a pure desire:
Come, sacred Spirit, from above,
And fill my soul with heavenly love.

3 Blest Saviour, what delicious fare!
How sweet thy entertainments are!
Ne'er did the angels taste above
Redeeming grace and dying love.

4 Hail, great Immanuel, all divine!
In thee thy Father's glories shine;
Thy glorious name shall be adored,
And every tongue confess thee Lord.

57 C. M.

Prayer.

PRAYER is the soul's sincere desire
  Unuttered or expressed,
The motion of a hidden fire
  That trembles in the breast.

2 Prayer is the burden of a sigh,
  The falling of a tear,
The upward glancing of an eye
  When none but God is near.

3 Prayer is the simplest form of speech
  That infant lips can try;
Prayer, the sublimest strains that reach
  The majesty on high.

4 Prayer is the Christian's vital breath
  The Christian's native air,
His watchword at the gates of death;
  He enters heaven with prayer.

58 L. M.

With my whole heart.

MY Father, when I come to thee,
I would not only bend the knee,
But with my spirit seek thy face,
With my whole heart desire thy grace.

2 I plead the name of thy dear Son,
All he has said, all he has done;
O may I feel his love for me,
Who died from sin to set me free.

3 To guide me, Lord, be ever nigh;
My sins forgive, my wants supply;
With favor crown my youthful days,
And my whole life shall speak thy praise.

4 Thy Holy Spirit, Lord, impart;
Impress thy likeness on my heart;
Let me obey thy truth in love,
Till raised to dwell with thee above.

59 C. M.

My sins are known to God.

ALMIGHTY God, thy piercing eye
Strikes through the shades of night,
And our most secret actions lie
All open to thy sight.

2 There's not a sin that we commit,
Nor wicked word we say,
But in thy dreadful book 'tis writ
Against the judgment-day.

3 And must the crimes that I have done
Be read and published there?
Be all exposed before the sun,
While men and angels hear?

4 Lord, at thy feet ashamed I lie,
Upward I dare not look;
Pardon my sins before I die,
And blot them from thy book.

5 Remember all the dying pains
That my Redeemer felt,
And let his blood wash out my stains,
And answer for my guilt.

60 6s & 4s.

Worthy the Lamb.

COME, children, join to sing
Loud praise to Christ our King;
Worthy the Lamb!
Let all with heart and voice
Before his throne rejoice;
Praise is his gracious choice,
Worthy the Lamb!

2 Come, lift your hearts on high,
Let praises fill the sky,
Worthy the Lamb!
He is our guide and friend,
To us he'll condescend;
His love shall never end,
Worthy the Lamb!

3 Praise yet the Lord again;
Life shall not end the strain,
Worthy the Lamb!
On heaven's blissful shore
His goodness we'll adore;
Singing for evermore,
Worthy the Lamb!

61 S. M.

Glory begun below.

COME, ye that love the Lord,
And let your joys be known;
Join in a song with sweet accord,
While ye surround his throne.
Let those refuse to sing
Who never knew our God,
But servants of the heavenly King
May speak their joys abroad.

2 The God that rules on high,
  That all the earth surveys,
That rides upon the stormy sky,
  And calms the roaring seas;
This awful God is ours,
  Our Father and our Love;
He will send down his heavenly powers
  To carry us above.

3 There we shall see his face,
  And never, never sin;
There, from the rivers of his grace,
  Drink endless pleasures in.
Yea, and before we rise
  To that immortal state,
The thoughts of such amazing bliss
  Should constant joys create.

4 The men of grace have found
  Glory begun below:
Celestial fruit on earthly ground
  From faith and hope may grow;
Then let our songs abound,
  And every tear be dry:
We're marching through Immanuel's ground
  To fairer worlds on high.

62 L. M.

The Mercy-Seat.

FROM every stormy wind that blows,
  From every swelling tide of woes,
There is a calm, a sure retreat;
'Tis found before the mercy-seat.

2 There is a place where Jesus sheds
The oil of gladness on our heads;
A place of all on earth most sweet;
It is the blood-bought mercy-seat.

3 There is a scene where spirits blend,
Where friend holds fellowship with friend;
Though sundered far, by faith they meet
Around one common mercy-seat.

4 There, there, on eagle wings we soar,
And sin and sense molest no more;
And heaven comes down our souls to greet,
And glory crowns the mercy-seat.

63 L. M.

Sweet hour of prayer.

SWEET hour of prayer, sweet hour of prayer,
That calls me from a world of care,
And bids me at my Father's throne
Make all my wants and wishes known:
In seasons of distress and grief
My soul has often found relief,
And oft escaped the tempter's snare
By thy return, sweet hour of prayer.

2 Sweet hour of prayer, sweet hour of prayer,
May I thy consolations share,
Till from Mount Pisgah's lofty height
I view my home and take my flight:
This robe of flesh I'll drop, and rise
To seize the everlasting prize,
And shout, while passing through the air,
Farewell, farewell, sweet hour of prayer.

64 4 *lines* 7s.

Encouragements to pray.

COME, my soul, thy suit prepare;
Jesus loves to answer prayer;
He himself invites thee near,
Bids thee ask him, waits to hear.

2 Lord, I come to thee for rest;
Take possession of my breast;
There, thy blood-bought right maintain,
And without a rival reign.

3 While I am a pilgrim here,
Let thy love my spirit cheer;
As my guide, my guard, my friend,
Lead me to my journey's end.

4 Show me what I have to do;
Every hour my strength renew;
Let me live a life of faith,
Let me die thy people's death.

65 S. M

Morning Prayer.

COME to the morning prayer,
  Come, let us kneel and pray;
Prayer is the Christian pilgrim's staff,
  To walk with God all day.

2 At noon, beneath the Rock
  Of Ages, rest and pray;
Sweet is the shadow from the heat,
  When sunbeams smite by day.

3 At eve shut to the door,
  And round the altar pray,
And finding there "the house of God,"
  At "heaven's gate" close the day.

4 When midnight seals our eyes,
  Let each in spirit say,
I sleep, but my heart waketh, Lord,
  With thee to watch and pray.

66 C. M.

Evening Hymn.

WHOM thou dost guard, O King of kings,
  No evil shall molest;
Under the shadow of thy wings
  Shall they securely rest.

2 Thy angels shall around their beds
  Their constant stations keep;
Thy faith and trust shall shield their heads,
  For thou dost never sleep.

3 May we with calm and sweet repose,
  And heavenly thoughts refreshed,
Our eyelids with the morn unclose,
  And bless the Ever-blessed.

67

6s & 4s.

Worthy the Lamb.

GLORY to God on high!
Let heaven and earth reply,
Praise ye his name:
His love and grace adore,
Who all our sorrows bore;
Sing then for evermore,
"Worthy the Lamb!"

2 Jesus, our Lord and God,
Bore sin's tremendous load:
Praise ye his name:
Tell what his arm hath done,
What spoils from death he won;
Sing his great name alone:
"Worthy the Lamb!"

3 Join, all ye ransomed race,
Our Lord and God to bless;
Praise ye his name:
In him we will rejoice,
And make a cheerful noise,
Shouting with heart and voice,
"Worthy the Lamb!"

4 What though we change our place,
Yet we shall never cease
Praising his name:
To him our songs we bring,
Hail him our gracious King,
And without ceasing sing,
"Worthy the Lamb!"

5 Let all the hosts above
Join in our song of love,
Praising his name:
To him ascribed be
Honor and majesty
Through all eternity,
"Worthy the Lamb!"

68 L. M.

Impart thy grace.

O LORD, behold before thy throne
  A band of children lowly bend:
Thy face we seek, thy name we own,
  And pray that thou wilt be our friend.

2 Thou didst on earth the young receive,
  And gently fold them to thy breast,
And say that such in heaven should live
  Forever safe, forever blest.

3 Thy Holy Spirit's aid impart,
  That he may teach us how to pray;
Make us sincere, and let each heart
  Delight to tread in wisdom's way.

4 O, let thy grace our souls renew,
  And seal a sense of pardon there;
Teach us thy will to know and do,
  And let us all thine image bear.

69 C. M.

Morning Hymn.

THROUGH all the dangers of the night
  Preserved, O Lord! by thee,
Again we hail the cheerful light,
  Again we bow the knee.

2 Preserve us, Lord! throughout the day,
  And guide us by thy arm;
For they are safe, and only they,
  Whom thou dost keep from harm.

3 Let all our words, and all our ways,
  Declare that we are thine,
That so the light of truth and grace
  Before the world may shine.

4 Let us ne'er turn away from thee;
  Dear Saviour, hold us fast,
Till, with immortal eyes, we see
  Thy glorious face at last.

70

4 lines 7s.

Suffer us to come to thee.

LORD, before thy throne we stand,
 Once again thy children see;
Smile upon this youthful band,
 Suffer us to come to thee.

2 Whither else should children go,
 Weak and impotent as we?
Thou hast all things to bestow,
 Suffer us to come to thee.

3 While we here have life and breath,
 This our constant prayer should be,
This our latest sigh in death,
 Suffer us to come to thee.

71

8s & 7s.

Evening Prayer.

JESUS! tender Shepherd, hear me!
 Bless thy little lamb to-night!
Through the darkness be thou near me,
 Watch my sleep till morning light.

2 All this day thy hand has led me,
 And I thank thee for thy care;
Thou hast clothed me, warmed and fed me,
 Listen to my evening prayer.

3 Let my sins be all forgiven!
 Bless the friends I love so well!
Take me, when I die, to heaven,
 Happy there with thee to dwell.

72

S. M.

Evening Hymn.

THE day is past and gone;
 The evening shades appear;
O may we all remember well
 The night of death draws near.

2 We lay our garments by,
Upon our beds to rest;
So death shall soon disrobe us all
Of what we here possessed.

3 Lord, keep us safe this night,
Secure from all our fears;
May angels guard us while we sleep,
Till morning light appears.

73 C. M.

Keep us to day.

THE morning breaks; my voice I raise
To thee great God, above;
Accept my prayer, my feeble praise,
In kindness and in love.

2 Forgive the crimes that I have done;
My follies I deplore;
And since another day's begun,
O may I love thee more.

3 Preserve me from all ill I pray,
And guide me with thine eye,
And grant through every hour I may
On grace divine rely.

4 Keep me from sinful thoughts, O Lord,
And make my heart sincere;
Make me to read thy holy word
With reverence and fear.

74 L. M.

I renew my vows.

AWAKE, my soul, and with the sun
Thy daily stage of duty run;
Shake off dull sloth, and early rise,
To pay the morning sacrifice.

2 Glory to Thee, who safe hast kept,
And hast refreshed me, while I slept;
Grant, Lord, when I from death shall wake
I may of endless life partake.

3 Lord, I my vows to thee renew,
Scatter my sins as morning dew;
Guard my first springs of thought and will,
And with thyself my spirit fill.

4 Direct, control, suggest, this day,
All I design, or do, or say;
That all my powers, with all their might,
In thy sole glory may unite.

75 C. M.

Hymns for Saturday eve.

GOD over all, forever blest!
Grant me thy grace within;
That I may keep to-morrow's rest,
A rest indeed from sin;

2 A rest from all my usual play,
A holy rest in Thee;
Then will thy blessed Sabbath-day
Be a sweet rest to me.

3 Lord, sanctify my every thought
In these my days of youth;
Make me remember what I'm taught
Out of thy word of truth.

76 4 6s & 2 8s

Parting Hymn.

DEAR Father, ere we part,
Now let thy grace descend,
And fill our youthful heart
With peace from Christ our Friend;
May showers of blessings from above
Descend and fill our hearts with love.

2 May we in after years
With gratitude review
The service of this day,
The work we now pursue.
And speed our way to worlds above,
With hearts on fire with holy love.

3 We know that soon on earth
The fondest ties must end,
Our own most cherished hopes
To death's cold hand must bend;
The fairest flowers in all their bloom
Must soon lie withered in the tomb.

4 Then, when our spirits leave
These tenements of clay,
May they to God, who gave,
Ascend, in endless day,
And sing with parents, teachers, friends,
That anthem sweet which never ends.

77 6s & 5s.

The Lord's Prayer.

OUR Father in heaven,
We hallow thy name!
May thy kingdom holy
On earth be the same!
O give to us daily
Our portion of bread;
It is from thy bounty
That all must be fed.

2 Forgive our transgressions,
And teach us to know
That humble compassion
That pardons each foe:
Keep us from temptation,
From weakness and sin;
And thine be the glory
Forever, amen!

78 7s & 6s.

Sing to Jesus.

COME, let us sing of Jesus,
While hearts and accents blend;
Come, let us sing of Jesus,
The sinner's only friend:

His holy soul rejoices,
  Amid the choirs above,
To hear our youthful voices
  Exulting in his love.

2 We love to sing of Jesus
  Who wept our path along;
We love to sing of Jesus,
  The tempted and the strong:
None who besought his healing,
  He passed unheeded by;
And still retains his feeling
  For us above the sky.

3 We love to sing of Jesus,
  Who died our souls to save;
We love to sing of Jesus,
  Triumphant o'er the grave;
And in our hour of danger,
  We'll trust his love alone,
Who once slept in a manger,
  And now sits on the throne.

4 Then let us sing of Jesus,
  While yet on earth we stay,
And hope to sing of Jesus
  Throughout the eternal day:
For those who here confess him,
  He will in heaven confess;
And faithful hearts that bless him,
  He will forever bless.

79 — 8s, 7s, & 4s

Lord, dismiss us.

LORD, dismiss us with thy blessing,
  Fill our hearts with joy and peace;
Let us each, thy love possessing,
  Triumph in redeeming grace:
    O refresh us,
  Traveling through this wilderness.

2 Thanks we give, and adoration,
For thy Gospel's joyful sound;
May the fruits of thy salvation
In our hearts and lives abound;
May thy presence
With us evermore be found.

3 Then, whene'er the signal's given
Us from earth to call away,
Borne on angels' wings to heaven,
Glad the summons to obey,—
May we ever
Reign with Christ in endless day.

80 L. M.

Sing to the Redeemer's praise.

AWAKE, my soul, in joyful lays,
And sing thy great Redeemer's praise,
He justly claims a song from thee,—
His loving-kindness, O how free!

2 He saw me ruined in the fall,
Yet loved me notwithstanding all:
He saved me from my lost estate,—
His loving-kindness, O how great!

3 When trouble, like a gloomy cloud,
Has gathered thick and thundered loud,
He near my soul has always stood,—
His loving-kindness, O how good!

4 Often I feel my sinful heart
Prone from my Saviour to depart;
But though I oft have him forgot,
His loving-kindness changes not.

5 Soon shall I pass the gloomy vale,
Soon all my mortal powers must fail:
O may my last expiring breath
His loving-kindness sing in death.

81 C. M.

Evening Hymn.

GREAT God, to thee my evening song
With gratitude I raise;
O let thy mercy tune my tongue,
And fill my heart with praise.

2 My days, unclouded as they pass,
And every fleeting hour,
Are monuments of wondrous grace,—
Of mercy, love, and power.

3 Thy love and power, celestial guard,
Preserve me from all harm:
Can danger reach me while the Lord
Extends his mighty arm?

4 Let this blest hope mine eyelids close;
With sleep refresh my frame;
Safe in thy care may I repose,
And wake to praise thy name.

82 L. M.

God, my Father.

GREAT God! and wilt thou condescend
To be my Father and my Friend?
I a poor child, and thou so high,
The Lord of earth and air and sky!

2 Art thou my Father? Then I'll be
A meek, obedient child to thee;
And try, in word and deed and thought,
To serve and please thee as I ought.

3 Art thou my Father? I'll depend
Upon the care of such a friend;
And only wish to do and be
Whatever seemeth good to thee.

4 Art thou my Father? Then, at last
When all my days on earth are past,
Send down and take me, in thy love,
To be thy better child above.

83

4 *lines* 7s.

Saints and angels ever praising God.

SONGS of praise the angels sang,
  Heaven with halleluiahs rang,
When Jehovah's work begun,
When he spake and it was done.

2 Songs of praise awoke the morn
When the Prince of Peace was born;
Songs of praise arose, when he
Captive led captivity.

3 Saints below with heart and voice,
Still in songs of praise rejoice;
Learning here, by faith and love,
Songs of praise to sing above.

4 Borne upon their latest breath,
Songs of praise shall couquer death;
Then, amid eternal joy,
Songs of praise their powers employ.

84

C. M.

Lord, teach a child to pray.

LORD, teach a little child to pray,
  Thy grace betimes impart,
And grant thy Holy Spirit may
  Renew my infant heart.

2 A fallen creature I was born,
  And from thy grace I strayed;
I must be wretched and forlorn
  Without thy mercy's aid.

3 But Christ can all my sins forgive,
  And wash away their stain,
And fit my soul with him to live,
  And in his kingdom reign.

4 To him let little children come,
  For he hath said they may;
His bosom then shall be their home,—
  Their tears he'll wipe away.

5 For all who early seek his face
Shall surely taste his love;
Jesus shall guide them by his grace,
To dwell with him above.

85 S. M.

The Song of Moses and the Lamb.

AWAKE, and sing the song
Of Moses and the Lamb;
Wake, every heart and every tongue,
To praise the Saviour's name.

2 Sing of his dying love;
Sing of his rising power;
Sing how he intercedes above
For those whose sins he bore.

3 Sing on your heavenly way,
Ye ransomed sinners sing;
Sing on, rejoicing every day
In Christ, the exalted King.

4 Soon we shall hear him say,
"Ye blessed children, come;"
Soon will he call us hence away,
And take his wanderers home.

5 Soon shall our raptured tongue
His endless praise proclaim,
And sweeter voices tune the song
Of Moses and the Lamb.

THE SAVIOUR.

86 C. M.

We owe all to Christ.

MAJESTIC sweetness sits enthroned
Upon the Saviour's brow;
His head with radiant glories crowned,
His lips with grace o'erflow.

2 He saw me plunged in deep distress,
  And flew to my relief;
For me he bore the shameful cross,
  And carried all my grief.

3 To him I owe my life and breath,
  And all the joys I have;
He makes me triumph over death,
  And saves me from the grave.

4 Since from thy bounty I receive
  Such proofs of love divine,
Had I a thousand hearts to give,
  Lord, they should all be thine.

87 C. M.

Jesus near us.

DEAR Jesus, ever at my side,
  How loving must thou be,
To leave thy home in heaven to guard
  A little child like me!

2 Thy beautiful and shining face
  I see not, though so near;
The sweetness of thy soft low voice
  I am too deaf to hear.

3 I cannot feel thee touch my hand,
  With pleasure light and mild,
To check me, as my mother does
  Her erring little child.

4 But I have felt thee in my thought,
  Fighting with sin for me;
And when my heart loves God, I know
  The sweetness is from thee.

5 And when, dear Saviour, I kneel down,
  Morning and night, to prayer,
Something there is within my heart
  Which tells me thou art there.

6 Yes, when I pray, thou prayest too;
Thy prayer is all for me;
But when I sleep thou sleepest not,
But watchest patiently.

88 8s, 7s, & 4.

Halleluiah.

O THOU God of my salvation,
My Redeemer from all sin;
Moved by thy divine compassion,
Who hast died my heart to win,
I will praise thee:
Where shall I thy praise begin?

2 Though unseen, I love the Saviour;
He hath brought salvation near;
Manifests his pard'ning favor;
And when Jesus doth appear,
Soul and body
Shall his glorious image bear.

3 While the angel choirs are crying,—
Glory to the great I AM,
I with them will still be vying—
Glory! glory to the Lamb!
O how precious
Is the sound of Jesus' name!

4 Angels now are hovering round us,
Unperceived amid the throng;
Wondering at the love that crowned us,
Glad to join the holy song:
Halleluiah!
Love and praise to Christ belong.

89 7s & 6s.

I lay my sins on Jesus.

I LAY my sins on Jesus,
The spotless Lamb of God;
He bears them all, and frees us
From the accursed load.

I bring my guilt to Jesus,
  To wash my crimson stains
White in his blood most precious,
  Till not a spot remains.

2 I lay my wants on Jesus,
  All fullness dwells in him;
He healeth my diseases,
  He doth my soul redeem.
I lay my griefs on Jesus,
  My burdens and my cares;
He from them all releases,
  He all my sorrows shares.

3 I long to be like Jesus,
  Meek, loving, lowly, mild;
I long to be like Jesus,
  The Father's holy child.
I long to be with Jesus,
  Amid the heavenly throng,
To sing with saints his praises,
  And learn the angels' song.

90 — 8 *lines* 7s.

The only refuge.

JESUS, lover of my soul,
  Let me to thy bosom fly,
While the nearer waters roll,
  While the tempest still is high;
Hide me, O my Saviour, hide,
  Till the storm of life is past;
Safe into the haven guide,
  O receive my soul at last.

2 Other refuge have I none;
  Hangs my helpless soul on thee:
Leave, O leave me not alone;
  Still support and comfort me:
All my trust on thee is stayed;
  All my help from thee I bring;
Cover my defenseless head
  With the shadow of thy wing.

3 Thou, O Christ, art all I want;
More than all in thee I find:
Raise the fallen, cheer the faint,
Heal the sick, and lead the blind.
Just and holy is thy name;
I am all unrighteousness;
False and full of sin I am;
Thou art full of truth and grace.

91 C. M.

Thy child to be.

DEAR Jesus, let thy pitying eye
Look kindly down on me;
A sinful, weak, and helpless child,
I come thy child to be.

2 O blessed Saviour, take my heart,
This sinful heart of mine,
And wash it clean in every part;
Make me a child of thine.

3 My sins, though great, thou canst forgive,
For thou hast died for me;
Amazing love! Help me, O God,
Thine own dear child to be.

4 For thou hast said, "Forbid them not;
Let children come to me;"
I hear thy voice, and now, dear Lord,
I come thy child to be.

92 4 6s & 2 8s.

Proclaim his love.

COME, every pious heart,
That loves the Saviour's name!
Your noblest powers exert
To celebrate his fame;
Tell all above and all below
The debt of love to him you owe.

2 He left his starry crown,
And laid his robes aside;
On wings of love came down,
And wept and bled and died:
What he endured no tongue can tell,
To save our souls from death and hell.

3 From the dark grave he rose,
The mansion of the dead,
And thence his mighty foes
In glorious triumph led;
Up through the sky the conqueror rode
And reigns on high, the Saviour-God.

4 From thence he'll quickly come,
His chariot will not stay,
And bear our spirits home
To realms of endless day;
There we shall see his lovely face,
And ever be in his embrace.

93 C. M.

Crown him Lord of all.

ALL hail the power of Jesus' name!
Let angels prostrate fall;
Bring forth the royal diadem,
And crown him Lord of all.

2 Crown him, ye martyrs of our God,
Who from his altar call;
Extol the stem of Jesse's rod,
And crown him Lord of all.

3 Ye chosen seed of Israel's race,
Ye ransomed from the fall,
Hail him who saves you by his grace,
And crown him Lord of all.

4 Sinners, whose love can ne'er forget
The wormwood and the gall,
Go spread your trophies at his feet,
And crown him Lord of all

5 Let every kindred, every tribe,
On this terrestrial ball,
To him all majesty ascribe,
And crown him Lord of all.

94

8s, 7s, & 4.

The Good Shepherd.

SAVIOUR, like a shepherd lead us;
Much we need thy tender care;
In thy pleasant pastures feed us,
For our use thy folds prepare.
Blessed Jesus!
Thou hast bought us, thine we are.

2 We are thine; do thou befriend us,
Be the guardian of our way;
Keep thy flock, from sin defend us,
Seek us when we go astray.
Blessed Jesus!
Hear young children when they pray.

3 Thou hast promised to receive us,
Poor and sinful though we be;
Thou hast mercy to relieve us,
Grace to cleanse and power to free.
Blessed Jesus!
Let us early turn to thee.

4 Early let us seek thy favor,
Early let us do thy will;
Holy Lord, our only Saviour,
With thy grace our bosom fill.
Blessed Jesus!
Thou hast loved us, love us still.

95

7s & 6s.

The glory of his kingdom.

HAIL to the Lord's anointed,
Great David's greater Son!
Hail, in the time appointed,
His reign on earth begun!

He comes to break oppression,
  To set the captive free;
To take away transgression,
  And rule in equity.

2 He comes, with succor speedy
  To those who suffer wrong;
To help the poor and needy,
  And bid the weak be strong;
To give them songs for sighing,
  Their darkness turn to light,
Whose souls, condemned and dying,
  Were precious in his sight.

3 He shall descend like showers
  Upon the fruitful earth,
And love and joy, like flowers,
  Spring in his path to birth;
Before him, on the mountains,
  Shall peace, the herald, go,
And righteousness, in fountains,
  From hill to valley flow.

4 To him shall prayer unceasing,
  And daily vows ascend;
His kingdom still increasing,
  A kingdom without end;
The tide of time shall never
  His covenant remove;
His name shall stand forever;
  That name to us is Love.

96

8s, 7s, & 4.

Hosanna.

ONCE was heard the song of children
  By the Saviour when on earth;
Joyful in the sacred temple
  Shouts of youthful praise had birth,
    And hosannas
  Loud to David's Son broke forth.

2 Palms of victory strewn around him,
Garments spread beneath his feet,
Prophet of the Lord they crowned him,
In fair Salem's crowded street;
With hosannas,
Him the lips of children greet.

3 Blessed Saviour, now triumphant,
Glorified and throned on high,
Mortal lays, from man or infant,
Vain to tell thy praise essay;
But hosannas
Swell the chorus of the sky.

4 God o'er all in heaven reigning,
We this day thy glory sing;
Not with palms thy pathway strewing,
We would loftier tribute bring:
Glad hosannas
To our Prophet, Priest, and King.

5 O, though humble is our off'ring,
Deign accept our grateful lays;
These from children once proceeding
Thou didst deem "perfected praise."
Now hosannas,
Saviour, Lord, to thee we raise.

97 L. M.

Hosanna to the Son of David.

WHAT are those soul-reviving strains
Which echo thus from Salem's plains?
What anthems loud, and louder still,
So sweetly sound from Zion's hill?

2 Lo! 'tis an infant chorus sings
Hosanna to the King of kings;
The Saviour comes! and babes proclaim
Salvation, sent in Jesus' name.

3 Nor these alone their voice shall raise,
For we will join this song of praise;
Still Israel's children forward press
To hail the Lord their righteousness

4 Messiah's name shall joy impart
Alike to Jew and Gentile heart;
He bled for us, he bled for you,
And we will sing hosanna too.

5 Proclaim hosannas loud and clear,
See David's Son and Lord appear!
All praise on earth to him be given,
And glory shout through highest heaven.

98 S. M.

Attachment to the Church.

I LOVE thy kingdom, Lord,
  The house of thine abode,
The Church our blest Redeemer saved
  With his own precious blood.

2 I love thy Church, O God;
  Her walls before thee stand,
Dear as the apple of thine eye,
  And graven on thy hand.

3 For her my tears shall fall;
  For her my prayers ascend;
To her my cares and toils be given,
  Till toils and cares shall end.

4 Beyond my highest joy
  I prize her heavenly ways,
Her sweet communion, solemn vows,
  Her hymns of love and praise.

5 Jesus, thou Friend divine,
  Our Saviour and our King,
Thy hand, from every snare and foe,
  Shall great deliverance bring.

6 Sure as thy truth shall last,
  To Zion shall be given
The brightest glories earth can yield,
  And brighter bliss of heaven.

99 4 6s & 2 8s.

Christ a Prophet, Priest, and King.

JOIN all the glorious names
  Of wisdom, love, and power,
That ever mortals knew,
  Or angels ever bore:
All are too mean to speak his worth,
Too mean to set the Saviour forth.

2 Great Prophet of our God,
  Our tongues shall bless thy name;
By thee the joyful news
  Of our salvation came;
The joyful news of sins forgiven,
Of hell subdued, and peace with heaven.

3 Jesus, our great High Priest,
  Has shed his blood and died;
Our guilty conscience needs
  No sacrifice beside:
His precious blood did once atone,
And now it pleads before the throne.

4 O thou almighty Lord,
  Our Conqu'ror and our King,
Thy scepter and thy sword,
  Thy reigning grace, we sing.
Thine is the power; O make us sit
In willing bonds beneath thy feet.

100 C. M.

The children's Friend.

THOU guardian of our youthful days,
  To thee our prayers ascend;
To thee we'll tune our songs of praise,
  Jesus, the children's Friend.

2 From thee our daily mercies flow,
  Our life and health descend;
O save our souls from sin and woe:
  Thou art the children's Friend.

3 Teach us to prize thy holy Word,
And to its truths attend;
Thus shall we learn to fear the Lord,
And love the children's Friend.

4 O may we feel a Saviour's love,
To him our souls commend,
Who left his glorious home above
To be the children's Friend.

5 Lord, draw our youthful hearts to thee,
And when this life shall end,
Raise us to live above the sky
With thee, the children's Friend.

101 L. M.

The highway of holiness.

JESUS, my all, to heaven is gone,
He, whom I fix my hopes upon;
His track I see, and I'll pursue
The narrow way till him I view.

2 The way the holy prophets went,
The road that leads from banishment,
The King's highway of holiness,
I'll go, for all his paths are peace.

3 This is the way I long have sought,
And mourned because I found it not;
My grief a burden long has been,
Because I was not saved from sin.

4 The more I strove against its power,
I felt its weight and guilt the more;
Till late I heard my Saviour say,
Come hither, soul, I am the way.

5 Lo! glad I come; and thou, blest Lamb,
Shalt take me to thee as I am;
Nothing but sin have I to give,
Nothing but love shall I receive.

6 Then will I tell to sinners round
What a dear Saviour I have found;
I'll point to thy redeeming blood,
And say, Behold the way to God.

102 C. M.

The precious Name.

HOW sweet the name of Jesus sounds
In a believer's ear!
It soothes his sorrows, heals his wounds,
And drives away his fear.

2 It makes the wounded spirit whole,
And calms the troubled breast;
'Tis manna to the hungry soul,
And to the weary, rest.

3 Dear Name, the rock on which I build,
My shield and hiding-place;
My never-failing treasure, filled
With boundless stores of grace;

4 Jesus, my Shepherd, Saviour, Friend,
My Prophet, Priest, and King,
My Lord, my Life, my Way, my End,
Accept the praise I bring.

5 I would thy boundless love proclaim
With every fleeting breath;
So shall the music of thy name
Refresh my soul in death.

103 4 8s & 2 6s.

For power over temptation.

HELP, Lord, to whom for help I fly,
And still my tempted soul stand by
Throughout the evil day;
The sacred watchfulness impart,
And keep the issues of my heart,
And stir me up to pray.

2 My soul with thy whole armor arm;
In each approach of sin, alarm,
And show the danger near:
Surround, sustain, and strengthen me,
And fill with godly jealousy
And sanctifying fear.

3 Whene'er my careless hands hang down
O let me see thy gathering frown,
And feel thy warning eye;
And starting, cry, from ruin's brink,
Save, Jesus, or I yield, I sink;
O save me, or I die.

4 If near the pit I rashly stray,
Before I wholly fall away,
The keen conviction dart;
Recall me by that pitying look,
That kind, upbraiding glance, which broke
Unfaithful Peter's heart.

5 In me thine utmost mercy show,
And make me, like thyself below,
Unblamable in grace;
Ready prepared and fitted here,
By perfect holiness, to' appear
Before thy glorious face.

104 S. M.

The Lord, my Shepherd.

THE Lord my Shepherd is;
I shall be well supplied;
Since he is mine and I am his,
What can I want beside?

2 He leads me to the place
Where heavenly pasture grows,
Where living waters gently pass,
And full salvation flows.

3 If e'er I go astray,
He doth my soul reclaim,
And guides me in his own right way,
For his most holy name.

4 While he affords his aid,
I cannot yield to fear;
Though I should walk through death's dark shade,
My Shepherd's with me there.

105 L. M.

Jesus reigns.

COME, let us tune our loftiest song,
And raise to Christ our joyful strain;
Worship and thanks to him belong,
Who reigns, and shall forever reign.

2 His sovereign power our bodies made;
Our souls are his immortal breath;
And when his creatures sinned, he bled
To save us from eternal death.

3 Burn every breast with Jesus' love;
Bound every heart with rapturous joy;
And saints on earth, with saints above,
Your voices in his praise employ.

4 Extol the Lamb with loftiest song,
Ascend for him our cheerful strain;
Worship and thanks to him belong,
Who reigns, and shall forever reign.

106 7s, 8s, & 6s.

Like Jesus.

I WANT to be like Jesus,
So lowly and so meek;
For no one marked an angry word
That ever heard him speak.
I want to be like Jesus,
So frequently in prayer;
Alone upon the mountain-top
He met his Father there.

2 I want to be like Jesus;
I never, never find
That he, though persecuted, was
To any one unkind.
I want to be like Jesus,
Engaged in doing good,
So that of me it may be said,
"She hath done what she could."

3 I want to be like Jesus,
So lowly and so meek;
For no one marked an angry word
That ever heard him speak.
Alas! I'm not like Jesus,
As any one may see;
O gentle Saviour, send thy grace,
And make me like to thee.

107

4 *lines* 7s.

My Shepherd.

TO thy pastures green and fair,
Saviour, let a child repair:
I will never stray from thee,
But thy fold my home shall be.

CHORUS.—I will never stray from thee,
But thy fold my home shall be.
I will never, never stray from thee,
But thy fold my home shall be.

2 Like a gentle lamb, I'll stay
In the meadows fresh and gay;
Peaceful and contented there,
Guarded by my Shepherd's care.
CHORUS.—I will never stray, etc.

3 By the waters still and clear
I shall wander without fear:
Happy by my Shepherd's side,
All my wants shall be supplied.
CHORUS.—I will never stray, etc.

4 Lord, wilt thou my Shepherd be?
Help me then to follow thee;
At thy feet myself I cast,
Thee to serve while life shall last.

CHORUS—I will never stray, etc.

108

8s, 7s, & 4.

"My son, give me thine heart."

WELCOME, welcome, dear Redeemer,
Welcome to this heart of mine;
Lord, I make a full surrender,
Every power and thought be thine;
Thine entirely,
Through eternal ages thine.

2 Known to all to be thy mansion,
Earth and hell will disappear;
Or in vain attempt possession
When they find the Lord is near:
Shout, O Zion!
Shout, ye saints, the Lord is here!

109

4 *lines* 7s.

"Lovest thou me?"

HARK, my soul! it is the Lord;
'Tis the Saviour; hear his word:
Jesus speaks, and speaks to thee:
"Say, poor sinner, lov'st thou me?

2 "I delivered thee when bound,
And, when wounded, healed thy wound,
Sought thee wandering, set thee right,
Turned thy darkness into light.

3 "Can a woman's tender care
Cease toward the child she bare?
Yes, she may forgetful be;
Yet will I remember thee.

4 "Mine is an unchanging love,
Higher than the heights above.
Deeper than the depths beneath,
Free and faithful, strong as death.

5 "Thou shalt see my glory soon,
When the work of grace is done;
Partner of my throne shalt be:
Say, poor sinner, lov'st thou me?"

6 Lord, it is my chief complaint,
That my love's so weak and faint;
Yet I love thee, and adore;
O for grace to love thee more!

110

7s, 4s, & 6.

Seeking Christ's care.

SAVIOUR, listen to our prayer,
Poor and sinful though we are;
Guilt-confessing,
Give thy blessing,
Grant us thy loving care.

CHORUS.

O God, our Father, Christ, our King,
Now to thee our hearts we bring;
Keep them ever,
Blessed Saviour,
Till in heaven thy love we sing.

2 Strength is thine; we often stray
From thy pure and holy way;
Wilt thou guide us,
Walk beside us,
Nearer every day?
CHORUS.—O God, our Father, etc.

3 Then may we, when life is o'er,
Stand with thee on yonder shore:
Freed from sinning,
Heaven winning,
Praising evermore.
CHORUS.—O God, our Father, etc.

111

8s & 7s.

Jesus reigns.

HARK! ten thousand harps and voices
  Sound the note of praise above;
Jesus reigns, and heaven rejoices;
  Jesus reigns, the God of love.
See, he sits on yonder throne!
Jesus rules the world alone.
  Halleluiah, Amen!

2 Jesus, hail! whose glory brightens
  All above, and gives it worth:
Lord of love, thy smile enlightens,
  Cheers and charms thy saints on earth:
When we think of love like thine,
Lord, we own it love divine.

3 King of glory, reign forever,
  Thine an everlasting crown;
Nothing from thy love shall sever
  Those whom thou hast made thine own,
Happy objects of thy grace,
Chosen to behold thy face.

4 Saviour, hasten thine appearing,
  Bring, O bring the glorious day
When, the awful summons hearing,
  Heaven and earth shall pass away!
Then with golden harps we'll sing
Glory, glory to our King!

112

11s & 10s.

Shepherd of Israel.

O TELL me, thou life and delight of my soul,
  Where the flock of thy pasture are feeding;
I seek thy protection, I need thy control,
  I would go where my Shepherd is leading.

2 O tell me the place where thy flock are at rest,
  Where the noontide will find them reposing;
The tempest now rages, my soul is distressed,
  And the pathway of peace I am losing.

3 O why should I stray with the flocks of thy foes,
'Mid the desert where now they are roving,
Where hunger and thirst, where affliction and woes
And temptations, their ruin are proving?

4 O when shall my foes and my wanderings cease,
And the follies that fill me with weeping?
Thou Shepherd of Israel, restore me that peace
Thou dost give to the flock thou art keeping.

5 A voice from the Shepherd now bids thee return
By the way where the footprints are lying;
No longer to wander, no longer to mourn,
O lost one, now homeward be flying.

113 C. M.

Crown Jesus Lord of all.

COME, children, hail the Prince of peace,
Obey the Saviour's call;
Come, seek his face and taste his grace,
And crown him Lord of all.

2 Ye lambs of Christ your tribute bring,
Ye children great and small,
Hosanna sing to Christ your King;
O crown him Lord of all.

3 This Jesus will your sins forgive;
O haste! before him fall;
For you he died, that you might live
To crown him Lord of all.

4 All hail the Saviour, Prince of peace!
Let saints before him fall;
Let sinners seek his pard'ning grace,
And crown him Lord of all.

114 7s & 6s.

The need of Jesus.

I NEED thee, precious Jesus,
For I am full of sin;
My soul is dark and guilty,
My heart is dead within.

I need the cleansing fountain,
  Where I can always flee;
The blood of Christ most precious,
  The sinner's perfect plea.

2 I need thee, precious Jesus,
  For I am very poor;
A stranger and a pilgrim,
  I have no earthly store.
I need the love of Jesus
  To cheer me on my way,
To guide my doubting footsteps,
  To be my strength and stay.

3 I need thee, precious Jesus,
  I need a friend like thee;
A friend to soothe and sympathize,
  A friend to care for me.
I need the heart of Jesus
  To feel each anxious care,
To tell my every want,
  And all my sorrows share.

4 I need thee, precious Jesus,
  And hope to see thee soon,
Encircled with the rainbow,
  And seated on thy throne.
There with thy blood-bought children,
  My joy shall ever be,
To sing thy praises, Jesus,
  To gaze, my Lord, on thee.

115

4 8s & 2 6s.

Excellency of Christ.

O COULD we speak the matchless worth,
O could we sound the glories forth,
  Which in our Saviour shine,
We'd soar, and touch the heavenly strings,
And vie with Gabriel, while he sings
  In notes almost divine.

2 We'd sing the precious blood he spilt,
Our ransom from the dreadful guilt
Of sin and wrath divine;
We'd sing his glorious righteousness,
In which all-perfect heavenly dress
We shall forever shine.

3 We'd sing the characters he bears,
And all the forms of love he wears,
Exalted on his throne;
In loftiest songs of sweetest praise,
We would, to everlasting days,
Make all his glories known.

4 Well, the delightful day will come
When our dear Lord will bring us home,
And we shall see his face:
Then with our Saviour, Brother, Friend,
A blest eternity we'll spend,
Triumphant in his grace.

116 4 6s & 2 8s.

Christ seen of angels.

O YE immortal throng
Of angels round the throne,
Join with our feeble song
To make the Saviour known;
On earth ye knew his wondrous grace,
In heaven ye view his beauteous face.

2 Ye saw the holy child
In human flesh arrayed,
Supremely meek and mild,
While in the manger laid;
And praise to God and peace on earth,
Proclaimed aloud for such a birth.

3 Around the bloody tree
Ye pressed with strong desire,
That wondrous sight to see,
The Lord of life expire:
And could your eyes have known a tear,
In sad surprise had dropped it there.

4 Around his sacred tomb
  A willing watch ye keep,
Till the blest moment come
  To rouse him from his sleep:
Then rolled the stone, and all adored
With joy unknown your rising Lord.

5 When all arrayed in light
  The shining Conqu'ror rode,
Ye hailed his rapturous flight
  Up to the throne of God,
And waved your golden wings around,
And struck your strings of sweetest sound.

117

8 *lines* 7s.

Chiefest among ten thousand.

Tune.—"*Watchman, tell us of the night.*"

LORD of earth, thy forming hand
  Well this beauteous frame hath planned:
Woods that wave, and hills that tower,
Ocean rolling in its power;
Yet amid this scene so fair,
Should I cease thy smile to share,
What were all its joys to me?
Whom have I on earth but thee?

2 Lord of heaven, beyond our sight
Shines a world of purer light;
There, in love's unclouded reign,
Parted hands shall meet again:
O that world is passing fair!
Yet if thou wert absent there
What were all its joys to me?
Whom have I in heaven but thee?

3 Lord of earth and heaven, my breast
Seeks in thee its only rest;
I was lost; thy accents mild
Homeward lured thy wandering child:

O, should once thy smile divine
Cease upon my soul to shine,
What were earth or heaven to me?
Whom have I in each but thee?

118 S. M.

Thy way, not mine.

THY way, not mine, O Lord,
  However dark it be!
Lead me by thine own loving hand,
  Choose out the path for me.

2 Smooth let it be or rough,
  It will be still the best:
Winding or straight, it matters not,
  It leads me to thy rest.

3 I dare not choose my lot;
  I could not if I might;
Choose thou for me, my Saviour, God,
  So shall I walk aright.

4 Choose thou for me my friends,
  My sickness or my health;
Choose thou, my Lord, my cares for me,
  My poverty or wealth.

5 Not mine, not mine the choice,
  In things or great or small;
Be thou my guide, my shield, my strength,
  My wisdom, and my all.

6 The kingdom that I seek
  Is thine: so let the way
That leads to it be also thine,
  Else I must surely stray.

7 Take thou my cup, and it
  With joy or sorrow fill;
Mingle as best to thee may seem;
  Choose thou my good and ill.

119

8s, 7s, & 4.

Praise the Saviour.

PRAISE the Lord who died to save us;
Praise his name forever dear;
Praise his blessed name, who gave us
Eyes to see and ears to hear:
Praise the Saviour,
Object of our love and fear.

2 Grace it was, 'twas grace abounding
Brought him down to save the lost;
Ye above his throne surrounding,
Praise him, praise him, all his host:
Saints adore him!
Ye are they who owe him most.

3 Ye, of all his hand created,
Objects are of grace alone;
Aliens once, but reinstated,
Destined now to fill a throne;
Sing with wonder,
Sing of what our Lord hath done.

4 Praise his name who died to save us,
'Tis by him his people live;
And in him the Father gave us
All that boundless love could give:
Life eternal
In our Saviour we receive.

120

4 *lines* 11s.

A firm foundation.

HOW firm a foundation, ye saints of the Lord,
Is laid for your faith in his excellent word:
What more can he say than to you he hath said,
Who unto the Saviour for refuge have fled.

2 Fear not, I am with ye; O be not dismayed,
For I am thy God, and will still give thee aid:
I'll strengthen thee, help thee, and cause thee to stand,
Uphold by my righteous, omnipotent hand.

3 When through the deep waters I call thee to go,
The rivers of sorrow shall not overflow;
For I will be with thee thy trials to bless,
And sanctify to thee thy deepest distress.

4 The soul that on Jesus hath leaned for repose,
I will not, I will not desert to his foes:
That soul, though all hell should endeavor to shake,
I'll never—no, never—no, never forsake.

121 L. M.

The King of Salem.

WHEN Jordan hushed his waters still,
And silence slept on Zion's hill;
When Bethlehem's shepherds through the night
Watched o'er their flocks by starry light;

2 Hark! from the midnight hills around,
A voice of more than mortal sound
In distant halleluiahs stole,
Wild murmuring o'er the raptured soul.

3 On wheels of light, on wings of flame,
The glorious hosts of Zion came;
High heaven with songs of triumph rung,
While thus they struck their harps and sung:

4 "O Zion, lift thy raptured eye,
The long expected hour is nigh;
Renewed creation smiles again,
The Prince of Salem comes to reign.

5 "He comes to cheer the trembling heart,
Bid Satan and his host depart;
Again the Day-star gilds the gloom,
Again the bowers of Eden bloom."

122 S. M.

Jacob's Ladder.

WHAT doth the ladder mean,
Sent down from the Most High?
Fastened to earth its foot is seen,
Its summit to the sky.

Lo! up and down the scale
  The angels swiftly move;
And God, the great Invisible,
  Himself appears above!

2 Jesus that ladder is,
  The incarnate Deity,
Partaker of celestial bliss
  And human misery.
Sent from his high abode,
  To sleeping mortals given;
He stands, and man unites to God,
  And earth connects with heaven.

3 Redeemer of mankind,
  Who on thy name rely,
A constant intercourse we find
  Opened 'twixt earth and sky.
Mercy, and grace, and peace,
  Descend through thee alone;
And thou dost all our services
  Present before the throne.

4 On us thy Father's love
  Is for thy sake bestowed;
Thou art our Advocate above,
  Thou art our way to God:
Our way to God we trace,
  And through thy name forgiven,
From step to step, from grace to grace,
  On thee we climb to heaven.

123

6 lines 7s.

Faithful Shepherd.

FAITHFUL Shepherd, meek and mild;
  To thy pastures lead a child,
Where the tender verdure grows,
Where the peaceful streamlet flows.
Where thy flock, from danger free,
Hear thy voice, and follow thee.

2 There, beneath thy watchful eye,
They are safe, though danger's nigh;
There enfolded in thy arms,
They can smile at rude alarms;
Though a host their way oppose,
Thou wilt save them from their foes.

3 When the vale of grief they tread,
Thou dost mark the tears they shed;
By their side in pity stand,
Dry the tear with tender hand;
Gently quell the rising fear,
Make it sweet to suffer there.

4 Faithful Shepherd, meek and mild,
To thy pastures lead a child;
Weak and helpless, Lord, I am,
Gather in a wandering lamb;
Lest from thee I further stray,
Take me to thy fold, I pray.

124 8s & 7s.

The Friend above all others.

ONE there is above all others
  Well deserves the name of Friend;
His is love beyond a brother's,
  Costly, free, and knows no end.

2 Which of all our friends, to save us,
  Could or would have shed his blood
But the Saviour died to have us
  Reconciled in him to God.

3 When he lived on earth abased,
  Friend of sinners was his name
Now, above all glory raised,
  He rejoices in the same.

4 O for grace our hearts to soften!
  Teach us, Lord, at length to love,
We, alas! forget too often
  What a friend we have above.

125

4 6s & 2 8s.

Proclaiming the universal Saviour.

LET earth and heaven agree,
Angels and men be joined,
To celebrate with me
The Saviour of mankind:
To' adore the all-atoning Lamb,
And bless the sound of Jesus' name.

2 Jesus! transporting sound!
The joy of earth and heaven;
No other help is found,
No other name is given,
By which we can salvation have;
But Jesus came the world to save.

3 Jesus! harmonious name!
It charms the hosts above;
They evermore proclaim,
And wonder at his love:
'Tis all their happiness to gaze,
'Tis heaven to see our Saviour's face.

4 His name the sinner hears,
And is from sin set free;
'Tis music in his ears;
'Tis life and victory;
New songs do now his lips employ,
And dances his glad heart for joy.

126

4 *lines* 11s.

The Lord my Shepherd.

THE Lord is my Shepherd, how happy am I!
How tender and watchful my wants to supply!
He daily provides me with raiment and food;
Whate'er he denies me is meant for my good.

2 The Lord is my Shepherd, then I must obey
His gracious commandments, and walk in his way;
His fear he will teach me, my heart he'll renew,
And though I'm so sinful, my sins he'll subdue.

3 The Lord is my Shepherd, how happy am I!
I'm blest when I live, and I'm blest when I die;
In death's gloomy valley no evil I'll dread,
"For I will be with thee," my Shepherd has said.

4 The Lord is my Shepherd, I'll sing with delight,
Till called to adore him in regions of light;
Then praise him with angels to bright harps of gold,
And ever and ever his glory behold.

127

6s & 5s.

Praise to Christ.

JESUS, high in glory,
Lend a listening ear;
When we bow before thee,
Infant praises hear.

2 We are little children,
Weak and apt to stray;
Saviour, guide and keep us
In the heavenly way.

3 Save us, Lord, from sinning,
Watch us day by day;
Help us now to love thee,
Take our sins away.

4 Then when Jesus calls us
To our heavenly home,
We will answer gladly,
"Saviour, Lord, we come."

128

4 *lines* 11s.

Christ our friend.

HOW loving is Jesus who came from the sky,
In tenderest pity for sinners to die;
His hands and his feet were nailed to the tree,
And all this he suffered for you and for me.

2 How precious is Jesus to all who believe,
And out of his fullness what grace they receive:
When weak he supports them, when erring he guides,
And everything needful he kindly provides.

3 O give then to Jesus your earliest days;
They only are blessed who walk in his ways:
In life and in death he will still be your Friend,
For whom Jesus loveth, he loves to the end.

HIS DEATH FOR US.

129 4 lines 11s.

The Lamb that was slain.

IN the far better land of glory and light
The ransomed are singing in garments of white;
The harpers are harping, and all the bright train
Sing the song of Redemption, the Lamb that was slain.

2 Like the sound of the sea swells their chorus of praise,
Round the star-circled crown of the Ancient of days,
And thrones and dominions re-echo the strain
Of Glory eternal to Him that was slain.

3 Dear Saviour, may we, with our voices so faint,
Sing the chorus celestial with angel and saint?
Yes! yes! we will sing, and thine ear we will gain
With the song of Redemption the Lamb that was slain.

4 Now children and teachers and friends all unite
In a loud halleluiah with the ransomed in light;
To Jesus we'll sing that melodious strain
The song of Redemption, the Lamb that was slain.

130 C. M.

Bought with a price.

ALAS! and did my Saviour bleed?
And did my sovereign die?
Would he devote that sacred head
For such a worm as I?

2 Was it for crimes that I had done
He groaned upon the tree?
Amazing pity! grace unknown!
And love beyond degree!

3 Well might the sun in darkness hide,
And shut his glories in,
When God, the mighty Maker, died
For man the creature's sin.

4 Thus might I hide my blushing face
While his dear cross appears,
Dissolve my heart in thankfulness,
And melt mine eyes to tears.

5 But drops of grief can ne'er repay
The debt of love I owe:
Here, Lord, I give myself away;
'Tis all that I can do.

131 C. M.

Our ever-present Guide.

JESUS, the Lord of glory, died,
That we might never die;
And now he reigns supreme, to guide
His people to the sky.

2 Weak though we are, he still is near,
To lead, console, defend;
In all our sorrow, all our fear,
Our all-sufficient Friend.

3 From His high throne in bliss, he deigns
Our every prayer to heed;
Bears with our folly, soothes our pains
Supplies our every need.

4 And from his love's exhaustless spring
Joys like a river come,
To make the desert bloom and sing
O'er which we travel home.

5 O Jesus, there is none like thee,
Our Saviour and our Lord.
Through earth and heaven exalted be,
Beloved, obeyed, adored.

132 C. M.

He died for thee.

BEHOLD the Saviour of mankind
Nailed to the shameful tree;
How vast the love that him inclined
To bleed and die for thee!

2 Hark! how he groans, while nature shakes,
And earth's strong pillars bend:
The temple's vail in sunder breaks,
The solid marbles rend.

3 'Tis done! the precious ransom's paid!
Receive my soul! he cries:
See where he bows his sacred head,
He bows his head, and dies.

4 But soon he'll break death's envious chain,
And in full glory shine:
O Lamb of God, was ever pain,
Was ever love, like thine?

133 8s, 4s, & 4.

He pleads his death.

CHILDREN, hear the melting story
Of the Lamb that once was slain;
'Tis the Lord of life and glory:
Shall he plead with you in vain?
O receive him,
And salvation now obtain.

2 Yield no more to sin and folly,
So displeasing in his sight:
Jesus loves the pure and holy;
They alone are his delight:
Seek his favor,
And your hearts to him unite.

3 All your sins to him confessing
Who is ready to forgive,
Seek the Saviour's richest blessing,
On his precious name believe;
He is waiting:
Will you not his grace receive?

134 7s & 6s.

The Author of salvation.

THE Author of salvation,
The Saviour, meek and mild,
Once took a lowly station,
Became a little child;
In infancy a stranger,
How mean was his abode!
His cradle was a manger,
Himself the Son of God.

2 His earthly parents found him
Submissive day by day;
So meek to all around him,
So ready to obey;
No stain of sin or folly
Could ever cloud his brow;
His heart, so pure and holy,
With love would ever glow.

3 And when his foes assailed him,
He sought but to forgive;
When to the cross they nailed him
He died that they might live.
This bright example shows us
What duties to fulfill;
O let it now arouse us
To learn and do his will.

135 L. M.

Glorying only in the cross.

WHEN I survey the wondrous cross
On which the Prince of glory died,
My richest gain I count but loss,
And pour contempt on all my pride.

2 Forbid it, Lord, that I should boast,
Save in the death of Christ, my God;
All the vain things that charm me most,
I sacrifice them to his blood.

3 See, from his head, his hands, his feet,
Sorrow and love flow mingled down:
Did e'er such love and sorrow meet,
Or thorns compose so rich a crown?

4 Were the whole realm of nature mine,
That were a present far too small;
Love so amazing, so divine,
Demands my soul, my life, my all.

136 7s & 6s.

The precious story.

HOW precious is the story
Of our Redeemer's birth,
Who left the realms of glory,
And came to dwell on earth!
He saw our sad condition,
Our guilt and sin and shame;
To save us from perdition
The blessed Jesus came.

2 He came to earth from heaven,
To weep and bleed and die,
That we might be forgiven,
And raised to God on high.
His kindness and compassion
To children then were shown;
The heirs of his salvation,
He claimed them for his own.

3 O may I love this Saviour,
So good, so kind, so mild!
And may I find his favor,
A young but sinful child!
And in his blissful heaven
May I at last appear,
With all my sins forgiven,
To know and praise him there.

137 C. M.

Agony in the garden.

DARK was the night, and cold the ground
  On which the Lord was laid;
His sweat, like drops of blood, ran down;
  In agony he prayed:

2 "Father, remove this bitter cup,
  If such thy sacred will;
If not, content to drink it up,
  Thy pleasure I fulfill."

3 Go to the garden, sinner; see
  Those precious drops that flow;
The heavy load he bore for thee;
  For thee he lies so low.

4 Then learn of him the cross to bear;
  Thy Father's will obey;
And when temptations press thee near,
  Awake to watch and pray.

138 C. M.

Sufficiency of the atonement.

THERE is a fountain filled with blood,
  Drawn from Immanuel's veins;
And sinners, plunged beneath that flood,
  Lose all their guilty stains.

2 The dying thief rejoiced to see
  That fountain in his day;
O, may I there, though vile as he,
  Wash all my sins away.

3 Thou dying Lamb, thy precious blood
  Shall never lose its power,
Till all the ransomed Church of God
  Are saved, to sin no more.

4 E'er since, by faith, I saw the stream
  Thy flowing wounds supply,
Redeeming love has been my theme,
  And shall be, till I die.

5 And when this feeble, faltering tongue
  Lies silent in the grave,
Then, in a nobler, sweeter song,
  I'll sing thy power to save.

139 6 *lines* 7s.

Come and welcome.

FROM the cross uplifted high,
  Where the Saviour deigns to die,
What melodious sounds we hear,
Bursting on the ravished ear!
"Love's redeeming work is done;
Come and welcome, sinner, come.

2 "Sprinkled now with blood the throne,
Why beneath thy burdens groan?
On my piercèd body laid,
Justice owns the ransom paid:
Bow the knee, embrace the Son;
Come and welcome, sinner, come.

3 "Spread for thee, the festal board
See with richest dainties stored;
To thy Father's bosom pressed,
Yet again a child confessed,
Never from his house to roam,
Come and welcome, sinner, come.

4 "Soon the days of life shall end;
Lo, I come, your Saviour, Friend,
Safe your spirits to convey
To the realms of endless day;
Up to my eternal home,
Come and welcome, sinner, come."

140 C. M.

Voice from the Cross.

I SAW One hanging on a tree,
  In agony and blood,
Who fixed his languid eyes on me,
  As near the cross I stood.

2 Sure, never till my latest breath,
Can I forget that look;
It seemed to charge me with his death,
Though not a word he spoke.

3 Alas! I knew not what I did,
But now my tears are vain;
Where shall my trembling soul be hid?
For I the Lord have slain.

4 A second look he gave, that said,
"I freely all forgive;
This blood is for thy ransom paid,
I die, that thou may'st live."

141

6s & 4s.

Gethsemane.—TUNE, *I'm but a Traveler here.*

WITHIN the olive shade
The Saviour see,
As there he knelt and prayed,
My soul, for thee;
While cold and damp midnight,
Pale moon and dim starlight,
Beheld thy strange, sad sight,
Gethsemane!

2 Even the faithful fail
Vigils to keep;
They sink behind the vail
Of weary sleep.
Jesus is left alone,
Bowed on dark earth and stone,
And thou dost hear his moan,
Gethsemane!

3 Why is my Saviour there
In tears and cries?
Under a burdening prayer,
In groans and sighs?

While sorrow's dread control
O'erwhelms his holy soul,
His blood to thee doth roll,
Gethsemane!

4 Ah! there he took the cup
His Father gave,
Resigned, he drank it up,
My soul to save!
The world's deep guilt and hate,
Heart-crushing load so great,
How death-like was its weight,
Gethsemane!

5 Garden of love and woe,
How dear to me!
I oft in spirit go,
Jesus to see,
Who gives me heavenly aid
To pray as there he prayed,
Within thy sacred shade,
Gethsemane!

142 L. M.

In the garden.

'TIS midnight; and on Olive's brow
The star is dimmed that lately shone;
'Tis midnight; in the garden now,
The suffering Saviour prays alone.

2 'Tis midnight; and from all removed,
The Saviour wrestles lone with fears;
E'en that disciple whom he loved
Heeds not his Master's grief and tears.

3 'Tis midnight; and for others' guilt
The Man of sorrows weeps in blood;
Yet he that hath in anguish knelt,
Is not forsaken by his God.

4 'Tis midnight; and from ether-plains
Is borne the song that angels know;
Unheard by mortals are the strains
That sweetly soothe the Saviour's woe.

143

8s, 7s, & 4.

It is finished.

HARK! the voice of love and mercy
Sounds aloud from Calvary;
See, it rends the rocks asunder,
Shakes the earth and vails the sky!
"It is finished!"
Hear the dying Saviour cry.

2 "It is finished!" O, what pleasure
Do these precious words afford!
Heavenly blessings without measure
Flow to us from Christ, the Lord;
"It is finished!"
Saints, the dying words record.

3 Finished; all the types and shadows
Of the ceremonial law;
Finished; all that God had promised;
Death and hell no more shall awe:
"It is finished!"
Saints, from hence your comforts draw.

4 Tune your harps anew, ye seraphs,
Join to sing the pleasing theme;
All on earth and all in heaven,
Join to praise Immanuel's name;
Halleluiah!
Glory to the bleeding Lamb!

144

4 *lines* 11s.

A Fountain never dry.

O THERE is a fountain that never is dry,
The wounds of Immanuel that fountain supply:
From ages to ages the crimson stream flows,
To cleanse the polluted and lighten their woes.

2 'Tis there in his childhood a sinner may go,
And manhood may wash till he's whiter than snow;
And age, by his sins and his sorrows oppressed,
May find in the wounds of the Saviour a rest.

3 No vileness too vile for that fount to remove,
No sinner too sinful its virtues to prove;
If conscience reproaches, if terrors appall,
'Twas opened for you, for 'twas opened for all.

4 Then come to the fountain so gushing and red;
A tempest of wrath mutters over your head,
And the moments of mercy are passing away:
Then come to the fountain, poor sinner, to-day.

145

7s & 6s

To the Saviour crucified.

O SACRED Head, now wounded,
With grief and shame weighed down,
Now scornfully surrounded
With thorns, thy only crown;
O sacred head, what glory,
What bliss till now was thine!
Yet, though despised and gory,
I joy to call thee mine.

2 O noblest brow and dearest,
In other days, the world
All feared when thou appearedst,
What shame on thee is hurled!
How art thou pale with anguish,
With sore abuse and scorn;
How does that visage languish
Which once was bright as morn!

3 What language shall I borrow
To thank thee, dearest Friend,
For this thy dying sorrow,
Thy pity without end?
O make me thine forever;
And should I fainting be,
Lord, let me never, never,
Outlive my love to thee.

4 Be near me when I'm dying;
O show thy cross to me,
And for my succor flying,
Come, Lord, to set me free.
These eyes new faith receiving,
From Jesus shall not move;
For he who dies believing,
Dies safely through thy love.

CHRISTMAS.

146 8s & 7s.

Peace on earth, good-will to men.

HARK! what mean those holy voices,
Sweetly sounding through the skies?
Lo! the' angelic host rejoices;
Heavenly hallelujahs rise.

2 Listen to the wondrous story,
Which they chant in hymns of love:
Glory in the highest, glory,
Glory be to God above!

3 Peace on earth, good-will from heaven,
Reaching far as man is found;
Souls redeemed and sins forgiven!
Loud our golden harps shall sound.

4 Christ is born, the great Anointed;
Heaven and earth his praises sing;
O receive whom God appointed,
For your Prophet, Priest, and King.

5 Hasten, mortals, to adore him;
Learn his name and taste his love;
Till in heaven ye sing before him,
Glory be to God above.

147 C. M.

Glad tidings.

WHILE shepherds watched their flocks by night,
All seated on the ground,
The angel of the Lord came down,
And glory shone around.

2 Fear not, said he, (for mighty dread
Had seized their troubled mind,)
Glad tidings of great joy I bring
To you and all mankind.

3 To you, in David's town, this day
Is born, of David's line,
The Saviour, who is Christ the Lord;
And this shall be the sign:

4 The heavenly babe you there shall find
To human view displayed,
All meanly wrapped in swathing-bands,
And in a manger laid.

5 Thus spake the seraph; and forthwith
Appeared a shining throng
Of angels, praising God on high,
Who thus addressed their song:

6 All glory be to God on high,
And to the earth be peace;
Good-will henceforth from heaven to men,
Begin and never cease.

148 S. M.

The nativity of Christ.

BEHOLD the grace appear,
The blessing promised long;
Angels announce the Saviour near
In this triumphant song:

2 "Glory to God on high,
And heavenly peace on earth;
Good-will to men, to angels joy
At the Redeemer's birth."

3 In worship so divine
Let men employ their tongues;
With the celestial host we join,
And loud repeat their songs:

4 "Glory to God on high,
And heavenly peace on earth;
Good-will to men, to angels joy,
At our Redeemer's birth."

149 C. M.

Children recalling the example of Jesus.

WHEN Jesus left his Father's throne,
He chose an humble birth;
And, all unhonored and unknown,
He came to dwell on earth.

2 Like him may we be found below
In wisdom's path of peace;
Like him, in grace and knowledge grow,
As years and strength increase.

3 Sweet were his words, and kind his look,
When mothers round him pressed;
Their infants in his arms he took,
And on his bosom blest.

4 Safe from the world's alluring charms,
Beneath his watchful eye,
Thus, in the circle of his arms,
May we forever lie.

150 11s & 10s.

The star in the East.

BRIGHTEST and best of the sons of the morning,
Dawn on our darkness, and lend us thine aid;
Star of the East, the horizon adorning,
Guide where the infant Redeemer is laid.

2 Cold, on his cradle, the dew-drops are shining;
Low lies his bed with the beasts of the stall;
Angels adore him, in slumber reclining,
Maker, and Monarch, and Saviour of all.

3 Say, shall we yield him, in costly devotion,
  Odors of Eden and off'rings divine?
Gems of the mountains and pearls of the ocean,
  Myrrh from the forest and gold from the mine?

4 Vainly we offer each ample oblation;
  Vainly with gifts would his favor secure;
Richer by far is the heart's adoration;
  Dearer to God are the prayers of the poor.

151 — 7s & 6s.

Christmas morning.

LITTLE children, can you tell,
Do you know the story well,
Every girl and every boy,
Why the angels sing for joy
  On the Christmas morning?

2 Shepherds sat upon the ground,
Fleecy flocks were scattered round,
When the brightness filled the sky,
And a song was heard on high,
  On the Christmas morning.

3 "Joy and peace," the angels sang,
Far the pleasant echoes rang,
"Peace on earth, to men good-will!"
Hark! the angels sing it still
  On the Christmas morning.

4 For a little babe that day,
Christ, the Lord of angels, lay,
Born on earth our Lord to be:
This the wondering angels see
  On the Christmas morning.

5 Let us sing the angels' song,
And the pleasant sounds prolong:
This fair babe of Bethlehem
Children loves, and blesses them
  On the Christmas morning.

6 "Peace" our little hearts shall fill,
"Peace on earth, to men good-will."
Hear us sing the angels' song,
And the pleasant notes prolong,
On the Christmas morning.

152 — 4 lines 7s.

The Sun of Righteousness.

HARK! the herald angels sing,
Glory to the new-born King!
Peace on earth and mercy mild;
God and sinners reconciled.

2 Joyful all ye nations rise,
Join the triumphs of the skies;
With angelic hosts proclaim,
Christ is born in Bethlehem.

3 Christ, by highest heaven adored;
Christ, the everlasting Lord;
Vailed in flesh the Godhead see;
Hail, incarnate Deity!

4 Hail the heaven-born Prince of peace!
Hail the Sun of Righteousness!
Light and life to all he brings,
Risen with healing in his wings.

153 — 8s & 7s.

The Child Jesus.

LONG ago the Lord of glory
Lived on earth, a little child;
He was gentle, he was holy,
He was always kind and mild.

2 He was cradled in a manger,
Poor and humble was his bed;
Jesus, when on earth, a stranger,
Had not where to lay his head.

3 When he came, the angels, singing,
Told the shepherds of his birth:
"Christ," they said, "is come: he's bringing
Joy and peace to men on earth."

4 Let us love him, let us fear him,
Let us learn of him below;
Then in heaven we shall be near him;
More of him we then shall know.

154 4 6s & 2 8s.

The Song of Angels.

HARK! what celestial sounds,
What music fills the air!
Soft warbling to the morn,
It strikes the ravished ear:
Now all is still, now wild it floats,
Loud, sweet, and shrill, in tuneful notes.

2 Th' angelic hosts descend,
With harmony divine;
See how from heaven they bend,
And in full chorus join:
"Fear not, great joy we bring," they say;
"Jesus your King is born to-day."

3 He comes, your souls to save
From death's eternal gloom;
To realms of bliss and light
He lifts you from the tomb:
With sons of light your voices raise,
Your songs unite of endless praise.

4 Glory to God on high!
Ye mortals spread the sound,
And let your raptures fly
To earth's remotest bound:
For peace on earth from God in heaven,
At Jesus' birth to man is given.

155

6s & 4s.

Good-will to man.

GLORY to God on high!
Peace upon earth and joy!
Good-will to man.
Ye, who the blessing prove
Join with the hosts above;
Sing ye a Saviour's love,—
Too vast to scan.

2 Mercy and truth unite;
This is a joyful sight;
All sights above.
Jesus the curse sustains;
Bitter the cup he drains;
Nothing for us remains,
Nothing but love.

3 Love, that no tongue can teach,
Love, that no thought can reach,
No love like His!
Heaven is its blessed source,
Death could not stop his course,
Nothing can check its force,
Matchless it is.

4 Join then this love to sing,
Join to exalt our King,
Sinners forgiven.
To the great One in Three
Honor and majesty,
Now and for ever be,
Here and in heaven.

156

4 *lines* 7s.

A Bethlehem hymn.

HE has come! the Christ of God;
Left for us his glad abode;
Stooping from his throne of bliss,
To this darksome wilderness.

2 He has come! the Prince of Peace;
Come to bid our sorrows cease;
Come to scatter, with his light,
All the shadows of our night.

3 He has come, whose name of grace
Speaks deliverance to our race;
Left for us his glad abode;
Son of Mary, son of God!

4 Unto us a child is born!
Ne'er has earth beheld a morn
Among all the morns of time,
Half so glorious in its prime.

5 Unto us a Son is given!
He has come from God's own heaven:
Bringing with him from above,
Holy peace and holy love.

157 C. M.

Joy to the world.

JOY to the world, the Lord is come;
  Let earth receive her King;
Let every heart prepare him room,
  And heaven and nature sing.

2 Joy to the earth, the Saviour reigns;
  Let men their songs employ;
While fields and floods, rocks, hills and plains
  Repeat the sounding joy.

3 No more let sins and sorrows grow,
  Nor thorns infest the ground;
He comes to make his blessings flow
  Far as the curse is found.

4 He rules the world with truth and grace,
  And makes the nations prove
The glories of his righteousness,
  And wonders of his love.

158 L. M.

The Star of Bethlehem.

WHEN, marshaled on the nightly plain,
The glittering host bestud the sky,
One star alone, of all the train,
Can fix the sinner's wandering eye.

2 Hark! hark! to God the chorus breaks,
From every host, from every gem;
But one alone the Saviour speaks—
It is the Star of Bethlehem!

3 Once on the raging seas I rode;
The storm was loud, the night was dark,
The ocean yawned, and rudely blowed
The wind that tossed my foundering bark.

4 Deep horror then my vitals froze:
Death-struck, I ceased the tide to stem;
When suddenly a star arose—
It was the Star of Bethlehem!

5 It was my guide, my light, my all;
It bade my dark foreboding cease;
And through the storm and danger's thrall,
It led me to the port of peace.

6 Now, safely moored, my perils o'er,
I'll sing, first in night's diadem,
For ever and for ever more,
The Star—the Star of Bethlehem!

159 6s & 8s.

A Christmas carol.

JOY to the sons of men
On this bright Christmas morn!
List to the welcome words again
That charm our waiting hearts, as when
The shepherds heard with glad amaze
The announcement of angelic lays,
"A Saviour, Christ, is born."

2 Joy to earth's sorrowing child
  On this calm, peaceful morn!
The holy, harmless, undefiled,
Can soothe his breast with comfort mild,
The hymn that floats along the air
Shall find an answer echoing there—
  "The Saviour, Christ, is born."

3 Joy to the sick and poor,
  "Blessed are they that mourn;"
If they submissively endure,
And trust his holy promise sure:
He comes all sorrow to relieve,
To comfort all who will believe—
  "The Saviour, Christ, is born."

4 Love, joy, good-will, and peace,
  Since that first Christmas morn,
Have come to earth, and ne'er shall cease.
To Him who purchased our release,
Our hearts, redeemed from death, we'll bring
And humbly, gratefully we'll sing,
  "The Saviour, Christ, is born."

160 8s & 7s.

Christmas Hymn.

CHRIST is born, and heaven rejoices,
  Judah's plain is bathed in light;
Thousand, thousand harps and voices
  Break the silence of the night.

CHORUS.

Glory in the highest, glory,
  Peace on earth, good-will to men.

2 Christ is born, the Lord's Anointed
  Leaves the heavenly world a while,
Enters on the work appointed,
  God and man to reconcile,
    CHORUS.—Glory in the highest, etc.

3 To the lost he brings salvation,
Freedom to the captive slave;
Peace amid death's desolation,
Victory o'er the boasting grave.
CHORUS.—Glory in the highest, etc.

4 Christ is born, O wondrous story!
Lord of life, yet born to die;
Sorrow's child, yet King of glory:
Born to rule and reign on high.
CHORUS.—Glory in the highest, etc.

5 Royal babe, though few enthrone him,
Few their grateful offerings bring,
All the tribes of earth shall own him
Prince of peace, creation's King.
CHORUS.—Glory in the highest, etc.

161 8s & 7s.

Star of Bethlehem.

SAW you never in the twilight,
When the sun has left the skies,
Up in heaven the clear stars shining
Through the gloom like silver eyes?
So of old, the wise men watching,
Saw a little stranger star,
And they knew the King was given,
And they followed it from far.

2 Heard you never of the story
How they crossed the desert wild,
Journeyed on by plain and mountain,
Till they found the holy child—
How they opened all their treasure,
Kneeling to that infant King,
Gave the gold and fragrant incense,
Gave the myrrh in offering?

3 Know you not that lowly infant
Was the bright and Morning Star,
He who came to light the Gentiles
And the darkened isles afar?

And we too may seek his cradle,
  There our hearts' best treasure bring—
Love and faith and true devotion,
  For our Saviour, God, and King.

162

7s, 4s, & 6.

Christmas carol.

WE three Kings of Orient are;
  Bearing gifts we traverse afar
    Field and fountain,
    Moor and mountain,
Following yonder star.

CHORUS.

O star of wonder, star of night,
Star with royal beauty bright,
  Westward leading,
  Still proceeding,
Guide us to the perfect Light.

2 Born a King on Bethlehem's plain,
Gold I bring to crown him again—
    King for ever,
    Ceasing never
Over us all to reign.

CHORUS.—O star of wonder, etc.

3 Frankincense to offer have I:
Incense owns a deity nigh;
    Prayer and praising
    All men raising,
Worship him God on high.—

CHORUS.—O star of wonder, etc.

4 Myrrh is mine: its bitter perfume
Breathes a life of gathering gloom—
    Sorrowing, sighing,
    Bleeding, dying,
Sealed in the stone-cold tomb.

CHORUS.—O star of wonder, etc.

5 Glorious now behold him arise,
King and God and Sacrifice;
Heaven singing
Halleluiah;
Joyous the earth replies.
CHORUS.—O star of wonder, etc.

163 C. M.

The advent.

CALM on the list'ning ear of night
Come heaven's melodious strains,
Where wild Judea stretches far
Her silver-mantled plains.

2 Celestial choirs, from courts above,
Shed sacred glories there;
And angels, with their sparkling lyres,
Make music on the air.

3 The answering hills of Palestine
Send back the glad reply;
And greet from all their holy heights
The Day-spring from on high.

4 O'er the blue depths of Galilee
There comes a holier calm,
And Sharon waves, in solemn praise,
Her silent groves of palm.

5 "Glory to God!" the sounding skies
Loud with their anthems ring:
"Peace to the earth, good-will to men,
From heaven's eternal King!"

164 8s & 7s.

Christmas bells are ringing.

CHRISTMAS bells are ringing, ringing,
O'er the land triumphantly;
Children's voices singing, singing,
Sound a joyous jubilee.

'Tis the day the wondrous sign
Broke the wise men's calm repose;
Newly robed in rays divine
The Star of Bethlehem arose.

CHORUS.

Christmas bells are ringing, ringing,
O'er the land triumphantly;
Children's voices singing, singing,
Sound a joyous jubilee.

2 Soft the world lay dreaming, dreaming,
On the morning of his birth;
Its pure snow-vail gleaming, gleaming,
When the Christ-child came on earth.
He's the priceless pearl we hail,
Sent us from a Father's hand;
A fount of life that shall not fail,
A rock in a weary land.
CHORUS.—Christmas bells are ringing, etc

3 Angel hymns are pealing, pealing,
Through the depths of yonder sky;
Ransomed saints are kneeling, kneeling,
Kneeling at the throne on high.
With grateful voices come we now,
Come, both heart and hand to lift;
Lord of life, to thee we bow,
And thank thee for thy gift.
CHORUS.—Christmas bells are ringing, etc.

RESURRECTION OF JESUS.

165 — 4 lines 7s.

If we suffer with Him we shall reign with Him.

CHRIST, the Lord, is risen to-day,
Sons of men and angels say:
Raise your joys and triumphs high:
Sing, ye heavens, and earth, reply.

2 Love's redeeming work is done,
Fought the fight, the battle won:
Lo! the sun's eclipse is o'er;
Lo! he sets in blood no more.

3 Vain the stone, the watch, the seal;
Christ has burst the gates of hell;
Death in vain forbids his rise;
Christ hath opened paradise.

4 Lives again our glorious King;
Where, O death, is now thy sting?
Once he died our souls to save;
Where's thy vict'ry, boasting grave?

5 Soar we now where Christ has led,
Follow our exalted head;
Made like him, like him we rise;
Ours the cross, the grave, the skies.

166 — 4 lines 7s.

The Conqueror's welcome.

"WIDE, ye heavenly gates, unfold,
Closed no more by death and sin;
Lo! the conquering Lord behold;
Let the King of glory in."

2 Hark! th' angelic host inquire,
"Who is he, th' almighty King?"
Hark again! the answering choir
Thus in strains of triumph sing:

3 "He whose powerful arm, alone,
On his foes destruction hurled;
He who hath the victory won;
He who saved a ruined world;

4 "He who God's pure law fulfilled:
Jesus, the incarnate Word;
He whose truth with blood was sealed;
He is heaven's all-glorious Lord."

5 "Who shall up to that abode
  Follow in the Saviour's train?"
"They who in his cleansing blood
  Wash away each guilty stain;

6 "They whose daily actions prove
  Steadfast faith and holy fear,
Fervent zeal and holy love;
  They shall dwell forever here."

167 S. M.

Encouragement to faithfulness.

OUR Captain leads us on;
  He beckons from the skies;
He reaches out a starry crown,
  And bids us take the prize.

2 "Be faithful unto death,
  Partake my victory,
And thou shalt wear this glorious wreath.
  And thou shalt reign with me."

3 'Tis thus the righteous Lord
  To every soldier saith;
Eternal life is the reward
  Of all victorious faith.

4 Who conquer in his might
  The victor's meed receive;
They claim a kingdom in his right,
  Which God will freely give.

168 L. M.

Dying, rising, reigning.

HE dies! the Friend of sinners dies!
  Lo! Salem's daughters weep around;
A solemn darkness vails the skies,
  A sudden trembling shakes the ground;
Come, saints, and drop a tear or two
  For him who groaned beneath your load;
He shed a thousand drops for you,
  A thousand drops of richer blood.

2 Here's love and grief beyond degree:
The Lord of glory dies for man!
But lo! what sudden joys we see:
Jesus, the dead, revives again.
The rising God forsakes the tomb;
(In vain the tomb forbids his rise;)
Cherubic legions guard him home,
And shout him welcome to the skies.

3 Break off your tears, ye saints, and tell
How high your great Deliv'rer reigns;
Sing how he spoiled the hosts of hell,
And led the monster death in chains:
Say, Live forever, wondrous King!
Born to redeem, and strong to save;
Then ask the monster, Where's thy sting?
And, Where's thy vict'ry, boasting grave?

169 C. M.

Easter Sunday.

THE Lord of Sabbath let us praise,
In concert with the blest,
Who, joyful, in harmonious lays
Employ an endless rest.

2 Thus, Lord, while we remember thee,
We blest and pious grow;
By hymns of praise we learn to be
Triumphant here below.

3 On this glad day a brighter scene
Of glory was displayed
By the eternal Word, than when
This universe was made.

4 He rises, who mankind has bought,
With grief and pain extreme;
'Twas great to speak the world from naugh
'Twas greate to redeem.

170

8 *lines* 7s.

"He is risen."

"HE is risen, he is not here;
  Seek him not among the dead,
He is living, do not fear,"
  So the white-robed angel said.
He hath conquered every foe,
  He hath shown his power to save,
When he took the sting from death
  And the vict'ry from the grave.

CHORUS.

Then with one heart and voice
Let all the earth rejoice;
Let all the living join the strain,
And angels shout it back again:
The Lord is risen, rejoice.

2 He is risen, he is not here;
  On the earth he walks no more;
All his trials, all his toils,
  All his grief and shame are o'er;
All his purpose is fulfilled,
  All his work on earth is done:
He whom sinners put to death
  Sitteth on the great white throne.
    CHORUS.—Then with one heart, etc.

3 He is risen, he is not here—
  Not indeed to mortal eyes;
But we all who die with him
  Shall again with him arise.
'Tis in him alone we live;
  And because he lives again—
Blessed promise, glorious hope!
  We shall with him live and reign.
    CHORUS.—Then with one heart, etc.

171 C. M.

The ascension.

THE golden gates are lifted up,
The doors are opened wide,
The King of glory is gone in
Unto his Father's side.

2 Thou art gone up before us, Lord,
To make for us a place;
That we may be where now thou art,
And look upon God's face.

3 And ever on thine earthly path
A gleam of glory lies;
A light shall break behind the cloud
That vailed thee from our eyes.

4 Lift up your hearts, lift up your minds,
Let thy dear grace be given,
That while we tarry here below,
Our treasure be in heaven.

5 That where thou art, at God's right hand,
Our hope, our love may be;
Dwell thou in us, that we may dwell
For evermore in thee.

172 C. M.

The resurrection.

WHEN downward to the darksome tomb
I thoughtful turn my eyes,
Frail nature trembles at the gloom,
And anxious fears arise.

2 Why shrinks my soul? In death's embrace
Once Jesus captive slept;
And angels hovering o'er the place,
His lowly pillow kept.

3 Thus shall they guard my sleeping dust;
And, as the Saviour rose,
The grave again shall yield her trust,
And end my deep repose.

4 My Lord, before to glory gone,
Shall bid me come away;
And calm and bright shall break the dawn
Of heaven's eternal day.

5 Then let my faith each fear dispel,
And gild with light the grave;
To him my loftiest praises swell,
Who died from death to save.

INVITATIONS AND WARNINGS.

173 7s & 6s.

Go to Him early.

GO thou in life's fair morning,
Go in thy bloom of youth,
And seek, for thine adorning,
The precious pearl of truth:
Secure the heavenly treasure,
And bind it on thy heart;
And let no earthly pleasure
E'er cause it to depart.

2 Go, while the day-star shineth,
Go, while thy heart is light,
Go, ere thy strength declineth,
While every sense is bright:
Sell all thou hast, and buy it:
'Tis worth all earthly things—
Rubies, and gold, and diamonds,
Scepters and crowns of kings!

3 Go, ere the cloud of sorrow
Steals o'er thy bloom of youth;
Defer not till to-morrow:
Go now and buy the truth.

Go, seek thy great Creator;
  Learn early to be wise;
Go, place upon thy altar
  A morning sacrifice.

174 — 4 *lines* 7s.

Delay not.

HASTEN, sinner, to be wise,
  Stay not for the morrow's sun:
Wisdom if you still despise,
  Harder is it to be won.

2 Hasten, mercy to implore;
  Stay not for the morrow's sun,
Lest thy season should be o'er
  Ere this evening's stage be run.

3 Hasten, sinner, to return;
  Stay not for the morrow's sun,
Lest thy lamp should cease to burn
  Ere salvation's work is done.

4 Hasten, sinner, to be blest;
  Stay not for the morrow's sun,
Lest perdition thee arrest
  Ere the morrow is begun.

175 — L. M.

Jesus at the Door.

BEHOLD the Saviour at the door!
  He gently knocks, has knocked before;
Has waited long, is waiting still:
You treat no other friend so ill.

2 O, lovely attitude! he stands
With melting heart and loaded hands;
O, matchless kindness! and he shows
This matchless kindness to his foes!

3 But will he prove a friend indeed?
He will; the very friend you need;
The friend of sinners; yes, 'tis he,
With garments dyed on Calvary.

4 Rise, touch'd with gratitude divine,
Turn out his enemy and thine—
That soul-destroying monster, sin—
And let the heavenly stranger in.

5 Admit him ere his anger burn:
His feet departed ne'er return;
Admit him, or the hour's at hand
You'll at his door rejected stand.

176

4 *lines* 7s.

Come to-day.

HEAR ye not a voice from heaven,
To the listening spirit given?
"Children, come!" it seems to say,
"Give your hearts to me to-day."

2. Sweet as is a mother's love,
Tender as the heavenly Dove,
Thus it speaks a Saviour's charms;
Thus it wins us to his arms.

3 Lord, may we remember thee,
While from pains and sorrows free,
While our day is in its dew,
And the clouds of life are few,

4 Then when night and age appear,
Thou wilt chase each doubt and fear;
Thou our glorious leader be,
When the stars shall fade and flee.

5 Now to thee, O Lord, we come,
In our morning's early bloom;
Breathe on us thy grace divine:
Touch our hearts and make them thine.

177

7s & 6s.

Jesus, receive us.

WE bring no glittering treasures,
No gems from earth's deep mine;
We come, with simple measures,
To chant thy love divine.

Children, thy favors sharing,
Their voice of thanks would raise;
Father, accept our offering,
Our song of grateful praise.

2 The dearest gift of Heaven,
Love's written word of Truth,
To us is early given,
To guide our steps in youth:
We hear the wondrous story,
The tale of Calvary;
We read of homes in glory,
From sin and sorrow free.

3 Redeemer, grant thy blessing:
O, teach us how to pray,
That each, thy fear possessing,
May tread life's onward way:
Then, where the pure are dwelling
We hope to meet again,
And, sweeter numbers swelling,
Forever praise thy name.

178 C. M.

Early instruction.

HOW happy is the child who hears
Instruction's warning voice,
And who celestial Wisdom makes
His early, only choice!

2 For she has treasures greater far
Than east or west unfold,
And her rewards more precious are
Than all their stores of gold.

3 She guides the young with innocence
In pleasure's path to tread;
A crown of glory she bestows
Upon the hoary head.

4 According as her labors rise,
So her rewards increase;
Her ways are ways of pleasantness,
And all her paths are peace.

179 L. M.

The accepted time.

WHILE life prolongs its precious light,
Mercy is found and peace is given;
But soon, ah soon, approaching night
Shall blot out every hope of heaven.

2 While God invites, how blest the day!
How sweet the Gospel's charming sound!
Come, sinners, haste, O haste away,
While yet a pard'ning God is found.

3 Soon, borne on time's most rapid wing,
Shall death command you to the grave;
Before his bar your spirits bring,
And none be found to hear or save.

4 In that lone land of deep despair,
No Sabbath's heavenly light shall rise;
No God regard your bitter prayer,
No Saviour call you to the skies.

5 Now God invites, how blest the day!
How sweet the Gospel's charming sound!
Come, sinners, haste, O haste away,
While yet a pard'ning God is found!

180 S. M.

Seek Him while he may be found.

MY son, know thou the Lord;
Thy Father's God obey;
Seek his protecting care by night,
His guardian hand by day.

2 Call, while he may be found;
Seek him while he is near;
Serve him with all thy heart and mind,
And worship him with fear.

3 If thou wilt seek his face,
His ear will hear thy cry;
Then shalt thou find his mercy sure,
His grace forever nigh.

4 But if thou leave thy God,
Nor choose the path to heaven,
Then shalt thou perish in thy sins,
And never be forgiven.

181 C. M.

Remember now thy Creator.

REMEMBER thy Creator now,
In these thy youthful days;
He will accept thine earliest vow;
He loves thine earliest praise.

2 Remember thy Creator now,
Seek him while he is near;
For evil days will come, when thou
Shalt find no comfort here.

3 Remember thy Creator now,
His willing servant be;
Then, when thy head in death shall bow,
He will remember thee.

4 Almighty God, our hearts incline
Thy heavenly voice to hear;
Let all our future days be thine,
Devoted to thy fear.

182 8 *lines* 7s.

Early seek and you shall find.

CHILDREN! listen to the Lord,
And obey his gracious word;
Seek his face with heart and mind;
Early seek, and you shall find.

CHORUS.

Seek his face with heart and mind;
Early seek, and you shall find.

2 Sorrowful your sins confess;
Plead his perfect righteousness;
See the Saviour's bleeding side;—
Come! you will not be denied.

CHORUS.

See the Saviour's bleeding side;
Come! you will not be denied.

3 For his worship now prepare;
Kneel to him in fervent prayer;
Serve him with a perfect heart;
Never from his ways depart.

CHORUS.

Serve him with a perfect heart;
Never from his ways depart.

183 C. M.

The resolution.

COME, humble sinner, in whose breast
A thousand thoughts revolve,
Come, with your guilt and fear oppressed,
And make this last resolve:

2 I'll go to Jesus, though my sin
Like mountains round me close;
I know his courts, I'll enter in,
Whatever may oppose.

3 Prostrate I'll lie before his throne
And there my guilt confess;
I'll tell him I'm a wretch undone
Without his sovereign grace.

4 Perhaps he will admit my plea,
Perhaps will hear my prayer;
But, if I perish, I will pray,
And perish only there.

5 I can but perish if I go;
I am resolved to try;
For if I stay away, I know
I must forever die.

184 C. M.

The kind Shepherd.

SEE the Kind Shepherd, Jesus, stands,
And calls his sheep by name;
Gathers the feeble in His arms,
And feeds each tender lamb.

2 He leads them to the gentle stream,
Where living water flows;
And guides them to the verdant fields,
Where sweetest herbage grows.

3 When, wandering from the peaceful fold,
We leave the narrow way,
Our faithful Shepherd still is near,
To seek us when we stray.

4 The weakest Lamb amid the flock
Shall be its Shepherd's care;
While folded in our Saviour's arms,
We're safe from every fear.

185 C. M.

The Path of Life.

THERE is a path that leads to God,
All others go astray;
Narrow but pleasant is the road,
And Christians love the way.

2 It leads straight through this world of sin,
And dangers must be passed;
Bnt those who boldly walk therein
Will come to heaven at last.

3 While the broad road, where thousands go,
Lies near, and opens fair,
And many turn aside, I know,
To walk with sinners there.

4 But, lest my feeble steps should slide,
Or wander from thy way,
Lord, condescend to be my guide,
And I shall never stray.

186 S. M.

Salvation by grace.

GRACE! 'tis a charming sound—
Harmonious to the ear;
Heaven with the echo shall resound,
And all the earth shall hear.

2 Grace first contrived the way
To save rebellious man;
And all the steps that grace display
Which drew the wondrous plan.

3 Grace led my roving feet
To tread the heavenly road;
And new supplies each hour I meet
While pressing on to God.

4 Grace all the work shall crown,
Through everlasting days:
It lays in heaven the topmost stone,
And well deserves the praise.

187 C. M.

Religion.

RELIGION is the chief concern
Of mortals here below;
May I its great importance learn,
Its sovereign virtue know.

2 More needful this than glittering wealth
Or aught the world bestows;
Nor reputation, food or health
Can give us such repose.

3 Religion should our thoughts engage,
Amid our youthful bloom;
'Twill fit us for declining age,
And for the awful tomb.

4 O, may my heart, by grace renewed,
Be my Redeemer's throne,
And be my stubborn will subdued,
His government to own.

5 Let deep repentance, faith and love
Be joined with godly fear,
And all my conversation prove
My heart to be sincere.

188 C. M.

The Christian child.

BY cool Siloam's shady rill
How sweet the lily grows!
How sweet the breath, beneath the hill,
Of Sharon's dewy rose!

2 Lo! such the child whose early feet
The paths of peace have trod;
Whose secret heart, with influence sweet,
Is upward drawn to God.

3 By cool Siloam's shady rill
The lily must decay:
The rose that blooms beneath the hill
Must shortly fade away.

4 And soon, too soon, the wintry hour
Of man's maturer age
Will shake the soul with sorrow's power,
And stormy passion's rage.

5 O Thou who givest life and breath,
We seek thy grace alone,
In childhood, manhood, age, and death,
To keep us still thine own.

189 8s & 7s.

Come unto Me.

TO the wandering and the weary,
Everywhere on land and sea,
Jesus calls in tones of mercy,
"Come, dear children, come to me."

2 From our home, our household altar,
When our father bends the knee,
Oft we hear a voice inviting,
"Come, dear children, come to me."

3 When at night, upon our pillow,
We have prayed our prayer to thee,
Then we felt the word unspoken,
"Come, dear children, come to me."

4 Oft we hear it when our teachers
Talk to us of Calvary;
In our hearts its tones re-echo:
"Come, dear children, come to me."

5 When we pass death's troubled river,
Calm and peaceful it will be,
If we hear that voice of voices,
"Come, dear children, come to me."

190 L. M.

Return, O wanderer.

RETURN, O wanderer, return,
And seek an injured Father's face;
Those warm desires that in thee burn
Were kindled by reclaiming grace.

2 Return, O wanderer, return,
And seek a Father's melting heart;
His pitying eyes thy grief discern,
His hand shall heal thine inward smart.

3 Return, O wanderer, return,
Thy Saviour bids thy spirit live;
Go to his bleeding feet and learn
How freely Jesus can forgive.

4 Return, O wanderer, return,
And wipe away the falling tear;
'Tis God who says, "No longer mourn,"
'Tis mercy's voice invites thee near.

191 L. M.

One thing needful.

WHY will ye waste on trifling cares
That life which God's compassion spar*e*
While, in the various range of thought,
The one thing needful is forgot?

2 Shall God invite you from above?
Shall Jesus urge his dying love?
Shall troubled conscience give you pain
And all these pleas unite in vain?

3 Not so your eyes will always view
Those objects which you now pursue;
Not so will heaven and hell appear,
When death's decisive hour is near.

4 Almighty God, thy grace impart;
Fix deep conviction on each heart;
Nor let us waste on trifling cares
That life which thy compassion spares.

192 C. M.

A solemn point.

THERE is a time, we know not when,
  A point we know not where,
That marks the destiny of men
  To glory or despair.

2 And yet the doomed man's path below
  May bloom as Eden bloomed;
He did not, does not, will not know,
  Or feel that he is doomed.

3 How far may we go on in sin?
  How long will God forbear?
Where does hope end, and where begin
  The confines of despair?

4 An answer from the skies is sent:
  "Ye that from God depart,
While it is called to-day repent,
  And harden not your heart."

193 C. M.

A solemn hour.

THERE is an hour when I must part
  With all I hold most dear,
And life, with its best hopes, will then
  As nothingness appear.

2 There is an hour when I must sink
  Beneath the stroke of death,
And yield to Him who gave it first,
  My struggling vital breath.

3 There is an hour when I must stand
  Before the judgment-seat,
And all my sins and all my foes
  In awful vision meet.

4 There is an hour when I must look
  On one eternity,
And nameless woe or blissful life
  My endless portion be.

5 O Saviour, then, in all my need,
  Be near, be near to me;
And let my soul, by steadfast faith,
  Find life and heaven in thee.

194 C. M.

Say not, I will delay.

O SAY not, "I will yet delay
  To seek God's offered grace;"
When Jesus, with a voice of love,
  Says now, "Seek thou my face."

2 Say not, "To-morrow I will turn;"
  To thee it may not come;
For e'en this night thy soul may hear
  Its everlasting doom.

3 Say not, "When sickness lays me low
  I will begin to pray,"
For swift disease or sudden death
  May call thy soul away.

4 But say, with earnestness and faith,
  "Jesus, I come to thee;
Now, from this moment, by thy grace,
  Help me from sin to flee.

5 "Now, for thy tender mercy's sake,
Forgive my past delay,
And in thine own redeeming blood
Wash all my sins away.

6 "Now, by thy Holy Spirit's power,
Renew this heart of mine;
And may the life which thou hast spared
Be henceforth wholly thine."

195 L. M.

God and his law.

THERE is a God who reigns above,
The Lord of heaven and earth and seas;
I fear his wrath, I ask his love,
And with my lips I sing his praise.

2 There is a law which he hath made,
To teach us all what we must do;
And his commands must be obeyed,
For they are holy, just, and true.

3 There is an hour when I must die,
Nor do I know how soon 'twill come;
Thousands of children young as I
Are called by death to hear their doom.

4 Let me improve the hours I have,
Before the day of grace is fled;
There's no repentance in the grave,
Nor pardon offered to the dead.

196 L. M.

All things are now ready.

SINNERS, obey the Gospel word;
Haste to the supper of the Lord:
Be wise to know your gracious day;
All things are ready, come away.

2 Ready the Father is to own,
And kiss his late-returning son;
Ready your loving Saviour stands,
And spreads for you his bleeding hands.

3 Ready the Spirit of his love,
Just now the stony to remove;
To' apply and witness with the blood,
And wash and seal the sons of God

4 Ready for you the angels wait,
To triumph in your blest estate;
Tuning their harps, they long to praise
The wonders of redeeming grace.

5 The Father, Son, and Holy Ghost,
Are ready with their shining host:
All heaven is ready to resound,
The dead's alive! the lost is found!

197 C. M. D.

I heard the voice of Jesus say.

I HEARD the voice of Jesus say,
"Come unto me and rest;
Lay down, thou weary one, lay down
Thy head upon my breast."
I came to Jesus as I was,
Weary and worn and sad;
I found in him a resting-place,
And he has made me glad.

2 I heard the voice of Jesus say,
"Behold, I freely give
The living water; thirsty one
Stoop down, and drink and live."
I came to Jesus, and I drank
Of that life-giving stream;
My thirst was quenched, my soul revived,
And now I live in him.

3 I heard the voice of Jesus say,
"I am this dark world's light;
Look unto me, thy morn shall rise,
And all thy day be bright."

I looked to Jesus, and I found
In him my star, my sun;
And in that light of life I'll walk
Till traveling days are done.

REPENTANCE.

198 8s & 6.

Just as I am.

JUST as I am—without one plea,
But that thy blood was shed for me,
And that thou bidd'st me come to thee,
O Lamb of God, I come!

2 Just as I am—and waiting not
To rid my soul of one dark blot,
To thee, whose blood can cleanse each spot,
O Lamb of God, I come!

3 Just as I am—though tossed about
With many a conflict, many a doubt—
"Fightings within, and fears without,"
O Lamb of God, I come!

4 Just as I am—poor, wretched, blind—
Sight, riches, healing of the mind,
Yea, all I need, in thee to find:
O Lamb of God, I come!

5 Just as I am—thou wilt receive,
Wilt welcome, pardon, cleanse, relieve,
Because thy promise I believe:
O Lamb of God, I come!

6 Just as I am—thy love, I own,
Has broken every barrier down;
Now, to be thine, yea, thine alone,
O Lamb of God, I come!

199 C. M.

The returning prodigal.

THE long-lost son, with streaming eyes,
  From folly just awake,
Reviews his wanderings with surprise;
  His heart begins to break.

2 I starve, he cries, nor can I bear
  The famine in this land,
While servants of my Father share
  The bounty of his hand.

3 With deep repentance I'll return,
  And seek my Father's face:
Unworthy to be called a son,
  I'll ask a servant's place.

4 Far off the Father saw him move,
  In pensive silence mourn,—
And quickly ran, with arms of love,
  To welcome his return.

5 Through all the courts the tidings flew,
  And spread the joy around;
The angels tuned their harps anew,—
  The long-lost son is found!

200 S. M. D.

The wandering sheep.

I WAS a wandering sheep,
  I did not love the fold:
I did not love my Father's voice,
  I would not be controlled.
I was a wayward child,
  I did not love my home,
I did not love my Shepherd's voice,
  I loved afar to roam.

2 The Shepherd sought his sheep,
  The Father sought his child;
They followed me o'er vale and hill,
  O'er deserts waste and wild;

They found me nigh to death,
  Famished and faint and lone;
They bound me with the bands of love,
  They saved the wandering one.

3 Jesus my Shepherd is:
  'Twas he that loved my soul,
'Twas he that washed me in his blood,
  'Twas he that made me whole;
'Twas he that sought the lost,
  That found the wandering sheep,
'Twas he that brought me to the fold,
  'Twas he that still doth keep.

4 No more a wandering sheep,
  I love to be controlled,
I love my tender Shepherd's voice,
  I love the peaceful fold;
No more a wayward child,
  I seek no more to roam;
I love my heavenly Father's voice,
  I love, I love his home.

201 *6 lines* 7s.

Clinging to the Cross.

ROCK of ages, cleft for me,
  Let me hide myself in thee;
Let the water and the blood,
From thy wounded side which flowed,
Be of sin the double cure,
Save from wrath and make me pure.

2 Could my tears forever flow,
Could my zeal no languor know,
These for sin could not atone;
Thou must save, and thou alone:
In my hand no price I bring;
Simply to the cross I cling,

3 While I draw this fleeting breath,
When my eyes shall close in death,
When I rise to worlds unknown,
And behold thee on thy throne,—
Rock of ages, cleft for me,
Let me hide myself in thee.

202 L. M.

Condemned, but pleading the promises.

SHOW pity, Lord: O Lord, forgive;
Let a repenting rebel live;
Are not thy mercies large and free?
May not a sinner trust in thee?

2 My crimes are great, but don't surpass
The power and glory of thy grace;
Great God, thy nature hath no bound,
So let thy pard'ning love be found.

3 O wash my soul from every sin,
And make my guilty conscience clean;
Here on my heart the burden lies,
And past offenses pain my eyes.

4 O save a trembling sinner, Lord,
Whose hope, still hovering round thy Word,
Would light on some sweet promise there,—
Some sure support against despair.

203 C. M.

Pleading His gracious word.

LORD, I approach the mercy seat,
Where thou dost answer prayer;
There humbly fall before thy feet,—
For none can perish there.

2 Thy promise is my only plea;
With this I venture nigh;
Thou callest burdened souls to thee,
And such, O Lord, am I.

3 Bowed down beneath a load of sin,
By Satan sorely pressed;
By wars without, and fears within,
I come to thee for rest.

4 Be thou my shield and hiding-place;
That, sheltered near thy side,
I may rejoice in Jesus' grace,
In Jesus crucified.

5 O wondrous love! to bleed and die,
To bear the cross and shame,
That guilty sinners, such as I,
Might plead thy gracious name.

204 C. M.

Pleading the promises.

MERCY alone can meet my case;
For mercy, Lord, I cry:
Jesus, Redeemer, show thy face
In mercy, or I die:

2 I perish, and my doom were just;
But wilt thou leave me? No:
I hold thee fast, my hope, my trust:
I will not let thee go.

3 Still sure to me thy promise stands,
And ever must abide:
Behold it written on thy hands,
And graven in thy side.

4 To this, this only will I cleave;
Thy Word is all my plea;
That Word is truth, and I believe:
Have mercy, Lord, on me.

205 S. M.

Where shall rest be found?

O WHERE shall rest be found?
Rest for the weary soul?
'Twere vain the ocean's depths to sound,
Or pierce to either pole.

2 The world can never give
The bliss for which we sigh;
'Tis not the whole of life to live,
Nor all of death to die.

3 Beyond this vale of tears
There is a life above,
Unmeasured by the flight of years,
And all that life is love.

4 There is a death, whose pang
Outlasts the fleeting breath:
O, what eternal horrors hang
Around the second death!

5 Lord God of truth and grace,
Teach us that death to shun,
Lest we be driven from thy face,
For evermore undone.

206 S. M.

Jesus weeps for sinners.

DID Christ o'er sinners weep,
And shall our cheeks be dry?
Let floods of penitential grief
Burst forth from every eye.

2 The Son of God in tears,
Angels with wonder see;
Be thou astonished, O my soul,
He shed those tears for me.

3 He wept that we might weep,
Each sin demands a tear;
In heaven alone no sin is found,
And there's no weeping there.

207 C. M.

Thy face will I seek.

SOON as I heard my Father say,
"Ye children, seek my grace,"
My heart replied without delay,
"I'll seek my Father's face."

2 Let not thy face be hid from me,
Nor frown my soul away;
God of my life, I fly to thee
In each distressing day.

3 Should friends and kindred, near and dear,
Leave me to want or die.
My God will make my life his care,
And all my need supply.

4 Wait on the Lord, ye trembling saints,
And keep your courage up;
He'll raise your spirit when it faints,
And far exceed your hope.

208 C. M.

A warning from the grave.

BENEATH our feet and o'er our head
Is equal warning given;
Beneath us lie the countless dead,
Above us is the heaven.

2 Death rides on every passing breeze,
And lurks in every flower;
Each season has its own disease,
Its peril every hour.

3 Turn, mortal, turn; thy danger know;
Where'er thy foot can tread,
The earth rings hollow from below,
And warns thee by her dead.

4 Turn, mortal, turn: thy soul apply
To truths divinely given;
The dead who underneath thee lie
Shall live for hell or heaven.

209 4 *lines* 11s.

Delay not.

DELAY not, delay not; O sinner, draw near;
The waters of life are now flowing for thee;
No price is demanded; the Saviour is here;
Redemption is purchased, salvation is free.

2 Delay not, delay not; why longer abuse
The love and compassion of Jesus, thy God?
A fountain is opened; how canst thou refuse
To wash and be cleansed in his pardoning blood?

3 Delay not, delay not, O sinner, to come,
For mercy still lingers, and calls thee to-day;
Her voice is not heard in the shades of the tomb;
Her message, unheeded, will soon pass away.

4 Delay not, delay not; the Spirit of grace,
Long grieved and resisted, may take his sad flight,
And leave thee in darkness to finish thy race,
To sink in the gloom of eternity's night.

5 Delay not, delay not; the hour is at hand;
The earth shall dissolve, and the heavens shall fade;
The dead, small and great, in the judgment shall stand;
What helper, then, sinner, shall lend thee his aid?

210 L. M.

Firm resolve.

MAY I resolve with all my heart,
With all my powers to serve the Lord;
Nor from his precepts e'er depart,
Whose service is a rich reward.

2 O be his service all my joy!
Around let my example shine,
Till others love the blest employ,
And join in labors so divine.

3 Be this the purpose of my soul,
My solemn, my determined choice,
To yield to his supreme control,
And in his kind commands rejoice.

4 O may I never faint nor tire,
Nor, wandering, leave his sacred ways;
Great God, accept my soul's desire,
And give me strength to live thy praise.

211 — 4 lines 7s.

The penitent inquirer.

DEPTH of mercy! can there be
Mercy still reserved for me?
Can my God his wrath forbear,
And the chief of sinners spare?

2 I have long withstood his grace;
Long provoked him to his face;
Would not hear his gracious calls,
Grieved him by a thousand falls.

3 Jesus, answer from above:
Is not all thy nature love?
Wilt thou not the wrong forget?
Lo! I fall before thy feet.

4 Now incline me to repent;
Let me now my fall lament;
Deeply my revolt deplore;
Weep, believe, and sin no more.

212 — S. M.

To-morrow is not ours.

TO-MORROW, Lord, is thine,
Lodged in thy sov'reign hand,
And if its sun arise and shine,
It shines by thy command.

2 The present moment flies,
And bears our life away;
O make thy servants truly wise,
That they may live to-day.

3 Since on this fleeting hour
Eternity is hung,
Waken by thine almighty power
The aged and the young.

4 One thing demands our care,
O be it still pursued,
Lest, slighted once, the season fair
Should never be renewed.

5 To Jesus may we fly,
  Swift as the morning light;
Lest life's bright dreams at once should die
  In sudden, endless night.

213

4 lines 7s.

Child's prayer.

HOLY Father! hear my cry;
  Holy Saviour! bend thine ear;
Holy Spirit! come thou nigh;
  Father, Saviour, Spirit, hear.

2 Father, save me from my sin;
  Saviour, I thy mercy crave;
Gracious Spirit, make me clean;
  Father, Son, and Spirit, save.

3 Father, let me taste thy love;
  Saviour, fill my soul with peace;
Spirit, come, my heart to move;
  Father, Son, and Spirit, bless.

4 Father, Son, and Spirit, thou,
  One Jehovah, shed abroad
All thy grace within me now;
  Be my Father and my God.

214

C. M.

Love not the world.

O STREAMS of earthly love and joy,
  On whose green banks we dwell,
Gleaming in beauty to the eye,
  Ye promise fair and well.

2 Too deep and strong for us! We glide
  Down your deceiving wave;
Like men by siren song beguiled
  On to a siren grave.

3 O world, with all thy smiles and loves,
  With all thy song and wine,
What mockery of human hearts,
  What treachery, is thine!

4 Thou woundest, but thou canst not heal;
Thy words are warbled lies;
Thy hand contains the poisoned cup,
And he who drinks it dies.

5 O world, there's fever in thy touch,
And frenzy in thine eye;
To lose and shun thee is to live,
To win thee is to die.

215

7s & 6s.

First commandment.

I WANT to love my Saviour,
And worship him alone;
And have no earthly idol
Upon my spirit's throne.
I want, with pure devotion,
To serve him all my days;
And, for his countless blessings,
To yield him grateful praise.

2 It is his hand hath made me;
His power upholds me still;
And he will always aid me
To do his holy will.
Dear Saviour, be thou near me,
And guide my feet aright;
And make my thoughts and actions
Both blameless in thy sight.

3 There are many heathen children
Who yet thy name have known;
And many other idols
Than those of wood and stone.
O! if our hearts were opened
That other eyes might see,
How like a heathen temple
Would they be found to be!

4 And yet to him who formed them,
Each secret thought is known;
He sees each separate object
That occupies his throne.
Lord, in thy name appearing,
We come on bended knee;
O! teach us how to worship
No other God but thee!

216 C. M.

First commandment.

THERE are no gods but One; yet we
A thousand things may take,
And set them on our spirit's throne,
And thus a god may make.

2 That is our god which most we love;
And which, could we possess,
Would make us all the fullness prove
Of earthly happiness.

3 Pleasure, or dress, or selfish ease
May be a god to me;
For thousands, Lord, bestow on these
The love they owe to thee!

4 But how shall these our spirits cheer
When care or sorrow's nigh?
How can they bring the Saviour near
When we are called to die?

5 Then rule thou only in my mind!
Thine only let me be!
And, loving all men, let me find
No other God but thee!

217 7s & 6s.

Second commandment.

WHILE angels bow before thee,
And sing thy praise above;
Lord, teach us to adore thee,
And seek thy pardoning love.

And while our lips are singing
  The notes we love to raise,
O! may our hearts be bringing
  A tribute to thy praise.

2 Thou art a God who beareth
  No rival near thy throne;
Yet many a creature shareth
  The love that is thine own.
A thousand things around us
  Our idol gods may be:
And many a tie hath bound us
  That binds us not to thee.

3 But in His name appealing
  Who died that we might live;
Before thy footstool meeting,
  We pray thee to forgive.
O! help us now and ever,
  Our hearts on thee to place;
And every tie to sever
  That draws us from thy face.

218 4 6s & 2 8s.

Third commandment.

ALMIGHTY God, while we
  Our youthful voices raise,
And offer up to thee
  The tribute of our praise,
O! may thy love our hearts inflame,
And teach us to adore thy name.

2 Thy name in beauteous lines
  Of light, of life, and love,
Throughout creation shines,
  Around, beneath, above—
And all on earth, in air, and sea,
Pour forth a song of praise to thee!

3 O! may we never dare
  To act that wicked part;
Nor offer up a prayer
  That comes not from the heart:
Or speak that name in careless phrase,
That heaven adores and earth obeys.

4 Dear Saviour, to our hearts,
  Thy name in mercy show,
The blessings it can give,
  O! may we early know.
Thus shall we yield it honor due,
And others win to love it too.

219

8 *lines* 8s.

Fourth commandment.

THIS day is the day of the Lord!
  And we to his temple repair;
We come at the call of his Word,
  To thank him with praise and with prayer.
O! may we remember that he,
  The God of our spirit, is near;
Our actions he clearly can see,
  Our thoughts, ere they're spoken, can hear.

2 We'll think not of work or of play,
  Nor talk of our meat or our drink;
But find all our pleasure to-day
  In thoughts he would have us to think.
We'll talk of his works and his ways,
  We'll tell o'er the marks of his love;
And learn the first notes of that praise
  We would sing with the ransomed above.

3 Thus best shall we hallow the day
  That tells us that Jesus arose;
We'll welcome its earliest ray,
  And keep it in peace till it close.
And then, when these Sabbaths are o'er,
  We'll hope, at the last, to ascend
Where sin shall disturb us no more,
  And the Sabbath of God have no end.

220

4 *lines* 11s.

Fifth commandment.

THOU shalt honor thy father, the guide of thy youth,
And yield him the homage of love and of truth;
Thou shalt honor thy mother, whose love unto thee
The greatest of God's earthly blessings shall be.

2 My father! my mother! how true should I prove!
How well should I serve you, how faithfully love!
How yield to each wish the regard that is due;
And do all the things you would have me to do!

3 How sweet, when we hear this commandment, to say,
"Lord, if thou wilt help me, I'll strive to obey;
I'll bend down the force of my own stubborn will,
And bid every passionate feeling, *Be still!*"

4 The love of a parent, O! who can repay?
From life's early dawn to the close of its day
It shines on each pathway, it blesses each lot,
And remembers us still, though by all else forgot!

5 If thus earthly parents regard us with love,
O! what shall we say of our Father above?
Lord, make us thy children, in spirit, that we
May be always *just what thou wouldst have us to be!*

221

6s & 8s.

Fifth commandment.—He makes his mother sad.

HE makes his mother sad,
The proud, unruly child,
Who will not brook her warning look,
Nor hear her counsels mild.
He makes his mother sad
Who, in his thoughtless mirth,
Can e'er forget his mighty debt
To her who gave him birth.

2 He makes his mother sad
Who turns from wisdom's way,
Whose stubborn will, rebelling still,
Refuses to obey

He makes his mother sad,
  And sad his lot must prove;
A mother's fears, a mother's tears,
  Are marked by God above.

3 O! who so sad as he
  Who, o'er a parent's grave,
Too late repents, too late laments,
  The bitter pain he gave?
May we ne'er know such grief,
  Nor cause one feeling sad;
Let our delight be to requite,
  And make our parents glad.

222 C. M.

Sixth commandment.

OUR hands may not be red with blood,
  Yet we may murderers be;
For every causeless, angry thought
  Is murder, Lord, with thee.

2 There's many a deed of murder done,
  Where blood has ne'er been spilt;
For angry thoughts and words are one
  With deeds of crimson guilt.

3 Yes! in our hearts we often kill,
  And think the deed unknown;
Forgetting that each secret thought
  Is spoken at thy throne.

4 Great God! we cannot fully tell
  How such a thing can be;
We only feel how much of sin
  Within us thou must see!

5 O! then to Christ, the living stream,
  We'll come without delay;
And in the fountain of his blood
  Wash all our guilt away.

223 S. M.

Ninth commandment.

I MUST not let my tongue
A word of falsehood speak,
Which may my humblest neighbor wrong,
And God's commandment break.

2 I must not harshly judge,
When others go astray,
Or in my spirit bear a grudge,
To prompt the words I say.

3 For when I look within
And see the evil there,
I scarcely think another's sin
Can with my own compare.

4 Then let the law of love
My guide in all things be;
And may I by its judgment prove
The good and ill I see.

5 Dear Saviour, let me keep
Thy pattern in my view,
And always strive to think and speak
As thou wouldst have me do.

224 4 6s & 2 8s.

Ninth commandment.

FULL oft does Satan try
To draw my steps aside;
Now bids me tell a lie
My faults from all to hide;
And tempts me soon to sin again,
That I new pleasures may obtain.

2 Whenever I consent
To walk in Satan's ways,
It is as though I bent
My knee before his face.
And what reward will Satan give.
In his own place with him to live?

3 How shall my feeble heart
Be kept from Satan's power?
O Lord, thy strength impart
In every tempted hour.
That I may sinful joys refuse,
And with delight thy service choose.

225 L. M.

Tenth commandment.

I MUST not nurse within my soul
One spark of sin's unhallowed fire,
Or yield my heart to the control
Of aught that speaks a wrong desire.

2 If others in the flush of health
Can richly dress and brightly shine,
I must not envy them their wealth,
Or wish that aught of theirs was mine.

3 I must not turn with envious eyes
On aught that others may possess;
Or wish, whatever God denies,
To make their sum of blessings less.

4 Is there, then, naught beneath, above,
That I may covet to possess?
Yes, there's the Saviour's boundless love,
With which he waits my soul to bless.

5 To me this treasure, Lord, impart;
Thy pard'ning grace O let me prove;
Write thou thy laws upon my heart,
And make me covet all thy love.

226 11s & 8s.

Be kind to thy father.

BE kind to thy father; for when thou wast young
Who loved thee so fondly as he?
He caught the first accents that fell from thy tongue,
And joined in thy innocent glee.

Be kind to thy father, for now he is old,
  His locks intermingled with gray;
His footsteps are feeble, once fearless and bold;
  Thy father is passing away.

2 Be kind to thy mother; for lo! on her brow
  May traces of sorrow be seen;
O well mayst thou cherish and comfort her now,
  For loving and kind she hath been.
Remember thy mother; for thee will she pray
  As long as God giveth her breath;
With accents of kindness, then, cheer her lone way,
  E'en to the dark valley of death.

3 Be kind to thy brother; his heart will have dearth
  If the smiles of thy joy be withdrawn;
The flowers of feeling will fade at the birth
  If love and affection be gone.
Be kind to thy brother wherever you are:
  The love of a brother shall be
An ornament purer and richer by far
  Than pearls from the depths of the sea.

4 Be kind to thy sister; not many may know
  The depths of true sisterly love;
The wealth of the ocean lies fathoms below
  The surface that sparkles above.
Thy kindness shall bring to thee many sweet hours,
  And blessings thy pathway shall crown;
Affection shall weave thee a garland of flowers
  More precious than wealth or renown.

227 7s & 6s.

Repentance.

WE stand in deep repentance
  Before the throne of love;
O God of grace forgive us,
  The stain of guilt remove.
Behold us while with weeping
  We lift our eyes to thee,
And all our sins subduing,
  Our Father set us free.

2 O shouldst thou from us fallen,
Withhold thy grace to guide,
Forever we should wander
From thee and peace, aside;
But thou to spirits contrite
Dost light and life impart,
That man may learn to serve thee
With thankful, joyous heart.

3 Our souls, on thee we cast them;
Our only refuge thou;
Thy cheering words revive us,
When pressed with grief we bow:
Thou bear'st the trusting spirit
Upon thy loving breast,
And givest all thy ransomed
A sweet, unending rest.

228 L. M.

The Spirit's call.

SAY, sinner, hath a voice within
Oft whispered to thy secret soul?
Urged thee to leave the ways of sin,
And yield thy heart to God's control?

2 Sinner, it was a heavenly voice;
It was the Spirit's gracious call;
It bade thee make the better choice,
And haste to seek in Christ thine all.

3 Spurn not the call to life and light;
Regard in time the warning kind;
That call thou mayst not always slight,
And yet the gate of mercy find.

4 God's Spirit will not always strive
With hardened, self-destroying man;
Ye who persist his love to grieve,
May never hear his voice again.

5 Sinner, perhaps this very day
  Thy last accepted time may be,
O shouldst thou grieve him now away,
  Then hope may never beam on thee.

229 S. M.

The Holy Spirit.

THE Comforter has come,
  We feel his presence here;
Our hearts would now no longer roam,
  But bow in filial fear.

2 This tenderness of love,
  This hush of solemn power;
'Tis heaven descending from above
  To fill this favored hour.

3 Earth's darkness all has fled,
  Heaven's light serenely shines,
And every heart, divinely led,
  To holy thought inclines.

4 No more let sin deceive,
  Nor earthly cares betray;
O let us never, never grieve
  The Comforter away.

230 4 6s & 2 8s.

A broken heart.

A BROKEN heart, O Lord,
  Thou never wilt despise;
'Tis written in thy word,
  This is the sacrifice;
The sacrifice that thou wilt own,
It is the broken heart alone.

2 Break thou my heart, O Lord;
  The rock within me break;
To tremble at thy word,
  And at thine anger quake;
Let me in deep contrition lie,
And heave the penitential sigh.

3 For mercy dwells with thee;
  Compassion, all divine;
That mercy show to me,
  Be that compassion mine:
For sinners did not Jesus bleed?
And Jesus' blood alone I plead.

231

8 lines 7s.

Knock, weep, watch, wait.

PILGRIM, burdened with thy sin,
  Come the way to Zion's gate;
There, till mercy speaks within,
  Knock, and weep, and watch, and wait:
Knock, he knows the sinner's cry;
  Weep, he loves the mourner's tears;
Watch, for saving grace is nigh;
  Wait, till heavenly grace appears.

2 Hark! it is the Saviour's voice,
  "Welcome, pilgrim, to thy rest!"
Now within the gate rejoice,
  Safe, and owned, and bought, and blest.
Safe, from all the lures of vice;
  Owned, by joys the contrite know;
Bought, by love, and life the price;
  Blest, the mighty debt to owe.

232

C. M.

Come to the ark.

COME to the ark, come to the ark;
  To Jesus come away;
The pestilence walks forth by night,
  The arrow flies by day.

2 Come to the ark, the waters rise,
  The seas their billows rear;
While darkness gathers o'er the skies,
  Behold a refuge near.

3 Come to the ark all, all that weep
Beneath the sense of sin;
Without, deep calleth unto deep,
But all is peace within.

4 Come to the ark ere yet the flood
Your lingering steps oppose;
Come, for the door which open stood
May soon forever close.

233 L. M.

Linger not.

HASTE, traveler, haste! the night comes on,
And many a shining hour is gone;
The storm is gathering in the west,
And thou far off from home and rest.

2 The rising tempest sweeps the sky,
The rains descend, the winds are high,
The waters swell, and death and fear
Beset thy path, nor refuge near.

3 O yet a shelter you may gain,
A covert from the wind and rain,
A hiding-place, a rest, a home,
A refuge from the wrath to come.

4 Then linger not in all the plain;
Flee for thy life, the mountain gain,
Look not behind, make no delay,
O speed thee, speed thee on thy way.

234 8s & 7s.

Youthful consecration.

SAVIOUR, while my heart is tender,
I would yield that heart to thee;
All my powers to thee surrender,
Thine, and only thine, to be.
Take me now, Lord Jesus, take me;
Let my youthful heart be thine;
Thy devoted servant make me;
Fill my soul with love divine.

2 Send me, Lord, where thou wilt send me,
Only do thou guide the way;
May thy grace through life attend me,
Gladly then shall I obey.
Let me do thy will, or bear it,
I would know no will but thine;
Shouldst thou take my life, or spare it,
I that life to thee resign.

3 May this solemn dedication
Never once forgotten lie;
Let it know no revocation,
Published and confirmed on high.
Thine I am, O Lord, forever,
To thy service set apart;
Suffer me to leave thee never;
Seal thine image on my heart.

235 C. M.

Put not religion by.

O 'TIS a folly and a crime
To put religion by;
For now is the accepted time,
To-morrow we may die.

2 Our hearts grow harder every day,
And more depraved the mind;
The longer we neglect to pray,
The less we feel inclined.

3 Yet sinners trifle, young and old,
Until the dying day;
Then they would give a world of gold
To have an hour to pray.

4 O, then, lest we should perish thus,
We would no longer wait;
For time will soon be past with us,
And death will fix our state.

236 C. M. D.

Jesus, remember me.

JESUS, thou art the sinner's Friend;
As such I look to thee;
Now, in the fullness of thy love,
O Lord, remember me.
Remember thy pure word of grace,
Remember Calvary;
Remember all thy dying groans,
And then remember me.

2 Thou wondrous Advocate with God,
I yield myself to thee;
While thou art sitting on thy throne,
Dear Lord, remember me.
I own I'm guilty, own I'm vile,
Yet thy salvation's free;
Then, in thy all-abounding grace,
Dear Lord, remember me.

3 Howe'er forsaken or distressed,
Howe'er oppressed I be,
Howe'er afflicted here on earth,
Do thou remember me.
And when I close my eyes in death,
And creature helps all flee,
Then, O my great Redeemer-God,
Jesus, remember me.

237 L. M.

O that my load of sin were gone!

O THAT my load of sin were gone,
O that I could at last submit
At Jesus' feet to lay it down,
To lay my soul at Jesus' feet!

2 Rest for my soul I long to find:
Saviour of all, if mine thou art,
Give me thy meek and lowly mind,
And stamp thine image on my heart.

3 Break off the yoke of inbred sin,
And fully set my spirit free;
I cannot rest till pure within,
Till I am wholly lost in thee.

4 Fain would I learn of thee, my God;
Thy light and easy burden prove;
The cross, all stained with hallowed blood
The labor of thy dying love.

5 I would, but thou must give the power;
My heart from every sin release;
Bring near, bring near the joyful hour,
And fill me with thy perfect peace.

THE RELIGIOUS LIFE.

238 L. M.

Vows remembered and renewed.

O HAPPY day that fixed my choice
On thee, my Saviour and my God!
Well may this glowing heart rejoice,
And tell its raptures all abroad.

2 O happy bond, that seals my vows,
To Him who merits all my love;
Let cheerful anthems fill his house,
While to that sacred shrine I move.

3 'Tis done; the great transaction's done;
I am my Lord's, and he is mine;
He drew me, and I followed on,
Charmed to confess the voice divine.

4 Now rest, my long-divided heart;
Fixed on this blissful center, rest;
Nor ever from thy Lord depart:
With him of every good possessed.

5 High heaven, that heard the solemn vow,
That vow renewed shall daily hear,
Till in life's latest hour I bow,
And bless in death a bond so dear.

239 8s & 7s.

Taking up the cross.

JESUS, I my cross have taken,
All to leave and follow thee:
Naked, poor, despised, forsaken,
Thou, from hence, my all shalt be.
Perish, every fond ambition;
All I've sought, or hoped, or known:
Yet how rich is my condition;
God and heaven are still my own!

2 Soul, then know thy full salvation;
Rise o'er sin, and fear, and care;
Joy to find in every station
Something still to do or bear.
Think what Spirit dwells within thee;
Think what Father's smiles are thine;
Think that Jesus died to win thee;
Child of heaven, canst thou repine?

3 Haste thee on from grace to glory,
Armed by faith, and winged by prayer;
Heaven's eternal day's before thee,
God's own hand shall guide thee there.
Soon shall close thy earthly mission,
Soon shall pass thy pilgrim days;
Hope shall change to glad fruition,
Faith to sight, and prayer to praise.

240 L. M.

The vow sealed at the Cross.

LORD, I am thine, entirely thine,
Purchased and saved by blood divine;
With full consent thine I would be,
And own thy sovereign right in me.

2 Thine would I live, thine would I die;
Be thine through all eternity;
The vow is past beyond repeal,
And now I set the solemn seal.

3 Here at the cross where flows the blood
That bought my guilty soul for God,
Thee, my new Master, now I call,
And consecrate to thee my all.

4 Do thou assist a feeble worm
The great engagement to perform;
Thy grace can full assistance lend,
And on that grace I dare depend.

241 C. M.

Victory over death.

O FOR an overcoming faith
To cheer my dying hours,
To triumph o'er the monster Death,
And all his frightful powers!

2 Joyful, with all the strength I have,
My quivering lips should sing—
"Where is thy boasted victory, Grave?
And where, O Death, thy sting?"

3 If sin be pardoned, I'm secure;
Death has no sting beside:
The law gives sin its damning power,
But Christ, my ransom, died.

4 Now to the God of victory
Immortal thanks be paid,
Who makes us conquerors, while we die,
Through Christ, our living head.

242 L. M.

Heavenly bliss in prospect.

ARISE, my soul, on wings sublime,
Above the vanities of time;
Let faith now pierce the vail, and see
The glories of eternity.

2 Born by a new, celestial birth,
Why should I grovel here on earth?
Why grasp at vain and fleeting toys,
So near to heaven's eternal joys?

3 Shall aught beguile me on the road,
The narrow road that leads to God?
Or can I love this earth so well,
As not to long with God to dwell?

4 To dwell with God, to taste his love,
Is the full heaven enjoyed above:
The glorious expectation now
Is heavenly bliss begun below.

243 S. M

My times in God's hands.

MY times are in thy hand:
  O God, I wish them there:
My life, my soul, my friends, I leave
  Entirely to thy care.

2 My times are in thy hand,
  Whatever they may be,
Pleasing or painful, dark or bright,
  As best may seem to thee.

3 My times are in thy hand:
  Why should I doubt or fear?
My Father's hand will never cause
  His child a needless tear.

4 My times are in thy hand,
  Jesus the Crucified;
The hand our many sins have pierced
  Is now my guard and guide.

5 My times are in thy hand:
  I'll always trust in thee,
Till I have left this weary land,
  And all thy glory see.

244 C. M.

For victorious faith.

O FOR a faith that will not shrink,
Though pressed by every foe;
That will not tremble on the brink
Of any earthly woe;

2 That will not murmur nor complain
Beneath the chastening rod,
But in the hour of grief or pain,
Will lean upon its God;

3 A faith that shines more bright and clear,
When tempests rage without;
That when in danger knows no fear,
In darkness feels no doubt;

4 Lord, give us such a faith as this,
And then, whate'er may come,
We'll taste, e'en here, the hallowed bliss
Of an eternal home.

245 7s & 6s.

Stand up for Jesus.

STAND up! stand up for Jesus!
Ye soldiers of the cross;
Lift high his royal banner,
It must not suffer loss:
From victory unto victory
His army shall be led,
Till every foe is vanquished,
And Christ is Lord indeed.

2 Stand up! stand up for Jesus!
The trumpet call obey:
Forth to the mighty conflict
In this his glorious day:
Ye are the men, now serve him
Against unnumbered foes:
Your courage rise with danger,
And strength to strength oppose.

3 Stand up! stand up for Jesus!
Stand in his strength alone;
The arm of flesh will fail you,
Ye dare not trust your own;
Put on the Gospel armor,
And, watching unto prayer,
Where duty calls, or danger,
Be never wanting there.

4 Stand up! stand up for Jesus!
The strife will not be long:
This day the noise of battle,
The next the victor's song:
To him that overcometh
A crown of life shall be:
He with the King of glory
Shall reign eternally.

246 C. M.

Entire purification.

FOREVER here my rest shall be,
Close to thy bleeding side;
This all my hope and all my plea—
For me the Saviour died.

2 My dying Saviour, and my God,
Fountain for guilt and sin,
Sprinkle me ever with thy blood,
And cleanse, and keep me clean.

3 Wash me, and make me thus thine own;
Wash me, and mine thou art;
Wash me, but not my feet alone—
My hands, my head, my heart.

4 The atonement of thy blood apply,
Till faith to sight improve;
Till hope in full fruition die,
And all my soul be love.

247

6s.

Nearer home.

ONE sweetly solemn thought
  Comes to me o'er and o'er:
I'm nearer my home to-day
  Than I've ever been before.

2 Nearer my Father's house,
  Where the many mansions be;
Nearer the great white throne,
  Nearer the jasper sea:

3 Nearer the bound of life
  Where we lay our burdens down,
Nearer leaving my cross,
  Nearer wearing my crown.

4 But lying darkly between,
  Winding down through the night,
Is that dim and unknown stream
  Which leads at last to light.

5 Father, perfect my trust,
  Strengthen my feeble faith,
Let me feel as if I trod
  The shore of the river Death.

6 For even now my feet
  May stand upon its brink;
I may be nearer my home,
  Nearer now than I think.

248

S. M.

Sow beside all waters.

SOW in the morn thy seed;
  At eve hold not thy hand;
To doubt and fear give thou no heed,
  Broadcast it o'er the land.

2 Thou know'st not which shall thrive,
  The late or early sown;
Grace keeps the precious germ alive,
  When and wherever strown:

3 And duly shall appear,
In verdure, beauty, strength.
The tender blade, the stalk, the ear,
And the full corn at length.

4 Thou canst not toil in vain:
Cold, heat, and moist, and dry,
Shall foster and mature the grain
For garners in the sky.

249 C. M.

The race for glory.

AWAKE, my soul, stretch every nerve,
And press with vigor on;
A heavenly race demands thy zeal,
And an immortal crown.

2 'Tis God's all-animating voice
That calls thee from on high;
'Tis he whose hand presents the prize
To thine aspiring eye.

3 A cloud of witnesses around
Hold thee in full survey;
Forget the steps already trod,
And onward urge thy way.

4 Blest Saviour! introduced by thee,
Our race have we begun;
And crowned with vict'ry, at thy feet
We'll lay our trophies down.

250 5s & 6s.

Breast the wave, Christian.

BREAST the wave, Christian,
When it is strongest;
Watch for day, Christian,
When the night's longest.
Onward and onward still
Be thine endeavor;
The rest that remaineth
Shall be forever.

2 Fight the fight, Christian,
  Jesus is o'er thee;
Run the race, Christian,
  Heaven is before thee.
He that hath promised
  Faltereth never;
The love of eternity
  Flows on forever.

3 Lift the eye, Christian,
  Just as it closeth;
Raise the heart, Christian,
  Ere it reposeth.
Thee from the love of Christ
  Nothing shall sever,
Mount when thy work is done;
  Praise him forever!

251 C. M.

Prayer for thankfulness.

FATHER, whate'er of earthly bliss
  Thy sovereign will denies,
Accepted at thy throne of grace
  Let this petition rise:

2 Give me a calm, a thankful heart,
  From every murmur free;
The blessings of thy grace impart,
  And make me live to thee.

3 Let the sweet hope that thou art mine
  My life and death attend;
Thy presence through my journey shine,
  And crown my journey's end.

252 S. M.

The whole armor of God.

SOLDIERS of Christ, arise,
  And put your armor on,
Strong in the strength which God supplies
  Through his eternal Son;

Strong in the Lord of hosts,
  And in his mighty power,
Who in the strength of Jesus trusts,
  Is more than conqueror.

2 Stand then in his great might,
  With all his strength endued;
But take, to arm you for the fight,
  The panoply of God;
That having all things done,
  And all your conflicts past,
Ye may o'ercome, through Christ alone,
  And stand entire at last.

253 C. M.

There is a cross and a crown for me.

MUST Jesus bear the cross alone,
  And all the world go free?
No; there's a cross for every one,
  And there's a cross for me.

2 How happy are the saints above,
  Who once went sorrowing here!
But now they taste unmingled love
  And joy without a tear.

3 The consecrated cross I'll bear
  Till death shall set me free,
And then go home, my crown to wear;
  For there's a crown for me.

4 Upon the crystal pavement, down
  At Jesus' pierced feet,
Joyful I'll cast my golden crown,
  And his dear name repeat;

5 And palms shall wave, and harps shall ring
  Beneath heaven's arches high;
The Lord that lives, the ransomed sing,
  That lives no more to die.

254

6s & 4s

Christ our confidence.

MY faith looks up to thee,
Thou Lamb of Calvary;
Saviour divine,
Now hear me while I pray;
Take all my guilt away;
O let me, from this day,
Be wholly thine.

2 May thy rich grace impart
Strength to my fainting heart;
My zeal inspire:
As thou hast died for me,
O may my love to thee
Pure, warm, and changeless be;
A living fire.

3 While life's dark maze I tread,
And griefs around me spread,
Be thou my guide;
Bid darkness turn to day,
Wipe sorrow's tears away,
Nor let me ever stray
From thee aside.

4 When ends life's transient dream,
When death's cold, sullen stream
Shall o'er me roll,
Blest Saviour, then in love,
Fear and distress remove;
O bear me safe above,
A ransomed soul.

255

C. M.

Triumphant joy.

MY God, the spring of all my joys,
The life of my delights,
The glory of my brightest days,
And comfort of my nights;

2 In darkest shades, if thou appear,
My dawning is begun;
Thou art my soul's bright morning star,
And thou my rising sun.

3 The opening heavens around me shine
With beams of sacred bliss,
If Jesus shows his mercy mine,
And whispers I am his.

4 My soul would leave this heavy clay
At that transporting word,
Run up with joy the shining way,
To see and praise my Lord.

5 Fearless of hell and ghastly death,
I'd break through every foe;
The wings of love and arms of faith
Would bear me conqu'ror through.

256

8s & 7s.

Desiring sanctification.

LOVE divine, all love excelling,
Joy of heaven, to earth come down;
Fix in us thy humble dwelling;
All thy faithful mercies crown:
Jesus, thou art all compassion:
Pure, unbounded love thou art;
Visit us with thy salvation;
Enter every trembling heart.

2 Breathe, O breathe thy Holy Spirit
Into every troubled breast;
Let us all thy grace inherit;
Let us find thy promised rest:
Take away the love of sinning;
Let our love be fixed on thee;
End the work of thy beginning;
Set our hearts at liberty.

3 Finish then thy new creation;
Pure and holy may we be;
Let us see thy great salvation
Perfectly restored in thee;
Changed from glory into glory,
Till in heaven we take our place,
Till we cast our crowns before thee,
Lost in wonder, love, and praise.

257 C. M.

At evening time it shall be light.

WE journey through a vale of tears,
By many a cloud o'ercast;
And worldly cares and worldly fears
Go with us to the last.

2 Not to the last! Thy word hath said,
Could we but read aright,
Poor pilgrim, lift in hope thy head;
At eve it shall be light.

3 Though earth-born shadows now may shroud
Thy thorny path a while,
God's blessed word can part each cloud,
And bid the sunshine smile.

4 Only believe, in living faith,
His love and power divine,
And ere thy sun shall set in death,
His light shall round thee shine.

5 When tempest clouds are dark on high,
His bow of love and peace
Shines sweetly in the vaulted sky,
A pledge that storms shall cease.

6 Hold on thy way, with hope unchilled,
By faith and not by sight,
And thou shalt own his word fulfilled;
At eve it shall be light.

258

6s & 4s.

Nearer, my God, to thee.

NEARER, my God, to thee,
Nearer to thee!
E'en though it be a cross
That raiseth me!
Still all my song shall be,
Nearer, my God, to thee,
Nearer to thee!

2 Though like the wanderer,
The sun gone down,
Darkness be over me,
My rest a stone;
Yet in my dreams I'd be
Nearer, my God, to thee,
Nearer to thee.

3 Then, with my waking thoughts
Bright with thy praise,
Out of my stony griefs
Bethel I'll raise;
So by my woes to be
Nearer, my God, to thee,
Nearer to thee!

4 Or, if on joyful wing,
Cleaving the sky,
Sun, moon, and stars forgot,
Upward I fly;
Still all my song shall be,
Nearer, my God, to thee,
Nearer to thee!

259

C. M.

Purity of heart.

O FOR a heart to praise my God!
A heart from sin set free!
A heart that's sprinkled with the blood
So freely shed for me.

2 O for a heart submissive, meek,
  My great Redeemer's throne,
Where only Christ is heard to speak,
  Where Jesus reigns alone!

3 O for an humble, contrite heart,
  Believing, true, and clean,
Which neither life nor death can part
  From him that dwells within!

4 Thy temper, gracious Lord, impart;
  Come quickly from above;
O write thy name upon my heart;
  Thy name, O God, is love.

260 8s & 7s.

Mercies gratefully acknowledged.

COME, thou Fount of every blessing,
  Tune my heart to sing thy grace;
Streams of mercy, never ceasing,
  Call for songs of loudest praise.

2 Teach me some melodious measure,
  Sung by raptured saints above;
Fill my soul with sacred pleasure,
  While I sing redeeming love.

3 By thy hand sustained, defended,
  Safe through life, thus far, I've come;
Safely, Lord, when life is ended,
  Bring me to my heavenly home.

4 Jesus sought me when a stranger,
  Wandering from the fold of God;
He to save my soul from danger,
  Interposed his precious blood.

5 O, to grace how great a debtor
  Daily I'm constrained to be!
Let thy goodness, like afetter,
  Bind my wandering heart to thee.

6 Prone to wander, Lord, I feel it;
Prone to leave the God I love;
Here's my heart; O, take and seal it;
Seal it from thy courts above.

261 C. M.

A throne of grace.

A THRONE of grace! then let us go
And offer up our prayer;
A gracious God will mercy show
To all that worship there.

2 A throne of grace! O, at that throne
Our knees have often bent,
And God has showered his blessings down
As often as we went.

3 A throne of grace! rejoice, ye saints,
That throne is open still;
To God unbosom your complaints,
And then inquire his will.

4 A throne of grace we yet shall need
Long as we draw our breath,
A Saviour, too, to intercede,
Till we are changed by death.

5 The throne of glory then shall glow
With beams from Jesus' face,
And we no longer want shall know,
Nor need a throne of grace.

262 8s & 7s.

Seal my heart.

TAKE my heart, O Father! take it;
Make and keep it all thine own:
Let thy Spirit melt and break it:
Turn to flesh this heart of stone.
Heavenly Father, deign to mould it
In obedience to thy will;
And as passing years unfold it,
Keep it meek and childlike still.

2 Father, make it pure and lowly,
 Peaceful, kind, and far from strife,
Turning from the paths unholy
 Of this vain and sinful life.
May the blood of Jesus heal it,
 And its sins be all forgiven:
Holy Spirit, take and seal it;
 Guide it in the path to heaven.

263 L. M.

The Gospel exemplified in the conduct.

SO let our lips and lives express
 The holy Gospel we profess;
So let our works and virtues shine,
To prove the doctrine all divine.

2 Thus shall we best proclaim abroad
The honors of our Saviour God,
When his salvation reigns within,
And grace subdues the power of sin.

3 Our flesh and sense must be denied,
Ambition, envy, lust, and pride;
While justice, temperance, truth, and love,
Our inward piety approve.

4 Religion bears our spirits up,
While we expect that blessed hope,
The bright appearance of the Lord,
And faith stands leaning on his word.

264 6s & 4s.

Heaven is my home.

I'M but a stranger here,
 Heaven is my home.
Earth is a desert drear,
 Heaven is my home.
Dangers and sorrows stand
Round me on every hand,
Heaven is my Father-land,
 Heaven is my home.

2 What though the tempest rage?
Heaven is my home.
Short is my pilgrimage,
Heaven is my home.
Time's cold and wintry blast
Soon will be overpast,
I shall reach home at last,
Heaven is my home.

3 There at the Saviour's side,
Heaven is my home.
I shall be glorified,
Heaven is my home.
There are the good and blest,
Those I love most and best;
There, too, I soon shall rest,
Heaven is my home.

265 C. M.

Soldier of the Cross.

AM I a soldier of the cross,
A follower of the Lamb,
And shall I fear to own his cause
Or blush to speak his name?

2 Shall I be carried to the skies
On flowery beds of ease,
While others fought to win the prize
And sailed through bloody seas?

3 Are there no foes for me to face?
Must I not stem the flood?
Is this vain world a friend to grace,
To help me on to God?

4 Sure I must fight, if I would reign:
Increase my courage, Lord!
I'll bear the toil, endure the pain,
Supported by thy word.

5 Thy saints, in all this glorious war,
Shall conquer, though they die;
They see the triumph from afar,
By faith they bring it nigh.

6 When that illustrious day shall rise,
And all thy armies shine
In robes of victory through the skies,
The glory shall be thine.

266 S. M.

Prayer for watchfulness.

A CHARGE to keep I have,
A God to glorify;
A never-dying soul to save
And fit it for the sky.
To serve the present age,
My calling to fulfill,
O may it all my powers engage,
To do my Master's will.

2 Arm me with jealous care,
As in thy sight to live;
And O, thy servant, Lord, prepare,
A strict account to give.
Help me to watch and pray,
And on thyself rely,
Assured, if I my trust betray,
I shall forever die.

267 L. M.

Not ashamed of Christ.

JESUS, and shall it ever be
A mortal man ashamed of thee?
Ashamed of thee, whom angels praise,
Whose glories shine through endless days?

2 Ashamed of Jesus! that dear Friend
On whom my hopes of heaven depend?
No! when I blush, be this my shame:
That I no more revere his name.

3 Ashamed of Jesus! yes, I may,
When I've no guilt to wash away,
No tear to wipe, no good to crave,
No fears to quell, no soul to save.

4 Till then, nor is my boasting vain;
Till then, I boast a Saviour slain;
And O, may this my glory be,
That Christ is not ashamed of me.

268 C. M.

Purposes of God developed by his providence.

GOD moves in a mysterious way,
His wonders to perform;
He plants his footsteps in the sea,
And rides upon the storm.

2 Ye fearful saints, fresh courage take;
The clouds ye so much dread
Are big with mercy, and shall break
With blessings on your head.

3 Judge not the Lord by feeble sense,
But trust him for his grace;
Behind a frowning providence
He hides a smiling face.

4 His purposes will ripen fast,
Unfolding every hour;
The bud may have a bitter taste,
But sweet will be the flower.

5 Blind unbelief is sure to err,
And scan his work in vain;
God is his own interpreter,
And he will make it plain.

269 S. M.

The well-fought day.

PRAY without ceasing, pray,
(Your Captain gives the word;)
His summons cheerfully obey,
And call upon the Lord:

To God your every want
  In instant prayer display;
Pray always; pray, and never faint;
  Pray, without ceasing, pray.

2 From strength to strength go on;
  Wrestle, and fight, and pray;
Tread all the powers of darkness down,
  And win the well-fought day;
Still let the Spirit cry,
  In all his soldiers, Come,
Till Christ, the Lord, descend from high,
  And take the conqu'rors home.

270

4 6s & 2 8s.

"Abba, Father."

ARISE, my soul, arise;
  Shake off thy guilty fears;
The bleeding Sacrifice
  In my behalf appears;
Before the throne my Surety stands;
My name is written on his hands.

2 Five bleeding wounds he bears,
  Received on Calvary;
They pour effectual prayers,
  They strongly plead for me:
Forgive him, O forgive, they cry,
Nor let that ransomed sinner die.

3 The Father hears him pray,
  His dear anointed One;
He cannot turn away
  The presence of his Son:
His Spirit answers to the blood,
And tells me I am born of God.

4 My God is reconciled;
  His pard'ning voice I hear;
He owns me for his child;
  I can no longer fear:
With confidence I now draw nigh,
And Father, Abba, Father, cry.

271 C M.

Earthly pleasures dangerous.

HOW vain are all things here below!
How false, and yet how fair!
Each pleasure hath its poison too,
And every sweet a snare.

2 The brightest things below the sky
Shine with deceiving light;
We should suspect some danger nigh,
Where we possess delight.

3 Our dearest joys, our nearest friends,
The partners of our blood,
How they divide our wavering minds,
And leave but half for God!

4 The fondness of a creature's love,
How strong it strikes the sense!
Thither the warm affections move,
Nor can we call them thence.

5 Dear Saviour, let thy beauties be
My soul's eternal food,
And grace command my heart away
From all created good.

272 8s, 7s, & 4.

O, be my guide.

GUIDE me, O thou great Jehovah,
Pilgrim through this barren land;
I am weak, but thou art mighty;
Hold me with thy powerful hand;
Bread of heaven,
Feed me till I want no more.

2 Open thou the crystal fountain
Whence the healing waters flow;
Let the fiery, cloudy pillar
Lead me all my journey through:
Strong Deliverer,
Be thou still my strength and shield

3 When I tread the verge of Jordan,
Bid the swelling stream divide;
Death of death, and hell's destruction,
Land me safe on Canaan's side;
Songs of praises
I will ever give to thee.

273 C. M.

Exhortation to Christian activity.

MY drowsy powers, why sleep ye so?
Awake, my sluggish soul!
Nothing has half thy work to do,
Yet nothing's half so dull.

2 Go to the ants! for one poor grain
See how they toil and strive;
Yet we, who have a heaven t' obtain,
How negligent we live!

3 We, for whose sake all nature stands,
And stars their courses move;
We, for whose guard the angel bands
Come flying from above;

4 We, for whom God the Son came down,
And labored for our good,
How careless to secure that crown
He purchased with his blood!

5 Lord, shall we lie so sluggish still,
And never act our parts?
Come, holy Dove, from th' heavenly hill,
And warm our frozen hearts.

274 7s & 6s.

Press for the prize.

RISE, my soul, and stretch thy wings.
Thy better portion trace;
Rise from transitory things
Toward heaven, thy native place:

Sun, and moon, and stars decay,
  Time shall soon this earth remove;
Rise, my soul, and haste away
  To seats prepared above.

2 Rivers to the ocean run,
  Nor stay in all their course;
Fire, ascending, seeks the sun,
  Both speed them to their source:
So the soul that's born of God
  Pants to see his glorious face,
Upward tends to his abode,
  To rest in his embrace.

3 Cease, ye pilgrims, cease to mourn;
  Press onward to the prize;
Soon our Saviour will return
  Triumphant in the skies;
Yet a season, and you know
  Happy entrance will be given;
All our sorrows left below,
  And earth exchanged for heaven.

275 6s & 5s.

Little drops of water.

LITTLE drops of water,
  Little grains of sand,
Make the mighty ocean
  And the beauteous land;

2 And the little moments,
  Humble though they be,
Make the mighty ages
  Of eternity

3 So our little errors
  Lead the soul away
From the paths of virtue,
  Oft in sin to stray.

4 Little deeds of kindness,
Little words of love,
Make our earth an Eden,
Like the heaven above.

5 Little seeds of mercy,
Sown by youthful hands,
Grow to bless the nations
Far in heathen lands.

276 8s, 7s, & 4.

Daily work to do.

IN the vineyard of our Father
Daily work we find to do;
Scattered gleanings we may gather,
Though we are but young and few;
Little clusters
Help to fill the garners, too.

2 Toiling early in the morning,
Catching moments through the day,
Nothing small or lowly scorning,
As along our path we stray:
Gathering gladly
Free-will offerings by the way.

3 Up and ever at our calling,
Till in death our lips are dumb;
Or till, sin's dominion falling,
Christ shall in his kingdom come,
And his children
Reach their everlasting home.

4 Steadfast, then, in our endeavor,
Heavenly Father, may we be;
And forever and forever
We will give the praise to thee.
Halleluiah!
Singing all eternity.

277 L. M.

He liveth long who liveth well.

HE liveth long who liveth well!
All other life is short and vain;
He liveth longest who can tell
Of living most for heavenly gain.

2 He liveth long who liveth well!
All else is being flung away;
He liveth longest who can tell
Of true things truly done each day.

3 Waste not thy being; back to Him
Who freely gave it, freely give;
Else is that being but a dream,
'Tis but to be, and not to live.

4 Fill up each hour with what will last;
Buy up the moments as they go;
The life above when this is past
Is the ripe fruit of life below.

278 C. M.

The shadow of the Cross.

OPPRESSED with noonday's scorching heat,
To yonder cross I flee;
Beneath its shelter take my seat:
No shade like this for me!

2 Beneath that cross clear waters burst,
A fountain sparkling free;
And there I quench my desert thirst;
No spring like this for me!

3 For burdened ones a resting-place
Beside that cross I see;
Here I cast off my weariness;
No rest like this for me!

4 A stranger here, I pitch my tent
Beneath this spreading tree;
Here shall my pilgrim life be spent,
No home like this for me!

279 8s & 7s.

The elder brother.

YES, for me, for me he careth
With a brother's tender care;
Yes, with me, with me he shareth
Every burden, every fear.

2 Yes, o'er me, o'er me he watcheth,
Ceaseless watcheth, night and day;
Yes, e'en me, e'en me he snatcheth
From the perils of the way.

3 Yes, for me he standeth pleading,
At the mercy-seat above;
Ever for me interceding,
Constant in untiring love.

4 Yes, in me abroad he sheddeth
Joys unearthly, love and light;
And to cover me he spreadeth
His paternal wing of night.

5 Yes, in me, in me he dwelleth;
I in him, and he in me!
And my empty soul he filleth
Here and through eternity.

6 Thus I wait for his returning,
Singing all the way to heaven;
Such the joyful song of morning,
Such the tranquil song of even.

280 L. M.

The useful life.

GO labor on; spend and be spent,
Thy joy to do the Father's will;
It is the way the Master went,
Should not the servant tread it still?

2 Go labor on; 'tis not for naught;
Thy earthly loss is heavenly gain;
Men heed thee, love thee, praise thee not;
The Master praises—what are men?

3 Go labor on; enough while here,
If he shall praise thee, if he deign
Thy willing heart to mark and cheer;
No toil for him shall be in vain.

4 Toil on; faint not; keep watch, and pray;
Be wise the erring soul to win;
Go forth into the world's highway,
Compel the wanderer to come in.

5 Toil on, and in thy toil rejoice;
For toil comes rest, for exile home;
Soon shalt thou hear the bridegroom's voice,
The midnight peal, "Behold, I come!"

281 C. M.

Mine and thine.

ALL that I was; my sin, my guilt,
My death, was all my own;
All that I am I owe to thee,
My gracious God, alone.

2 The evil of my former state
Was mine and only mine;
The good in which I now rejoice
Is thine and only thine.

3 The darkness of my former state,
The bondage, all was mine;
The light of life in which I walk,
The liberty, is thine.

4 All that I am, even here on earth,
All that I hope to be
When Jesus comes and glory dawns,
I owe it, Lord, to thee.

282 C. M.

'Tis I, be not afraid.

WHEN waves of sorrow round me swell,
My soul is not dismayed;
I hear a voice I know full well,
"'Tis I, be not afraid."

2 When black the threat'ning clouds appear,
And storms my path invade,
That voice shall tranquilize each fear,
"'Tis I, be not afraid."

3 There is a gulf that must be crossed;
Saviour! be near to aid;
Whisper when my frail bark is tossed,
"'Tis I, be not afraid."

4 There is a dark and fearful vale
Death hides within its shade;
O say when flesh and heart shall fail,
"'Tis I, be not afraid."

283 8s & 6.

Thy will be done.—TUNE, "*Just as I am.*"

MY God, my Father, while I stray
Far from my home on life's rough way,
O teach me from my heart to say,
"Thy will, let it be done."

2 If thou shouldst call me to resign
What most I prize, it ne'er was mine;
I only yield thee what was thine!
"Thy will, let it be done."

3 If but my fainting heart be blest
With thy sweet Spirit for its guest,
My God, to thee I leave the rest—
"Thy will, let it be done."

4 And when on earth I breathe no more
The prayer oft mixed with tears before,
I'll sing upon a happier shore,
"Thy will, let it be done."

284 8s & 6.

Plead for me.—TUNE, "*Just as I am.*"

O THOU, the contrite sinner's friend,
Who, loving, lov'st them to the end,
On this alone my hopes depend,
That thou wilt plead for me.

2 When, weary in the Christian race,
Far off appears my resting-place,
And, fainting, I mistrust thy grace,
Then, Saviour, plead for me.

3 When I have erred and gone astray,
Afar from thine and wisdom's way,
And see no glimm'ring, guiding ray,
Still, Saviour, plead for me.

4 And when my dying hour draws near,
Darkened with conflict, pain, and fear,
Then to my fainting sight appear,
Pleading in heaven for me.

285 7s & 6s.

The Cross of Jesus.

I SAW the cross of Jesus
When burdened with my sin;
I sought the cross of Jesus
To give me peace within:
I brought my sin to Jesus;
He cleansed it in his blood;
And in the cross of Jesus
I found my peace with God.

2 I love the cross of Jesus,
It tells me what I am;
A vile and guilty creature,
Saved only through the Lamb.
No righteousness, no merit,
No beauty can I plead;
Yet in the cross I glory,
My title there I read.

3 I clasp the cross of Jesus
In every trying hour,
My sure and certain refuge,
My never-failing tower.

In every fear and conflict,
  I more than conqu'ror am,
Living I'm safe, or dying,
  Through Christ the risen Lamb.

4 Sweet is the cross of Jesus!
  There let my weary heart
Still rest in perfect peace,
  Till life itself depart.
And then in strains of glory
  I'll sing thy wondrous power,
Where sin can never enter,
  And death is known no more.

286 C. M.

Prayer.

PRAYER is the breath of God in man,
  Returning whence it came;
Love is the sacred fire within,
  And prayer the rising flame.

2 It gives the burdened spirit ease,
  And soothes the troubled breast:
Yields comfort to the mourning soul,
  And to the weary rest.

3 The prayers and praises of the saints
  Like precious odors sweet,
Ascend and spread a rich perfume
  Around the mercy seat.

4 When God inclines the heart to pray,
  He hath an ear to hear;
To him there's music in a groan,
  And beauty in a tear.

5 The humble suppliant cannot fail
  To have his wants supplied,
Since He for sinners intercedes
  Who once for sinners died.

287

4 6s & 2 8s.

The Lord our Refuge.

THE Lord our refuge is,
  And ever will remain;
Since he hath made us his,
  He will our cause maintain;
In vain our enemies oppose,
For God is stronger than his foes.

2 The Lord our portion is,
  What can we wish for more?
As long as we are his,
  We never can be poor:
In vain do earth and hell oppose,
For God is stronger than his foes.

3 The Lord our Shepherd is,
  He knows our every need;
And since we now are his,
  His care our souls will feed:
In vain do sin and death oppose,
For God is stronger than his foes.

4 Our God our Father is,
  Our names are on his heart;
We ever shall be his,
  He ne'er from us will part:
In vain the world and flesh oppose,
For God is stronger than his foes.

288

6s & 4s.

Jesus, my Lord.

JESUS, thy name I love,
  All other names above,
    Jesus, my Lord!
O! thou art all to me,
Nothing to please I see,
Nothing apart from thee,
    Jesus, my Lord!

2 Thou blessed Son of God
Hast bought me with thy blood,
Jesus, my Lord!
How great to me thy love,
All other loves above,
Love that I daily prove,
Jesus, my Lord!

3 When unto thee I flee,
Thou wilt my refuge be,
Jesus, my Lord!
What need I now to fear,
What earthly grief or care,
Since thou art ever near?
Jesus, my Lord!

4 Soon wilt thou come again;
I shall be happy then,
Jesus, my Lord!
Then thine own face I'll see,
Then I shall like thee be,
Then evermore with thee,
Jesus, my Lord!

289 C. M.

Thy will be mine.

ONE prayer I have, all prayers in one,
When I am wholly thine;
Thy will, my God, thy will be done,
And let that will be mine.

2 All-wise, Almighty, and All-good,
In thee I firmly trust;
Thy ways, unknown or understood,
Are merciful and just.

3 May I remember, that to thee
Whate'er I have I owe;
And back in gratitude from me
May all thy bounties flow.

4 Thy gifts are only then enjoyed
When used as talents lent;
Those talents only well employed
When in thy service spent.

5 Write but my name upon the roll
Of thy redeemed above;
Then heart, and mind, and strength, and soul,
I'll love thee for thy love.

290 C. M.

A pilgrim here.

A PILGRIM through this lonely world,
The blessed Saviour passed;
A mourner all his life was he,
A dying Lamb at last.

2 That tender heart that felt for all,
For all its life-blood gave;
It found on earth no resting-place,
Save only in the grave.

3 Such was our Lord; and shall we fear
The cross, with all its scorn?
Or love a faithless evil world,
That wreathed his brow with thorn?

4 No! facing all its frowns or smiles,
Like him obedient still,
We homeward press through storm or calm,
To Zion's blessed hill.

291 S. M.

My sins are blotted out.

MY sins are blotted out
Since Jesus died for me;
My times are in a Father's hand,
My steps in his decree.

2 Jesus in heaven appears,
For me to intercede;
And countless benefits proclaim
"The Lord is risen indeed."

3 A little child is free
  From carefulness and guile,
Rests in a mother's guardian love,
  And waits a father's smile.

4 Father of spirits, hear,
  Make me this little child;
May I delight myself in thee,
  By no mistrust defiled.

292 S. M.

The ark of God.

LIKE Noah's weary dove
  That soared the earth around,
But not a resting-place above
  The cheerless waters found,

2 O cease, my wandering soul,
  On restless wing to roam;
All the wide world, to either pole,
  Has not for thee a home.

3 Behold the ark of God;
  Behold the open door;
Hasten to gain that dear abode,
  And rove, my soul, no more.

4 There, safe thou shalt abide;
  There, sweet shall be thy rest;
And every longing satisfied,
  With full salvation blessed.

293 C. M.

The pilgrim.

STILL onward through the land of foes
  I pass in pilgrim guise;
I may not stop to seek repose
  Where cool the shadow lies;
I may not stoop amid the grass
  To pluck earth's fairest flowers,
Nor by her springing fountains pass
  The sultry noontide hours.

2 Yet flowers I wear upon my breast
  That no earth-garden knows,
White lilies of immortal peace,
  And love's deep-tinted rose;
And there the blue-eyed flowers of faith,
  And hope's bright buds of gold,
As lone I tread the upward path,
  In richest hues unfold.

3 Painful and dark the pathway seems
  To distant earthly eyes;
They only see the hedging thorns
  On either side that rise;
They cannot know how soft between
  The flowers of love are strewn—
The sunny ways, the pastures green,
  Where Jesus leads his own;

4 They cannot see, as dark'ning clouds
  Behind the pilgrim close,
How far adown the western glade
  The golden glory flows;
They cannot hear, 'mid earthly din,
  The song to pilgrims known,
Still blending with the angels' hymn
  Around the wondrous throne.

294

4 6s & 2 8s.

Who is my brother?

MUST I my brother keep
  And share his pains and toil?
And weep with those that weep,
  And smile with those that smile?
Is he my brother to whose grief
I may have power to bring relief?

2 Must I his burden bear,
  As though it were my own?
And do as I would care
  Should to myself be done?
And faithful to his interests prove,
And as myself my neighbor love?

3 Then Jesus, at thy feet,
A student let me be,
And learn as it is meet,
My duty, Lord, of thee:
For thou didst come on mercy's plan,
And all thy life was love to man.

4 O make me as thou art;
Thy Spirit, Lord, bestow;
The kind and gentle heart
That feels another's woe;
That thus I may be like my Head,
And in my Saviour's footsteps tread.

295

7s & 6s.

Near Jesus.

I WANT to live near Jesus,
And never go astray;
To feel that I am growing
More like him every day;
That I am always laying
My treasure up above,
And gaining more the spirit
Of his gentleness and love.

2 I want such steadfast purpose
My mission to fulfill,
That it may be my meat and drink
To do my Father's will;
To follow in his footsteps,
Who never turned aside
From the path that leads to heaven,
Though often sorely tried.

3 O may I live near Jesus,
And never go astray,
And every sin-defiling stain
Shall soon be washed away;
And I'll bear my Master's image,
When I see him face to face,
Then earth shall lose the power
Its brightness to deface.

296

4 *lines* 7s.

The Christian.

WHO is as the Christian great?
  Bought and washed with sacred blood;
Crowns he sees beneath his feet,
  Soars aloft and walks with God.

2 Who is as the Christian wise?
  He his naught for all hath given;
Bought the pearl of greatest price,
  Nobly bartered earth for heaven.

3 Who is as the Christian blest?
  He hath found the long-sought stone;
He is joined to Christ, his rest,
  He and happiness are one.

4 Earth and heaven together meet,
  Gifts in him and graces join;
Make the character complete,
  All immortal, all divine.

297

C. M.

I'll turn to Thee.

JESUS, in sickness and in pain,
  Be near to succor me;
My sinking spirit still sustain;
  To thee I turn, to thee.

2 When cares and sorrows thicken round,
  And nothing bright I see,
In thee alone can help be found;
  To thee I turn, to thee.

3 Should strong temptations fierce assail,
  And Satan buffet me,
Then in thy strength will I prevail,
  While still I turn to thee.

4 Through all my pilgrimage below,
  Whate'er my lot may be,
In joy or sadness, weal or woe,
  Jesus, I'll turn to thee.

298

4 *lines* 7s.

Conflict with sin.

BRETHREN, while we sojourn here,
  Fight we must, but should not fear;
Foes we have, but we've a Friend,
One that loves us to the end;
Forward, then, with courage go;
Long we shall not dwell below;
Soon the joyful news will come,
"Child, your Father calls, Come home."

2 In the way a thousand snares
Lie to takes us unawares;
Satan, with malicious art,
Watches each unguarded part:
But from Satan's malice free,
Saints shall soon victorious be;
Soon the joyful news will come,
"Child, your Father calls, Come home."

3 But of all the foes we meet,
None so oft mislead our feet,
None betray us into sin
Like the foes that dwell within;
Yet let nothing spoil our peace,
Christ shall also conquer these;
Soon the joyful news will come,
"Child, your Father calls, Come home."

299

C. M.

The example of the faithful.

RISE, O my soul, pursue the path
  By ancient worthies trod;
Aspiring, view those holy men
  Who lived and walked with God.

2 Though dead, they speak in reason's ear
  And in example live;
Their faith, and hope, and mighty deeds
  Still fresh instruction give.

3 'Twas through the Lamb's most precious blood
They conquered every foe;
And to his power and matchless grace
Their crowns of life they owe.

4 Lord, may I ever keep in view
The patterns thou hast given,
And ne'er forsake the blessed road
That led them safe to heaven.

300 C. M.

The hour of prayer.

I LOVE to steal a while away
From every cumbering care,
And spend the hours of setting day
In humble, grateful prayer.

2 I love in solitude to shed
The penitential tear,
And all his promises to plead,
Where none but God can hear.

3 I love to think on mercies past,
And future good implore;
And all my cares and sorrows cast
On Him whom I adore.

4 I love by faith to take a view
Of brighter scenes in heaven;
The prospect doth my strength renew,
While here by tempests driven.

5 Thus, when life's toilsome day is o'er,
May its departing ray
Be calm as this impressive hour,
And lead to endless day.

SHORTNESS OF TIME.

301 C. M.

Man frail—God eternal.

O GOD, our help in ages past,
Our hope for years to come,
Our shelter from the stormy blast,
And our eternal home:—

2 Under the shadow of thy throne
Still may we dwell secure;
Sufficient is thine arm alone,
And our defence is sure.

3 Before the hills in order stood,
Or earth received her frame,
From everlasting thou art God,
To endless years the same.

4 A thousand ages, in thy sight,
Are like an evening gone;
Short as the watch that ends the night,
Before the rising sun.

5 Time, like an ever-rolling stream,
Bears all its sons away;
They fly, forgotten, as a dream
Dies at the opening day.

6 O God, our help in ages past,
Our hope for years to come;
Be thou our guide while life shall last,
And our perpetual home!

302 C. M.

Time the Period to prepare for Eternity.

THEE we adore, Eternal Name,
And humbly own to thee
How feeble is our mortal frame,
What dying worms are we.

2 The year rolls round, and steals away
The breath that first it gave;
Whate'er we do, where'er we be,
We're traveling to the grave.

3 Great God, on what a slender thread
Hang everlasting things!
The final state of all the dead
Upon life's feeble strings!

4 Eternal joy, or endless woe,
Attends on every breath;
And yet how unconcerned we go
Upon the brink of death!

5 Awake, O Lord, our drowsy sense,
To walk this dangerous road;
And if our souls are hurried hence,
May they be found with God.

303 C. M.

Time and Eternity.

LIFE is a span—a fleeting hour:
How soon the vapor flies!
Man is a tender, transient flower,
That e'en in blooming dies.

2 The once-loved form, now cold and dead,
Each mournful thought employs;
And nature weeps her comforts fled,
And withered all her joys.

3 Hope looks beyond the bounds of time,
When what we now deplore
Shall rise in full, immortal prime,
And bloom to fade no more.

4 Cease, then, fond Nature, cease thy tears,
Thy Saviour dwells on high;
There everlasting spring appears;
There joys shall never die.

304 C. M.

Deliverance is at hand.

MY span of life will soon be done,
The passing moments say;
As length'ning shadows o'er the mead
Proclaim the close of day.

2 O that my heart might dwell aloof
From all created things;
And learn that wisdom from above,
Whence true contentment springs.

3 Courage, my soul; thy bitter cross,
In every trial here,
Shall bear thee to thy heaven above,
Bnt shall not enter there.

4 The sighing ones, that humbly seek
In sorrowing paths below,
Shall in eternity rejoice,
Where endless comforts flow.

5 Courage, my soul, on God rely;
Deliv'rance soon will come;
A thousand ways has Providence
To bring believers home.

305 7s & 6s.

Time is winging us away.

TIME is winging us away
To our eternal home;
Life is but a winter's day,
A journey to the tomb:
Youth and vigor soon will flee,
Blooming beauty lose its charms;
All that's mortal soon will be
Enclosed in death's cold arms.

2 Time is winging us away
To our eternal home;
Life is but a winter's day,
A journey to the tomb:

But the Christian shall enjoy
  Health and beauty soon above,
Far beyond the world's alloy,
  Secure in Jesus' love.

306 S. M.

Our fathers, where are they?

HOW swift the torrent rolls
  That bears us to the sea;
The tide that hurries thoughtless souls
  To vast eternity!

2 Our fathers, where are they,
  With all they called their own?
Their joys and griefs, and hopes and cares,
  And wealth and honor? Gone.

3 God of our fathers, hear,
  Thou everlasting Friend!
While we, as on life's utmost verge,
  Our souls to thee commend.

4 Of all the pious dead
  May we the footsteps trace,
Till with them, in the land of light,
  We dwell before thy face.

307 C. M.

Life short, and man frail.

TEACH me the measure of my days,
  Thou Maker of my frame:
I would survey life's narrow space,
  And learn how frail I am.

2 A span is all that we can boast;
  How short the fleeting time!
Man is but vanity and dust
  In all his flower and prime.

3 What can I wish or wait for then,
  From creatures, earth and dust?
They make our expectations vain,
  And disappoint our trust.

4 Now I forbid my carnal hope,
My fond desire recall;
I give my mortal interest up,
And make my God my all.

DEATH.

308 C. M.

A sister's death.

DEATH has been here, and borne away
A sister from our side;
Just in the morning of her day,
As young as we, she died.

2 Not long ago she filled her place,
And sat with us to learn;
But she has run her mortal race,
And never can return.

3 Perhaps our time may be as short,
Our days may fly as fast:
O Lord, impress the solemn thought,
That this may be our last!

4 We cannot tell who next may fall
Beneath thy chastening rod;
One must be first; O, may we all
Prepare to meet our God!

5 All needful help is thine to give;
To thee our souls apply
For grace to teach us how to live
And make us fit to die.

309 L. M.

Death and burial of a Christian.

UNVEIL thy bosom, faithful tomb;
Take this new treasure to thy trust;
And give these sacred relics room
To slumber in the silent dust.

2 Nor pain, nor grief, nor anxious fear
Invades thy bounds; no mortal woes
Can reach the peaceful sleeper here,
While angels watch the soft repose.

3 So Jesus slept; God's dying Son
Passed through the grave, and blessed the bed
Rest here, blest saint, till from his throne
The morning break, and pierce the shade.

4 Break from his throne, illustrious morn;
Attend, O earth, his sovereign word;
Restore thy trust; a glorious form
Shall then arise to meet the Lord.

310 L. M.

The Christian's parting hour.

HOW sweet the hour of closing day,
When all is peaceful and serene,
And when the sun, with cloudless ray,
Sheds mellow luster o'er the scene!

2 Such is the Christian's parting hour;
So peacefully he sinks to rest;
When faith, endued from heaven with power,
Sustains and cheers his languid breast.

3 Mark now that radiance of his eye;
That smile upon his wasted cheek;
They tell us of his glory nigh
In language that no tongue can speak.

4 A beam from heaven is sent to cheer
The pilgrim on his gloomy road;
And angels are attending near
To bear him to their bright abode.

5 Who would not wish to die like those
Whom God's own Spirit deigns to bless?
To sink into that soft repose,
Then wake to perfect happiness?

311

6s, & 8.

At rest.

BROTHER, thou art gone to rest;
We will not weep for thee;
For thou art now where oft on earth
Thy Spirit longed to be.

2 Brother, thou art gone to rest;
Thine is an early tomb;
But Jesus summoned thee away;
Thy Saviour called thee home.

3 Brother, thou art gone to rest;
Thy toils and cares are o'er;
And sorrow, pain, and suffering, now
Shall ne'er distress theo more.

4 Brother, thou art gone to rest;
Thy sins are all forgiven;
And saints in light have welcomed thee
To share the joys of heaven.

5 Brother, thou art gone to rest,
And this shall be our prayer:
That when we reach our journey's end,
Thy glory we may share.

312

8s & 7s.

Peaceful slumber.

PEACEFUL be thy silent slumber,
Peaceful in the grave so low;
Thou no more wilt join our number,
Thou no more our songs shalt know.

2 Dearest brother, thou hast left us;
Here thy loss we deeply feel;
But 'tis God that hath bereft us,
He can all our sorrow heal.

3 Yet again we hope to meet thee
When the day of life is fled;
Then, in heaven, with joy to greet thee,
Where no farewell tear is shed.

313 C. M.

Peaceful death of the pious.

BEHOLD the western evening light!
  It melts in deepening gloom;
So calmly Christians sink away,
  Descending to the tomb.

2 The winds breathe low; the yellow leaf
  Scarce whispers from the tree;
So gently flows the parting breath
  When good men cease to be.

3 How beautiful, on all the hills,
  The crimson light is shed!
'Tis like the peace the Christian gives
  To mourners round his bed.

4 How mildly on the wandering cloud
  The sunset beam is cast!
So sweet the memory left behind
  When loved ones breathe their last.

5 And lo! above the dews of night
  The vesper star appears;
So faith lights up the mourner's heart
  Whose eyes are dim with tears.

314 L. M.

Asleep in Jesus.

ASLEEP in Jesus! blessed sleep!
  From which none ever wake to weep;
A calm and undisturbed repose,
Unbroken by the last of foes.

2 Asleep in Jesus! O how sweet
To be for such a slumber meet!
With holy confidence to sing
That death has lost his cruel sting.

3 Asleep in Jesus! peaceful rest!
Whose waking is supremely blest;
No fear, no woe, shall dim that hour
That manifests the Saviour's power.

4 Asleep in Jesus! O for me
May such a blissful refuge be!
Securely shall my ashes lie,
Waiting the summons from on high.

5 Asleep in Jesus! far from thee
Thy kindred and their graves may be;
But there is still a blessed sleep,
From which none ever wake to weep.

315 S. M.

The peaceful death of the righteous

O FOR the death of those
  Who slumber in the Lord!
O be like theirs my last repose,
  Like theirs my last reward.

2 Their bodies in the ground,
  In silent hope may lie;
Till the last trumpet's joyful sound
  Shall call them to the sky.

3 Their ransomed spirits soar
  On wings of faith and love,
To meet the Saviour they adore,
  And reign with him above.

4 With us their names shall live
  Through long-succeeding years,
Embalmed with all our hearts can give,
  Our praises and our tears.

5 O for the death of those
  Who slumber in the Lord!
O be like theirs my last repose,
  Like theirs my last reward!

316 4 lines 7s.

The Christian's burial.

BROTHER, though from yonder sky
  Cometh neither voice nor cry,
Yet we know for thee to-day
Every pain hath passed away.

2 Not for thee shall tears be given,
Child of God, and heir of heaven;
For he gave thee sweet release;
Thine the Christian's death of peace.

3 Well we know thy living faith
Had the power to conquer death;
As a living rose may bloom
By the border of the tomb.

4 Brother, in that solemn trust
We commend thee, dust to dust;
In that faith we wait, till, risen,
Thou shalt meet us all in heaven.

5 While we weep as Jesus wept,
Thou shalt sleep as Jesus slept;
With thy Saviour thou shalt rest,
Crowned, and glorified, and blest.

317

12s & 11s.

Farewell to a friend departed.

THOU art gone to the grave; but we will not deplore thee,
Though sorrows and darkness encompass the tomb;
The Saviour has passed through its portals before thee,
And the lamp of his love is thy guide through the gloom.

2 Thou art gone to the grave; we no longer behold thee,
Nor tread the rough paths of the world by thy side;
But the wide arms of mercy are spread to enfold thee,
And sinners may hope since the Saviour hath died.

3 Thou art gone to the grave; and, its mansion forsaking,
Perchance thy weak spirit in doubt lingered long;
But the sunshine of heaven beamed bright on thy waking,
And the sound thou didst hear was the seraphim's song.

4 Thou art gone to the grave; but we will not deplore thee,
Since God was thy ransom, thy guardian, thy guide
He gave thee, he took thee, and he will restore thee;
And death has no sting since the Saviour hath died.

318 C. M.

Preparation for death.

IF I must die, O let me die
With hope in Jesus' blood;
The blood that saves from sin and guilt,
And reconciles to God.

2 If I must die, O let me die
In peace with all mankind,
And change these fleeting joys below
For pleasures more refined.

3 If I must die, and die I must,
Let some kind seraph come
And bear me on his friendly wing
To my celestial home.

4 Of Canaan's land, from Pisgah's top,
May I but have a view,
Though Jordan should o'erflow its banks,
I'll boldly venture through.

319 8s & 7s.

Burial of a Christian brother.

BROTHER, rest from sin and sorrow;
Death is o'er, and life is won;
On thy slumber dawns no morrow;
Rest; thine earthly race is run.

2 Brother, wake; the night is waning;
Endless day is round thee poured;
Enter thou the rest remaining
For the people of the Lord.

3 Brother, wake; for He who loved thee,
He who died that thou mightst live,
He who graciously approved thee,
Waits thy crown of joy to give.

4 Fare thee well; though woe is blending
With the tones of earthly love,
Triumph high and joy unending
Wait thee in the realms above.

320 C. M.

Death of the young.

WHEN blooming youth is snatched away
By Death's resistless hand,
Our hearts the mournful tribute pay
Which pity must demand.

2 While pity prompts the rising sigh,
O may this truth, impressed
With awful power, "I too, must die,"
Sink deep in every breast.

3 The voice of this alarming scene
May every heart obey;
Nor be the heavenly warning vain
Which calls to watch and pray.

4 O let us fly, to Jesus fly,
Whose powerful arm can save;
Then shall our hopes ascend on high,
And triumph o'er the grave.

321 S. M.

Support in death.

WHEN on the brink of death
My trembling soul shall stand,
Waiting to pass that awful flood,
Great God! at thy command;

2 When every scene of life
Stands ready to depart,
And the last sigh that shakes the frame
Shall rend this bursting heart;

3 Then, Source of joy supreme
Whose arm alone can save,
Dispel the darkness that surrounds
The entrance to the grave.

4 Lay thy supporting hand
  Beneath my sinking head;
And with a ray of love divine
  Illume my dying bed.

322 7s & 5s.

A young Christian's burial.

COME, children, kindly gather
  Round this form beloved,
Whence so soon our heavenly Father
  Hath the soul removed.
Soul, leave the body mortal
  Safe with us at rest,
Pass beyond the golden portal
  To thy Saviour's breast.

CHORUS.

Bright angels, happy spirits,
  Watch with star-like eyes
O'er the spot whence at Christ's summons
  His beloved shall rise.

2 Eyes full of love and gladness,
  Quiet now in sleep,
Closed on all our sin and sadness,
  Never more to weep.
Unclose now with bliss amazing
  In the realms of peace;
Burst to sight, with rapture gazing
  On the Saviour's face.
    CHORUS.—Bright angels, etc.

3 Hark, 'mid the radiant dawning,
  Where night comes no more,
Sweet-toned bells of Sabbath morning
  Sound from that far shore.
Lo, cherub forms that hover,
  Bearing thee away;
So farewell, thy night is over,
  Lost in endless day.
    CHORUS.—Bright angels, etc.

323

8s, 7s, & 4.

One is gone.

WHERE we oft have met in gladness
  On the holy Sabbath-day,
Slowly, now, with tearful sadness,
  Each pursues his lonely way;
    Tears are falling
  On this holy Sabbath-day.

2 One we loved has left our number
  For the dark and silent tomb,—
Closed *his* eyes in deathless slumber,
  Faded in *his* early bloom;
    Hear us, Saviour!
  Thou hast blest the lonely tomb.

3 Through its dark and narrow portal
  Once they bore thee to thy rest;
There a ray of light immortal,
  Like a sunbeam from the west,
    Burst the shadows,
  And the grave thenceforth was blest.

4 By the light that thus was given
  To the darkness of the tomb;
By the blessed light of heaven,
  Gilding scenes of earthly gloom,
    Star of gladness!
  All our night with joy illume.

5 From our circle, dearest brother,
  Early hast thou passed away;
But the angels say, "Another
  Joins our holy song to-day."
    Weep no longer!
  Join with them the sacred lay.

HEAVEN.

324 8s & 6s.

Rest in heaven.

THERE is an hour of peaceful rest,
To mourning wanderers given:
There is a joy for souls distressed,
A balm for every wounded breast:
'Tis found alone in heaven.

2 There is a home for weary souls
By sin and sorrow driven,
When tossed on life's tempestuous shoals,
Where storms arise and ocean rolls,
And all is drear but heaven.

3 There Faith lifts up her cheerful eye,
To brighter prospects given,
And views the tempest passing by,
The evening shadows quickly fly,
And all serene in heaven.

4 There fragrant flowers immortal bloom,
And joys supreme are given;
There rays divine disperse the gloom;
Beyond the confines of the tomb
Appears the dawn of heaven.

325 C. M.

Children in heaven.

THERE is a glorious world of light
Above the starry sky,
Where saints departed, clothed in white,
Adore the Lord most high.

2 And hark, amid the sacred songs
Those heavenly voices raise,
Ten thousand thousand infant tongues
Unite in perfect praise.

3 Those are the hymns that we shall know
If Jesus we obey;
That is the place where we shall go,
If found in wisdom's way.

4 Soon will our earthly race be run,
Our mortal frame decay;
Children and teachers, one by one,
Must die and pass away.

5 Great God, impress this serious thought
To-day on every breast,
That both the teacher and the taught
May dwell among the blest.

326

4 *lines* 11s.

Longing for heaven.

I WOULD not live alway; I ask not to stay
Where storm after storm rises dark o'er the way
The few lurid mornings that dawn on us here
Are enough for its joys, full enough for its cheer.

2 I would not live alway, thus fettered by sin;
Temptation without and corruption within;
E'en the rapture of pardon is mingled with fears,
And the cup of thanksgiving with penitent tears.

3 I would not live alway; no, welcome the tomb:
Since Jesus hath lain there I dread not its gloom:
There sweet be my rest till he bid me arise
To hail him in triumph descending the skies.

4 Who, who would live alway, away from his God,
Away from yon heaven, that blissful abode,
Where rivers of pleasure flow bright o'er the plains,
And the noontide of glory eternally reigns?

5 There saints of all ages in harmony meet,
Their Saviour and brethren transported to greet;
While anthems of rapture unceasingly roll,
And the smile of the Lord is the feast of the soul.

327

6 *lines* 8s.

Beautiful Zion.

BEAUTIFUL Zion, built above,
Beautiful city, that I love,
Beautiful gates of pearly white,
Beautiful temple—God its light!
He who was slain on Calvary
Opens those pearly gates to me.

2 Beautiful heaven, where all is light,
Beautiful angels, clothed in white,
Beautiful strains, that never tire,
Beautiful harps through all the choir!
There shall I join the chorus sweet,
Worshiping at the Saviour's feet.

3 Beautiful crowns on every brow,
Beautiful palms the conquerors show,
Beautiful robes the ransomed wear,
Beautiful all who enter there!
Thither I press with eager feet;
There shall my rest be long and sweet.

4 Beautiful throne for Christ our King,
Beautiful songs the angels sing,
Beautiful rest, all wanderings cease,
Beautiful home of perfect peace!
There shall my eye the Saviour see:
Haste to this heavenly home with me.

328

C. M.

Everlasting life.

THERE is a fold where none can stray,
And pastures ever green,
Where sultry sun, or stormy day,
Or night, is never seen.

2 Far up the everlasting hills,
In God's own light it lies;
His smile its vast dimension fills
With joy that never dies.

3 One narrow vale, one darksome wave,
Divides that land from this;
I have a Shepherd pledged to save,
And bear me home to bliss.

4 Soon at his feet my soul will lie,
In life's last struggling breath;
But I shall only seem to die,
I shall not taste of death.

5 Far from this guilty world, to be
Exempt from toil and strife;
To spend eternity with thee,
My Saviour, this is life.

329 C. M.

Heavenly rest in anticipation.

WHEN I can read my title clear
To mansions in the skies,
I'll bid farewell to every fear,
And wipe my weeping eyes.

2 Should earth against my soul engage,
And fiery darts be hurled,
Then I can smile at Satan's rage,
And face a frowning world.

3 Let cares like a wild deluge come,
Let storms of sorrow fall,
So I but safely reach my home,
My God, my heaven, my all.

4 There I shall bathe my weary soul,
In seas of heavenly rest,
And not a wave of trouble roll
Across my peaceful breast.

330 C. M.

The heavenly Canaan.

THERE is a land of pure delight,
Where saints immortal reign;
Infinite day excludes the night,
And pleasures banish pain.

2 There everlasting spring abides,
And never-with'ring flowers;
Death, like a narrow sea, divides
This heavenly land from ours.

3 Sweet fields beyond the swelling flood
Stand dressed in living green;
So to the Jews old Canaan stood,
While Jordan rolled between.

4 Could we but climb where Moses stood,
And view the landscape o'er,
Not Jordan's stream, nor death's cold flood,
Should fright us from the shore.

331

4 *lines* 8s

A mansion above.

MY Saviour has gone to prepare
A place for the child of his love,
And now he's awaiting me there,
In the house of his Father above.

2 That house is beyond the blue sky,
More bright than I ever could tell:
I shall only go home when I die,
With my Brother and Father to dwell.

3 I have treasures laid up for me there,
A crown of the loveliest gold;
And my Father will give me to wear
A dress that will never grow old.

4 And perhaps he will give me bright wings,
To fly on long errands for him,
And a harp with its sweet-sounding strings,
Which never are tuneless or dim.

5 O, I long for those mansions so fair,
And to join with the angels in white,
You will hear me, perhaps, when I'm there
I shall sing out so loud with delight.

332 L. M.

How blest the righteous when he dies.

HOW blest the righteous when he dies,
When sinks a weary soul to rest!
How mildly beam the closing eyes!
How gently heaves the expiring breast!

2 So fades a summer cloud away,
So sinks the gale when storms are o'er,
So gently shuts the eye of day,
So dies a wave along the shore.

3 A holy quiet reigns around,
A calm which life nor death destroys;
Nothing disturbs that peace profound
Which his unfettered soul enjoys.

4 Farewell, conflicting hopes and fears,
Where lights and shades alternate dwell!
How bright th' unchanging morn appears!
Farewell, inconstant world, farewell!

5 Life's duty done, as sinks the clay,
Light from its load the spirit flies;
While heaven and earth combine to say,
"How blest the righteous when he dies!"

333 S. M.

A home above.

I HAVE a home above,
From sin and sorrow free;
A mansion which Eternal Love
Designed and formed for me.

2 My Father's gracious hand
Has built this sweet abode;
From everlasting it was planned;
My dwelling place with God.

3 My Saviour's precious blood
Has made my title sure;
He passed through death's dark raging flood,
To make my rest secure.

4 Bright angels guard my way,
His ministers of power,
And watching round me night and day,
Preserve in danger's hour.

5 Loved ones are gone before;
Whose pilgrim days are done;
I soon shall greet them on that shore
Where partings are unknown.

334 L. M.

Heavenly home.

MY heavenly home is bright and fair,
Nor pain nor death can enter there;
Its glittering flowers the sun outshine,
That heavenly mansion shall be mine:
CHORUS—I'm going home, I'm going home,
I'm going home to die no more.

2 My Father's house is built on high,
Far, far above the starry sky:
When from this earthly prison free,
That heavenly mansion mine shall be.
CHORUS—I'm going home, etc.

3 Let others seek a home below,
Which flames devour, or waves o'erflow;
Be mine the happier lot to own
A heavenly mansion near the throne.
CHORUS—I'm going home, etc.

4 Then fail this earth, let stars decline,
And sun and moon refuse to shine,
All nature sink and cease to be,
That heavenly mansion stands for me.
CHORUS—I'm going home, etc.

335 C. M.

City of God.

MY feet are weary with the march
Over the steep hill-side;
City of God! I fain would see
Thy peaceful waters glide!

2 My hands are weary, toiling on
For perishable meat;
City of God! I fain would reach
Thy glorious mercy seat

3 Patience, poor heart! His feet were worn,
His hands were weary too;
His garments stained and travel-torn,
His head wet with the dew.

4 Love thou the path thy Saviour trod,
And patient wait thy rest;
His holy city thou shalt see,
Home of the loved and blest!

336 C. M.

May I not fail of heaven.

THE roseate hues of early dawn,
The brightness of the day,
The crimson of the sunset sky,
How fast they fade away!

2 O for the pearly gates of heaven!
O for the golden floor!
O for the Sun of Righteousness,
That setteth nevermore!

3 The highest hopes we cherish here,
How soon they tire and faint!
How many a spot defiles the robe
That wraps an earthly saint!

4 O for a heart that never sins!
O for a soul washed white!
O for a voice to praise our King,
Nor weary day nor night!

5 Here faith is ours, and heavenly hope,
And grace to lead us higher;
But there are perfectness and peace,
Beyond our best desire.

6 O, by thy love and anguish, Lord,
And by thy life laid down,
Grant that we fall not from thy grace,
Nor fail to reach our crown.

337 S. M.

No night in heaven.

THERE is no night in heaven;
In that blest world above
Work never can bring weariness,
For work itself is love.
There is no grief in heaven;
For life is one glad day,
And tears are of those former things
Which all have passed away.

2 There is no want in heaven;
The Lamb of God supplies
Life's tree of twelvefold fruitage still,
Life's spring which never dries.
There is no sin in heaven;
Behold that blessed throng;
All holy is their spotless robe,
All holy is their song.

3 There is no death in heaven;
For they who gain that shore
Have won their immortality,
And they can die no more.
There is no death in heaven;
But when the Christian dies,
Angels await his parted soul,
And waft it to the skies!

338 C. M.

Jerusalem my happy home

JERUSALEM, my happy home!
Name ever dear to me!
When shall my labors have an end,
In joy and peace and thee?

2 O when, thou city of my God,
Shall I thy courts ascend,
Where congregations ne'er break up,
And Sabbaths have no end?

3 Why should I shrink at pain and woe,
Or feel at death dismay?
I've Canaan's goodly land in view,
And realms of endless day.

4 Apostles, martyrs, prophets, there
Around my Saviour stand;
And soon my friends in Christ below
Will join the glorious band.

5 Jerusalem, my happy home!
My soul still pants for thee;
Then will my labors have an end
When I thy joys shall see.

339 C. M.

Heaven in prospect.

ON Jordan's stormy banks I stand,
And cast a wishful eye
To Canaan's fair and happy land,
Where my possessions lie.

2 O the transporting, rapturous scene,
That rises to my sight!
Sweet fields arrayed in living green,
And rivers of delight.

3 O'er all those wide-extended plains
Shines one eternal day;
There God the Son forever reigns,
And scatters night away.

4 No chilling winds, nor poisonous breath,
Can reach that healthful shore;
Sickness and sorrow, pain and death,
Are felt and feared no more.

5 When shall I reach that happy place,
And be forever blest?
When shall I see my Father's face,
And in his bosom rest?

6 Filled with delight, my raptured soul
Would here no longer stay;
Though Jordan's waves around me roll,
Fearless, I'd launch away.

340

8 *lines* 8s.

"*Having a desire to depart, and to be with Christ.*"

YE angels who stand round the throne,
And view my Immanuel's face,
In rapturous songs make him known;
Tune, tune your soft harps to his praise.
He formed you the spirits you are,
So happy, so noble, so good;
When others sunk down in despair;
Confirmed by his power, ye stood.

2 Ye saints who stand nearer than they,
And cast your bright crowns at his feet,
His grace and his glory display,
And all his rich mercy repeat:
He snatched you from hell and the grave,
He ransomed from death and despair,
For you he was mighty to save,
Almighty to bring you safe there.

3 O, when will the period appear,
When I shall unite in your song?
I'm weary of lingering here,
And I to your Saviour belong!
I'm fettered and chained up in clay,
I struggle and pant to be free;
I long to be soaring away,
My God and my Saviour to see!

4 I want to put on my attire,
Washed white in the blood of the Lamb;
I want to be one of your choir,
And tune my sweet harp to his name.
I want, O, I want to be there
Where sorrow and sin bid adieu;
Your joy and your friendship to share,
To wonder and worship with you!

THE JUDGMENT.

341 C. M.

Secrets of the heart made known.

AND must I be to judgment brought,
And answer in that day
For every vain and idle thought,
And every word I say?

2 Yes, every secret of my heart
Shall shortly be made known,
And I receive my just desert
For all that I have done.

3 How careful then ought I to live;
With what religious fear;
Who such a strict account must give
For my behavior here?

4 Thou awful Judge of quick and dead,
The watchful power bestow;
So shall I to my ways take heed,
To all I speak or do.

5 If now thou standest at the door,
O let me feel thee near;
And make my peace with God before
I at thy bar appear.

342 8s, 7s, & 4.

Christ coming to judgment.

LO! he comes, with clouds descending,
Once for favored sinners slain;
Thousand thousand saints, attending,
Swell the triumph of his train:
Halleluiah!
Jesus shall forever reign.

2 Every eye shall now behold him,
Robed in dreadful majesty;
Those who set at naught and sold him,
Pierced, and nailed him to the tree,
Deeply wailing,
Shall the true Messiah see.

3 When the solemn trump has sounded,
Heaven and earth shall flee away;
All who hate him must, confounded,
Hear the summons of that day:
"Come to judgment!
Come to judgment, come away!"

4 Now the Saviour, long expected,
See, in solemn pomp, appear;
All his saints, by man rejected,
Now shall meet him in the air:
Halleluiah!
See the day of God appear.

343 S. M.

Preparation for the judgment.

AND will the Judge descend?
And must the dead arise?
And not a single soul escape
His all-discerning eyes?

2 How will my heart endure
The terrors of that day,
When earth and heaven, before his face,
Astonished, shrink away?

3 But, ere the trumpet shakes
  The mansions of the dead,
Hark! from the Gospel's cheering sound
  What joyful tidings spread!

4 Come, sinners, seek His grace
  Whose wrath ye cannot bear;
Fly to the shelter of his cross,
  And find salvation there.

344 4 8s & 2 6s.

Anxious desires.

THOU God of glorious majesty,
  To thee, against myself, to thee
  A sinful worm, I cry;
A half-awakened child of man,
An heir of endless bliss or pain,
  A sinner born to die.

2 Lo! on a narrow neck of land,
'Twixt two unbounded seas, I stand:
  Yet how insensible!
A point of time, a moment's space,
Removes me to that heavenly place,
  Or shuts me up in hell.

3 No matter which my thoughts employ,
A moment's misery or joy;
  But, O! when both shall end,
Where shall I find my destined place?
Shall I my everlasting days
  With fiends or angels spend?

345 4 8s & 2 6s.

Contemplation of judgment.

O GOD, my inmost soul convert,
  And deeply on my thoughtful heart
  Eternal things impress;
Cause me to feel their solemn weight,
And tremble on the brink of fate,
  And wake to righteousness.

2 Before me place, in dread array,
The pomp of that tremendous day,
When thou with clouds shalt come
To judge the nations at thy bar;
And tell me, Lord, shall I be there
To meet a joyful doom?

3 Be this my one great business here,
With serious industry and fear,
Eternal bliss t' insure;
Thine utmost counsel to fulfill,
And suffer all thy righteous will,
And to the end endure.

4 Then, Saviour, then my soul receive,
Transported from this vale, to live
And reign with thee above,
Where faith is sweetly lost in sight,
And hope in full, supreme delight,
And everlasting love.

346 L. M.

Eternity.

ETERNITY is just at hand!
And shall I waste my ebbing sand,
And careless view departing day,
And throw my inch of time away?

2 Eternity! tremendous sound!
To guilty souls a dreadful wound;
But O if Christ and heaven be mine,
How sweet the accents! how divine!

3 Be this my chief, my only care,
My high pursuit, my ardent prayer,
An interest in the Saviour's blood,
My pardon sealed, my peace with God.

4 Search, Lord, O search my inmost heart,
And light, and hope, and joy impart;
From guilt and error set me free,
And guide me safe to heaven and thee.

347

4 8s & 2 6s.

The momentous question.

AND am I only born to die?
And must I suddenly comply
With nature's stern decree?
What after death for me remains?
Celestial joys or hellish pains
To all eternity.

2 How then ought I on earth to live,
While God prolongs the kind reprieve,
And props the house of clay?
My sole concern, my single care,
To watch, and tremble, and prepare
Against that fatal day.

3 Nothing is worth a thought beneath,
But how I may escape the death
That never, never dies!
How make mine own election sure;
And when I fail on earth, secure
A mansion in the skies.

4 Jesus, vouchsafe a pitying ray;
Be thou my Guide, be thou my Way
To glorious happiness.
Ah! write the pardon on my heart;
And whensoe'er I hence depart,
Let me depart in peace.

348

12s & 8s.

When the harvest is past.

WHEN the harvest is past and the summer is gone,
And sermons and prayers shall be o'er,
When the beams cease to break of the sweet Sabbath morn,
And Jesus invites thee no more,
When the rich gales of mercy no longer shall blow,
The Gospel no message declare,
Sinner, how canst thou bear the deep wailings of woe,
How suffer the night of despair!

2 When the holy have gone to the regions of peace
To dwell in the mansions above;
When their harmony wakes, in the fullness of bliss,
Their song to the Saviour they love,
Say, O sinner who livest at rest and secure,
Who fearest no trouble to come,
Can thy spirit the swellings of sorrow endure
Or bear the impenitent's doom?

349

4 8s & 2 6s.

Save in that day.

WHEN thou, my righteous Judge, shalt come
To fetch thy ransomed people home,
Shall I among them stand?
Shall such a worthless worm as I,
Who sometimes am afraid to die,
Be found at thy right hand?

2 I love to meet among them now,
Before thy gracious feet to bow,
Though weakest of them all;
But can I bear the piercing thought,
What if my name should be left out
When thou for them shalt call?

3 O Lord, prevent it by thy grace;
Be thou my only hiding-place
In this accepted day:
Thy pard'ning voice, O let me hear,
To still my unbelieving fear,
Nor let me fall, I pray.

4 Let me among thy saints be found
Whene'er the archangel's trump shall sound,
To see thy smiling face:
Then loudest of the crowd I'll sing,
While heaven's resounding mansions ring
With shouts of sovereign grace.

THE SEASONS.

350

. lines 7s.

New Year's Day.

WHILE, with ceaseless course, the sun
  Hasted through the former year,
Many souls their race have run,
  Never more to meet us here:
Fixed in an eternal state,
  They have done with all below:
We a little longer wait,
  But how little none can know.

2 As the wingèd arrow flies,
  Speedily the mark to find;
As the lightning from the skies
  Darts and leaves no trace behind;
Swiftly thus our fleeting days
  Bear us down life's rapid stream:
Upward, Lord, our spirits raise;
  All below is but a dream.

3 Thanks for mercies past receive;
  Pardon of our sins renew;
Teach us, henceforth, how to live
  With eternity in view;
Bless thy word to old and young;
  Fill us with a Saviour's love:
When our life's short race is run,
  May we dwell with thee above.

351

C. M.

Reflections at the end of the year.

AND now, my soul, another yeai
  Of thy short life is past;
I cannot long continue here,
  And this may be my last.

2 Much of my hasty life is gone,
Nor will return again;
And swift my passing moments run,
The few that yet remain.

3 Awake, my soul; with utmost care
Thy true condition learn:
What are thy hopes? how sure? how fair?
What is thy great concern?

4 Behold, another year begins;
Set out afresh for heaven;
Seek pardon for thy former sins,
In Christ so freely given.

5 Devoutly yield thyself to God,
And on his grace depend;
With zeal pursue the heavenly road,
Nor doubt a happy end.

352 — 4 *lines* 7s.

Report of the Watchman.

WATCHMAN! tell us of the night,
What its signs of promise are?
Traveler, o'er yon mountain's height,
See that glory-beaming star.

2 Watchman! does its beauteous ray
Aught of hope or joy foretell?
Traveler! yes, it brings the day,
Promised day of Israel.

3 Watchman! tell us of the night;
Higher yet that star ascends?
Traveler! blessedness and light,
Peace and truth, its course portends.

4 Watchman! will its beams alone
Gild the spot that gave them birth?
Traveler! ages are its own;
See, it bursts o'er all the earth.

5 Watchman! tell us of the night,
For the morning seems to dawn?
Traveler! darkness takes its flight;
Doubt and terror are withdrawn.

6 Watchman! let thy wanderings cease;
Hie thee to thy quiet home.
Traveler! lo, the Prince of Peace,
Lo! the Son of God, is come.

353 C. M.

Spring.

WHEN verdure clothes the fertile vale,
And blossoms deck the spray,
And fragrance breathes in every gale,
How sweet the vernal day!

2 Hark! how the feathered warblers sing!
'Tis nature's cheerful voice;
Soft music hails the lovely spring,
And woods and fields rejoice.

3 O God of nature and of grace,
Thy heavenly gifts impart;
Then shall my meditation trace
Spring, blooming in my heart.

4 Inspired to praise, I then shall join
Glad nature's cheerful song,
And love and gratitude divine
Attune my joyful tongue.

354 C. M.

Praise and thanksgiving.

SING to the great Jehovah's praise;
All praise to him belongs;
Who kindly lengthens out our days
Demands our choicest songs:
His providence hath brought us through
Another various year;
We all, with vows and anthems new,
Before our God appear.

2 Father, thy mercies past we own,
  Thy still continued care,
To thee presenting, through thy Son,
  Whate'er we have or are:
Our lips and lives shall gladly show
  The wonders of thy love;
While on in Jesus' steps we go,
  To seek thy face above.

3 Our residue of days or hours
  Thine, wholly thine, shall be;
And all our consecrated powers
  A sacrifice to thee,
Till Jesus in the clouds appear,
  To saints on earth forgiven,
And bring the grand Sabbatic year,
  The jubilee of heaven.

355 L. M.

The year crowned with goodness.

ETERNAL source of every joy,
  Thy praise may well our lips employ,
While in thy temple we appear,
Whose goodness crowns the circling year.

2 Wide as the wheels of nature roll,
Thy hand supports the steady pole;
The sun is taught by thee to rise,
And darkness when to vail the skies.

3 The flowery spring, at thy command,
Embalms the air and paints the land;
The summer rays with vigor shine,
To raise the corn and cheer the vine.

4 Thy hand in autumn richly pours
Through all our coasts abundant stores;
And winters, softened by thy care,
No more a dreary aspect wear.

5 Still be the cheerful homage paid
With morning light and evening shade;
Seasons, and months, and weeks, and days
Demand successive songs of praise.

356 C. M.

New year.—Providential goodness.

GOD of our lives, thy various praise
Our voices shall resound:
Thy hand directs our fleeting days,
And brings the seasons round.

2 To thee shall grateful songs arise,
Our Father and our Friend,
Whose constant mercies from the skies
In genial streams descend.

3 In every scene of life, thy care.
In every age, we see;
And constant as thy favors are,
So let our praises be.

4 Still may thy love, in every scene,
In every age, appear;
And let the same compassion deign
To bless the opening year.

5 If mercy smile, let mercy bring
Our wandering souls to God:
In our affliction we shall sing,
If thou wilt bless the rod.

357 8s & 7s.

Autumn.

SEE the leaves around us falling,
Dry and withered, to the ground,
Thus to thoughtless mortals calling,
In a sad and solemn sound:

2 "Youth, on length of days presuming,
Who the paths of pleasure tread,
View us, late in beauty blooming,
Numbered now among the dead.

3 "What though yet no losses grieve you,
Gay with health and many a grace;
Let not cloudless skies deceive you;
Summer gives to autumn place."

4 On the tree of life eternal
Let our highest hopes be stayed:
This alone, forever vernal,
Bears a leaf that shall not fade.

358 4 6s & 2 8s.

Spring.

HOW pleasing is the voice
Of God, our heavenly king,
Who bids the frosts retire,
And wakes the lovely spring!
The mild wind blows; bright suns arise,
And beauty glows through earth and skies.

2 The morn, with glory crowned,
His hand arrays in smiles:
He bids the eve decline,
Rejoicing o'er the hills:
The evening breeze his breath perfumes,
In flowers and trees his beauty blooms.

3 With life he clothes the spring,
The earth with summer warms,
He spreads the autumnal feast,
And rides on wintry storms:
Through all appear his gifts divine,
And round the year his glories shine.

359 C. M.

The New Year.

OUR Father! through the coming year
We know not what shall be;
But we would leave without a fear
Its ordering all to thee.

2 It may be it shall darkly blend
Our love with anxious fears,
And snatch away the valued friend,
The tried of many years.

3 It may be it shall bring us days
And nights of lingering pain;
And bid us take a farewell gaze
Of these loved haunts of men.

4 But calmly, Lord, on thee we rest;
No fears our trust shall move;
Thou knowest what for each is best,
And thou art Perfect Love.

360 8 *lines* 7s.

The New Year.

THOU who roll'st the year around,
Crowned with mercies large and free,
Rich thy gifts to us abound,
Warm our thanks shall rise to thee;
Kindly to our worship bow,
While our grateful praises swell,
That, sustained by thee, we now
Bid the parting year farewell.

2 All its numbered days are sped,
All its busy scenes are o'er,
All its joys forever fled,
All its sorrows felt no more:
Mingled with th' eternal past,
Its remembrance shall decay,
Yet to be revived at last
At the solemn judgment day.

3 All our follies, Lord, forgive;
Cleanse each heart and make us thine;
Let thy grace within us live,
As our future suns decline;

Then when life's last eve shall come,
Happy spirits let us fly
To our everlasting home,
To our Father's house on high.

361

4 8s & 2 6s.

Voices of Spring.

SOFT are the fruitful showers that bring
The welcome promise of the spring;
And soft the vernal gale;
Sweet the wild warblings of the grove,
The voice of nature and of love,
That gladden every vale.

2 But softer in the mourner's ear
Sounds the mild voice of mercy near,
That whispers sins forgiven;
And sweeter far the music swells,
When to the raptured soul she tells
Of peace and promised heaven.

3 Fair are the flowers that deck the ground;
And groves and gardens blooming round,
Unnumbered charms unfold;
Bright is the sun's meridian ray,
And bright the beams of setting day,
That robe the clouds in gold.

4 But far more fair the pious breast,
In richer robes of goodness dressed;
When heaven's own graces shine;
And brighter far the prospects rise,
That burst on faith's delighted eyes,
From glories all divine.

362

7s & 6s.

Autumn.

THE leaves, around me falling,
Are preaching of decay;
The hollow winds are calling,
"Come, pilgrim, come away:"

The day, in night declining,
  Says I must, too, decline;
The year its bloom resigning,
  Its lot foreshadows mine.

2 The light my path surrounding,
  The loves to which I cling,
The hopes within me bounding,
  The joys that round me wing,
All, all, like stars at even,
  Just gleam and shoot away,
Pass on before to heaven,
  And chide at my delay.

3 The friends gone there before me
  Are calling from on high,
And happy angels o'er me
  Tempt sweetly to the sky.
"Why wait," they say, "and wither,
  'Mid scenes of death and sin?
O, rise to glory, hither,
  And find true life begin."

4 I hear the invitation,
  And fain would rise and come,
A sinner, to salvation,
  An exile to his home;
But while I must here linger,
  Thus, thus, let all I see
Point on, with faithful finger,
  To heaven, O Lord, and thee.

363 C. M.

Winter.

STERN winter throws his icy chains,
  Encircling nature round;
How bleak, how comfortless the plains,
  Late with gay verdure crowned!

2 The sun withholds his vital beams,
  And light and warmth depart;
And drooping, lifeless nature seems
  An emblem of my heart.

3 Return, O blissful sun, and bring
Thy soul-reviving ray:
This moral winter shall be spring,
This darkness cheerful day.

4 O happy state! divine abode,
Where spring eternal reigns,
And perfect day, the smile of God,
Fills all the heavenly plains.

5 Great Source of light, thy beams display,
My drooping joys restore,
And guide me to the seats of day,
Where winter frowns no more.

364 11s & 8s.

Flowers, sweet flowers.

HOW sweet are the flowers of the garden and field
When earth wears her summer array;
How laden the air with the fragrance they yield,
How varied the hues they display.

CHORUS.

Flowers of the wildwood, flowers of the garden,
Emblems of childhood, flowers, sweet flowers.

2 But frail is their texture and transient their stay,
For brief is the life of a flower;
Their fragrance and beauty too soon pass away,
They gladden the heart for an hour.
CHORUS.—Flowers of the wildwood, etc.

3 Some, plucked by the hand of the envious or rude,
Their life and their loveliness yield;
While some by the pitiless mower are strewed,
To wither like grass of the field.
CHORUS.—Flowers of the wildwood, etc.

4 Thus fair are the children in home's sunny ground,
Thus frail as the floweret are they;
The scythe of the mower is sweeping around,
They're fading and passing away.
CHORUS.—Flowers of the wildwood, etc.

5 We'll give them our prayers and the heart-cheering word;
Thus nurtured by sunshine and shower,
Their virtues may scatter a fragrance around,
Surviving the fall of the flower.
CHORUS.—Flowers of the wildwood, etc.

THANKSGIVING AND FASTS.

365 L. M.

Praises to God.

PRAISES to Him who built the hills;
Praises to Him the streams who fills;
Praises to Him who lights each star
That sparkles in the blue afar.

2 Praises to Him who makes the morn,
And bids it glow with beams new-born;
Who draws the shadows of the night
Like curtains o'er our wearied sight.

3 Praises to Him whose love has given,
In Christ his Son, the life of heaven;
Who for our darkness gives us light,
And turns to day our deepest night.

4 Praises to Him, in grace who came
To bear our woe and sin and shame;
Who lived to die, who died to rise,
The God-accepted sacrifice.

5 Praises to Him who sheds abroad
Within our hearts the love of God;
The Spirit of all truth and peace,
Fountain of joy and holiness.

6 To Father, Son, and Spirit now
The hands we lift, the knees we bow;
With voice and heart, O Lord, we raise
The sinner's endless song of praise.

366 6s & 4s.

Praise to the God of harvest.

THE God of harvest praise;
In loud thanksgiving raise
Hand, heart, and voice:
The valleys smile and sing,
Forests and mountains ring,
The plains their tribute bring,
The streams rejoice.

2 Yea, bless his holy name,
And purest thanks proclaim
Through all the earth;
To glory in your lot
Is duty; but be not
God's benefits forgot
Amid your mirth.

3 The God of harvest praise;
Hands, hearts, and voices raise
With sweet accord;
From field to garner throng,
Bearing your sheaves along,
And in your harvest song
Bless ye the Lord.

367 C. M.

A harvest hymn.

FOUNTAIN of mercy, God of love,
How rich thy bounties are!
The rolling seasons, as they move,
Proclaim thy constant care.

2 When in the bosom of the earth
The sower hid the grain,
Thy goodness marked its secret birth,
And sent the early rain.

3 The spring's sweet influence, Lord, was thine,
The plants in beauty grew;
Thou gavest refulgent suns to shine,
And the refreshing dew.

4 These various mercies from above
  Matured the swelling grain;
A kindly harvest crowns thy love,
  And plenty fills the plain.

5 We own and bless thy gracious sway;
  Thy hand all nature hails;
Seedtime nor harvest, night nor day,
  Summer nor winter, fails.

368 C. M.

Public supplication.

WHEN Abrah'm, full of sacred awe,
  Before Jehovah stood,
And with an humble, fervent prayer,
  For guilty Sodom sued,

2 With what success, what wondrous grace,
  Was his petition crowned!
The Lord would spare if in this place
  Ten righteous men were found.

3 And could a single pious soul
  So rich a boon obtain,
Great God, and shall a nation cry
  And plead with thee in vain?

4 Are not the righteous dear to thee
  Now, as in ancient times?
Or does this sinful land exceed
  Gomorrah in her crimes?

5 Still we are thine; we bear thy name;
  Here yet is thine abode;
Long has thy presence blessed our land:
  Forsake us not, O God.

369 C. M.

Prayer for our native land.

LORD, while for all mankind we pray,
  Of every clime and coast,
O hear us for our native land,
  The land we love the most.

2 O guard our shores from every foe;
With peace our borders bless;
Our cities with prosperity,
Our fields with plenteousness.

3 Unite us in the sacred love
Of knowledge, truth, and thee;
And let our hills and valleys chant
The songs of liberty.

4 Lord of the nations, thus to thee
Our country we commend;
Be thou her refuge and her trust,
Her everlasting friend.

370 L. M.

Public humiliation.

GREAT Maker of unnumbered worlds,
And whom unnumbered worlds adore,
Whose goodness all thy creatures share,
While nature trembles at thy power,

2 Thine is the hand that moves the spheres,
That wakes the wind and lifts the sea;
And man, who moves the lord of earth,
Acts but the part assigned by thee.

3 While suppliant crowds implore thine aid,
To thee we raise the humble cry;
Thine altar is the contrite heart,
Thine incense the repentant sigh.

4 O may our land, in this her hour,
Confess thy hand and bless the rod;
By penitence make thee her Friend,
And find in thee a guardian God.

371 C. M.

Humility under affliction.

O SINNER, bring not tears alone,
Or outward form of prayer;
But let it in thy heart be known
That penitence is there.

2 To smite the breast, the clothes to rend,
God asketh not of thee;
Thy secret soul he bids thee bend
In true humility.

3 O let us then, with heartfelt grief,
Draw near unto our God,
And pray to him to grant relief,
And stay the lifted rod.

4 O righteous Judge, if thou wilt deign
To grant us what we need,
We pray for time to turn again,
And grace to turn indeed.

372 7s & 6s.

Thanksgiving.

PRAISE the Lord who reigns above,
And keeps his courts below;
Praise him for his boundless love,
And all his greatness show:
Praise him for his noble deeds;
Praise him for his matchless power;
Him from whom all good proceeds,
Let earth and heaven adore.

2 Publish, spread to all around
The great Immanuel's name;
Let the Gospel trumpet sound;
Him the Prince of peace proclaim.
Praise him, every tuneful string;
All the reach of heavenly art,
All the power of music bring,
The music of the heart.

3 Him in whom they move and live,
Let every creature sing;
Glory to our Saviour give,
And homage to our King.

Hallowed be his name beneath,
As in heaven, on earth adored;
Praise the Lord in every breath,
Let all things praise the Lord.

373 — 8s & 8s.

Thanksgiving anthem.

LET every heart rejoice and sing;
Let choral anthems rise;
Ye rev'rend men and children bring
To God your sacrifice.

CHORUS.

For he is good; the Lord is good,
And kind are all his ways;
With songs and honors sounding loud,
The Lord Jehovah praise:
While the rocks and the rills,
While the vales and the hills
A glorious anthem raise,
Let each prolong the grateful song,
And the God of our fathers praise.

2 He bids the sun to rise and set;
In heaven his power is known;
And earth subdued to him, shall yet
Bow low before his throne,
CHORUS.—For he is good, etc.

NATIONAL HYMNS.

374 — L. M.

God acknowledged in national blessings.

GREAT God of nations, now to thee
Our hymn of gratitude we raise;
With humble heart and bending knee,
We offer thee our song of praise.

2 Thy name we bless, almighty God,
For all the kindness thou hast shown
To this fair land the pilgrims trod,
This land we fondly call our our own.

3 Here freedom spreads her banner wide,
And casts her soft and hallowed ray;
Here thou our fathers' steps didst guide
In safety through their dangerous way.

4 We praise thee that the Gospel's light
Through all our land its radiance sheds,
Dispels the shades of error's night,
And heavenly blessings round us spreads.

5 Great God, preserve us in thy fear:
In dangers still our guardian be:
O, spread thy truth's bright precepts here;
Let all the people worship thee.

375 6s & 4s.

My Country.

MY country, 'tis of thee,
Sweet land of liberty,
Of thee I sing;
Land where my fathers died,
Land of the pilgrim's pride,
From every mountain-side
Let freedom ring.

2 My native country, thee,
Land of the noble free,
Thy name I love;
I love thy rocks and rills,
Thy woods and templed hills;
My heart with rapture thrills,
Like that above.

3 Let music swell the breeze,
And ring from all the trees
Sweet freedom's song;

Let mortal tongues awake,
Let all that breathe partake,
Let rocks their silence break,
The sound prolong.

4 Our father's God, to thee,
Author of liberty,
To thee we sing;
Long may our land be bright
With freedom's holy light:
Protect us by thy might,
Great God, our King.

376 6s & 4s.

Hymn for the National Anniversary

AUSPICIOUS morning, hail!
Voices from hill and vale
Thy welcome sing:
Joy on thy dawning breaks;
Each heart that joy partakes,
While cheerful music wakes,
Its praise to bring.

2 When on the tyrant's rod
Our patriot fathers trod,
And dared be free,
They trusted not in zeal,
Firm nerves, and hearts of stee
Our country's joy to seal,
But, Lord, in thee.

3 Thou, as a shield of power,
In battle's awful hour,
Didst round us stand:
Our hopes were in thy throne
Strong in thy might alone,
By thee our banners shone,
God of our land.

4 Long o'er our native hills,
Long by our shaded rills,
May freedom rest;

Long may our shores have peace,
Our flag grace every breeze,
Our ships the distant seas,
From east to west.

5 Peace on this day abide
From morn till even-tide;
Wake tuneful song;
Melodious accents raise;
Let every heart, with praise,
Bring high and grateful lays,
Rich, full, and strong.

377 7s & 6s.

The Bible and Liberty.

ONCE more with hallowed feeling,
We join the blest employ,
Our nation's praises pealing
In songs of festive joy:
And back the loud hosanna
Shall roll from sea to sea,
Till mountain and savanna
Re-echo, "We are free."

2 We love the Book which lighted
The glow of patriot fires,
When Freedom was benighted
In the bosom of our sires.
They shed their blood to save us,
And gained our liberty:
The greatest boon they gave us,
The Bible was made free!

3 Our land is Virtue's dwelling;
Here Science builds her shrine;
And happy hearts are swelling
With joy almost divine:
And we in emulation
Here pledge ourselves to be
The guardians of our nation—
We'll keep the Bible free!

4 Then come, with hallowed feeling,
Join in the blest employ,
Our nation's praises pealing
In songs of festive joy.
Till back the loud hosanna
Shall roll from sea to sea,
From mountain and savanna,
We'll keep the Bible free!

378

11s & 12s.

The Star-Spangled Banner.

O SAY, can you see by the dawn's early light,
What so proudly we hail at the twilight's last gleaming,
Whose broad stripes and bright stars, through the perilous fight,
O'er the ramparts we watched, were so gallantly streaming?
And the rocket's red glare, bombs bursting in air,
Gave proof through the night that our flag was still there.

CHORUS.

O say, does that star-spangled banner yet wave
O'er the land of the free and the home of the brave?

2 On the shore, dimly seen through the mists of the deep,
Where the foe's haughty host in dread silence reposes,
What is that which the breeze o'er the towering steep,
As it fitfully blows, half conceals, half discloses?
Now it catches the gleam of the morning's first beam,
In full glory reflected now shines in the stream:

CHORUS.

'Tis the star-spangled banner: O long may it wave
O'er the land of the free and the home of the brave.

3 And where is that band who so vauntingly swore
That the havoc of war and the battle's confusion
A home and a country should leave us no more?
Their blood has washed out their foul footsteps' pollution.
No refuge can save the hireling and slave
From the terror of flight, or the gloom of the grave.

CHORUS.

And the star-spangled banner in triumph shall wave
O'er the land of the free and the home of the brave.

4 O thus be it ever when freemen shall stand
Between their loved home and the war's desolation;
Blest with victory and peace, may the heaven-rescued land
Praise the power that hath made and preserved us a nation.
Then conquer we must, when our cause it is just,
And this be our motto: "In God is our trust!"

CHORUS.

And the star-spangled banner in triumph shall wave
O'er the land of the free and the home of the brave.

379 — 8s & 4s.

God speed the right.

NOW to heaven our prayer ascending,
God speed the right;
In a noble cause contending,
God speed the right;
Be our zeal in heaven recorded,
With success on earth rewarded,
God speed the right.

2 Be that prayer again repeated,
God speed the right;
Ne'er despairing, though defeated,
God speed the right;
Like the great and good in story,
If we fail, we fail with glory,
God speed the right.

3 Patient, firm, and persevering,
God speed the right;
Ne'er th' event nor danger fearing,
God speed the right;
Pains, nor toils, nor trials heeding,
And in heaven's good time succeeding,
God speed the right.

4 Still our onward course pursuing,
God speed the right;
Every foe at length subduing,
God speed the right;
Truth our cause, whate'er delay it,
There's no power on earth can stay it;
God speed the right.

380 — 11s & 9s.

The Flag of our Union.

A SONG for our banner! the watchword recall
Which gave the Republic her station;
United we stand, divided we fall!
It made and preserved us a nation!

CHORUS.

The union of lakes, the union of lands,
The union of States none can sever;
The union of hearts, the union of hands,
And the flag of our Union forever.

2 What God in his infinite wisdom designed,
And armed with his weapon of thunder,
Not all the earth's despots and factions combined
Have the power to conquer or sunder.
CHORUS—The union of lakes, etc.

381 — C. M. D.

Unfurl the banner.

UNFURL the banner of the free;
True hearts should ne'er forget
The stars our fathers loved to see,
That sparkle on it yet;

The stars whose light in days gone by
Lit up the horizon
With the red fire of liberty,
Show freedom's cause was won

CHORUS.

The flag, the flag, the dear old flag,
The pride of all the free;
The flag, the flag, the dear old flag,
Emblem of liberty.

2 We need no trumpet-call to wake
The spirit of the past;
Spring to the halliard ropes, and shake
The old flag to the blast;
And loyal hearts shall greet the sight
And raise it to the sky;
And bear it bravely to the fight
Enwreathed with victory.
CHORUS—The flag, etc.

3 Behold its swelling glories wave
Above the eagle's nest,
Across the broad Atlantic's wave,
The prairies of the West,
The city spire, the gallant ship,
The highest mountain crag;
While blessings flow from every lip,
God bless our honored flag.
CHORUS—The flag, etc.

382 4 8s & 2 6s.

"Thou hast put all things under his feet."

O NORTH, with all thy vales of green,
O South, with all thy palms,
From peopled towns, and fields between,
Uplift the voice of psalms:
Raise, ancient East, the anthem high,
And let the youthful West reply.

2 Lo! in the clouds of heaven appears
  God's well-beloved Son;
He brings a train of brighter years,
  His kingdom has begun:
He comes a guilty world to bless
With mercy, truth, and righteousness.

3 O, Father, haste the promised hour
  When at his feet shall lie
All rule, authority, and power
  Beneath the ample sky:
When he shall reign from pole to pole,
The Lord of every human soul.

4 When all shall heed the words he said,
  Amid their daily cares,
And by the loving life he led
  Shall strive to pattern theirs:
And he who conquered death shall win
The mighty conquest over sin.

383 L. M.

Our beautiful banner.

OUR beautiful flag, O now we see,
  From every spot and blemish free,
The flag of our Union, bright and fair,
That waves in triumph everywhere.

CHORUS.

O! be true—O be true!
True, to our beautiful flag so free.

2 O, beautiful flag, so pure and bright,
Thy radiant stars are life and light,
The emblem of power, our guide alway,
Thy stars shall never fade away.
  CHORUS—O! be true, etc.

3 We see thy stripes and eagle bold,
And love thee more as we behold;
Forever wave on land and sea,
The Union flag of the brave and free.
  CHORUS—O! be true, etc

4 This beautiful flag we love to see
O'er every state unfurled and free;
Beneath its folds shall discord cease,
And North and South rejoice in peace
CHORUS—O! be true, etc.

MISCELLANEOUS SUBJECTS.

384 11s & 8s.

Do what you can.

DON'T think there is nothing for children to do,
Because they can't work like a man;
The harvest is great and the laborers few:
Then, children, do all that you can.

CHORUS.

Children, do all that you can;
Children, do all that you can;
The harvest is great and the laborers few,
Then, children, do all that you can.

2 You think, if great riches you had at command,
Your zeal would no weariness know;
You'd scatter your wealth with a liberal hand,
And succor the children of woe.
CHORUS—Children, do all, etc.

3 But what if you've naught but a penny to give?
Then give it, though scanty your store;
For those who give nothing when little they have,
When wealthy will do little more.
CHORUS--Children, do all, etc.

4 It was not the offering of pomp and of power,
It was not the golden bequest—
Ah, no! 'twas the mite from the hand of the poor
That Jesus applauded and blessed.
CHORUS—Children, do all, etc

5 Then don't be a sluggard and live at your ease,
And life with vain pleasures beguile;
But ever be active and busy as bees,
And God on your labors will smile.
CHORUS—Children do all, etc.

385

11s & 9s.

There's a crown for the young.

I KNOW there's a crown for the saints of renown,
And for saints whose good deeds are unsung;
But O say, is it true, if their days are but few,
That a crown is laid up for the young?

CHORUS.

Yes, I know there's a crown for the young;
If their lives daily prove that the Saviour they love,
I know there's a crown for the young.

2 The youthful shall stand in that beautiful land,
And the song of salvation shall sing;
And the infant of days strike its harp in the praise
Of Immanuel, its Saviour and king.
CHORUS—Yes, I know, etc.

3 The noble of birth, and the poor of the earth,
Both the man and the youth and the child,
If in Jesus they trust when they rise from the dust
Shall be crowned in the land undefiled.
CHORUS—Yes, I know, etc.

4 The soul of a child, though by folly defiled,
Is more precious than tongue can express;
And redeemed by the blood that on Calvary flowed,
It shall shine in the region of bliss.
CHORUS—Yes, I know, etc.

5 Then be it your care for that world to prepare;
Bear the cross, that the crown may be yours;
Never tire in the road that leads upward to God,
For the crown is for him who endures.
CHORUS—Yes, I know, etc.

386

8s, 7s & 5s.

There's rest for the weary.

IN the Christian's home in glory
  There remains a land of rest,
There my Saviour's gone before me,
  To fulfill my soul's request.

CHORUS.

There is rest for the weary,
  There is rest for you,
On the other side of Jordan,
In the sweet fields of Eden,
Where the tree of life is blooming,
  There is rest for you.

2 He is fitting up my mansion,
  Which eternally shall stand;
For my stay shall not be transient
  In that holy, happy land.
    CHORUS—There is rest, etc.

3 Pain and sickness ne'er shall enter,
  Grief nor woe my lot shall share,
But in that celestial center
  I a crown of life shall wear.
    CHORUS—There is rest, etc.

4 Sing, O sing, ye heirs of glory;
  Shout your triumphs as you go;
Zion's gates will open for you,
  You will find an entrance through.
    CHORUS—There is rest, etc.

387

8 *lines* 7s.

Little travelers.

LITTLE travelers Zionward,
  Each one entering into rest,
In the kingdom of your Lord,
  In the mansions of the blest.

There to welcome Jesus waits,
Gives the crowns his followers win:
Lift your heads, ye golden gates,
Let the little travelers in.

2 Who are those whose little feet,
Pacing life's dark journey through,
Now have reached that heavenly seat
They have ever kept in view?
"I, from Greenland's frozen land;"
"I, from India's sultry plain;"
"I, from Afric's barren sand;"
"I, from islands of the main."

3 "All our earthly journey past,
Every tear and pain gone by,
Here together met at last
At the portal of the sky!"
Each the welcome "Come!" awaits,
Conquerors over death and sin;
Lift your heads, ye golden gates,
Let the little travelers in!

388 7s & 6s.

The cry of the heathen.

FROM Greenland's icy mountains,
From India's coral strand;
Where Afric's sunny fountains
Roll down their golden sand;
From many an ancient river,
From many a palmy plain,
They call us to deliver
Their land from error's chain.

2 What though the spicy breezes
Blow soft o'er Ceylon's isle;
Though every prospect pleases,
And only man is vile:
In vain with lavish kindness
The gifts of God are strown;
The heathen in his blindness
Bows down to wood and stone.

3 Shall we, whose souls are lighted
With wisdom from on high,
Shall we to men benighted
The lamp of life deny?
Salvation! O salvation!
The joyful sound proclaim,
Till earth's remotest nation
Has learned Messiah's name.

4 Waft, waft, ye winds, his story,
And you, ye waters, roll,
Till, like a sea of glory,
It spreads from pole to pole:
Till o'er our ransomed nature
The Lamb for sinners slain,
Redeemer, King, Creator,
In bliss returns to reign.

389 7s & 6s.

Success of the Gospel.

THE morning light is breaking;
The darkness disappears;
The sons of earth are waking
To penitential tears:
Each breeze that sweeps the ocean
Brings tidings from afar
Of nations in commotion,
Prepared for Zion's war.

2 Rich dews of grace come o'er us
In many a gentle shower,
And brighter scenes before us
Are opening every hour:
Each cry, to heaven going,
Abundant answers brings,
And heavenly gales are blowing,
With peace upon their wings.

3 See heathen nations bending
Before the God we love,
And thousand hearts ascending
In gratitude above:

While sinners, now confessing,
The Gospel call obey,
And seek the Saviour's blessing—
A nation in a day.

4 Blest river of salvation,
Pursue thy onward way;
Flow thou to every nation,
Nor in thy riches stay:
Stay not till all the lowly
Triumphant reach their home;
Stay not till all the holy
Proclaim, "The Lord is come."

390 11s & 9s.

A light in the window.

THERE'S a light in the window for thee, brother,
There's a light in the window for thee;
A dear one has moved to the mansions above,
There's a light in the window for thee.
CHORUS—A mansion in heaven we see,
And a light in the window for thee;
A mansion in heaven we see,
And a light in the window for thee.

2 There's a crown, and a robe, and a palm, brother,
When from toil and from care you are free,
The Saviour has gone to prepare you a home,
With a light in the window for thee.
CHORUS—A mansion in heaven, etc.

3 O watch, and be faithful, and pray, brother,
All your journey o'er life's troubled sea;
Though afflictions assail you, and storms beat severe,
There's a light in the window for thee.
CHORUS—A mansion in heaven, etc.

4 Then on, perseveringly on, brother,
Till from conflict and suffering free,
Bright angels now beckon you over the stream,
There's a light in the window for thee.
CHORUS—A mansion in heaven, etc

391 8s & 7s.

Shall we meet beyond the river?

SHALL we meet beyond the river,
Where the surges cease to roll,
Where, in all the bright forever,
Sorrow ne'er shall press the soul?

CHORUS.
Shall we meet beyond the river,
Where the surges cease to roll?

2 Shall we meet in that blest harbor
When our stormy voyage is o'er;
Shall we meet and cast the anchor
By the fair celestial shore?
CHORUS—Shall we meet, etc.

3 Where the music of the ransomed
Rolls in harmony around,
And creation swells the chorus
With its sweet melodious sound?
CHORUS—Shall we meet, etc.

4 Shall we meet with many a loved one?
Torn on earth from our embrace?
Shall we listen to their voices,
And behold them face to face?
CHORUS—Shall we meet, etc.

5 Shall we meet with Christ our Saviour
When he comes to claim his own?
Shall we hear him bid us welcome,
And sit down upon his throne?
CHORUS—We shall meet, etc.

392 4 *lines* 11s.

We'll stand for the right.

THIS life is a battle with Satan and sin,
And we are the soldiers the vict'ry to win;
And Christ is the Captain of our little band;
Whatever opposes, for him we shall stand.
CHORUS—We will stand for the right.

2 To God for our armor we'll fail not to go,
He'll clothe us with truth and with righteousness too;
The "Gospel of peace" shall our footsteps attend,
The good "shield of faith" from all harm shall defend.
CHORUS—We will stand, etc.

3 Salvation our helmet, the Bible our sword,
Though wily our foes, we are "strong in the Lord;"
While watching and praying our armor keeps bright,
Our Saviour will help us to stand for the right.
CHORUS—We will stand, etc.

4 Though little temptations (the worst ones of all)
Will often beset us, to make us to fall;
We'll "stand up for Jesus," and when life is o'er,
For us he'll be standing on Jordan's bright shore.
CHORUS—We will stand, etc.

393 8s & 7s.

A home beyond the tide.

WE are out on an ocean sailing:
Homeward bound, we smoothly glide;
We are out on an ocean, sailing
To a home beyond the tide.

CHORUS.

All the storms will soon be over,
Then we'll anchor in the harbor;
We are out on an ocean sailing
To a home beyond the tide.

2 Millions now are safely landed
Over on the golden shore;
Millions more are on their journey,
Yet there's room for millions more.
CHORUS—All the storms, etc.

3 Come on board, O ship for glory!
Be in haste, make up your mind,
For our vessel's weighing anchor
And you may be left behind.
CHORUS—All the storms, etc.

4 When we all are safely anchored,
We will shout our passage o'er;
We will walk about the city,
And will sing for evermore.
CHORUS—All the storms, etc

394

4 lines 11s.

Happy greeting to all.

COME, children, and join in our festival song,
And hail the sweet joys which this day brings along;
We'll join our glad voices in one hymn of praise
To God, who has kept us, and lengthened our days.

CHORUS.

Happy greeting to all! happy greeting to all!
Happy greeting, happy greeting, happy greeting to all!

2 Our Father in heaven, we lift up to thee
Our voice of thanksgiving, our glad jubilee;
O bless us, and guide us, dear Saviour, we pray,
That from thy blest precepts we never may stray.
CHORUS—Happy greeting, etc.

3 And if, ere this glad year has drawn to a close,
Some loved one among us in death shall repose,
Grant, Lord, that the spirit in heaven may dwell,
In the bosom of Jesus, where all shall be well.
CHORUS—Happy greeting, etc.

4 Kind teachers, we children would thank you this day,
That faithfully, kindly, you've taught us the way,
How we may escape from the world's sinful charms,
And find a safe refuge in the Saviour's loved arms.
CHORUS—Happy greeting, etc.

395

6s & 5s.

Chide mildly the erring.

CHIDE mildly the erring;
Kind language endears;
Grief follows the sinful,
Add not to their tears,

Avoid with reproaches
  Fresh pain to bestow,
The heart which is stricken
  Needs never a blow.

2 Chide mildly the erring,
  Jeer not at their fall;
If strength be but human,
  How weakly were all!
What marvel that footsteps
  Should wander astray,
When tempests so shadow
  Life's wearisome way.

3 Chide mildly the erring,
  Entreat them with care;
Though sinful their natures,
  They need not despair.
We all have some frailty,
  We all are unwise;
The grace which redeems us
  Must come from the skies.

396

4 *lines* 11s.

Marching along.

THE children are gathering from near and from far
  The trumpet is sounding the call for the war;
The conflict is raging, our foes round us throng,
We'll gird on our armor and be marching along.

CHORUS.

Marching along, we are marching along;
Gird on the armor, and be marching along;
The conflict is raging, 'twill be fearful and long;
Then gird on the armor and be marching along

2 The foe is before us in battle array,
But let us not waver nor turn from the way;
The Lord is our strength, be this ever our song;
With courage and faith we are marching along.
  CHORUS.—Marching along, etc.

3 We've listed for life, and will camp on the field;
With Christ as our Captain we never will yield.
The "sword of the Spirit," both trusty and strong,
We'll hold in our hands as we're marching along.
CHORUS.—Marching along, etc.

4 Through conflicts and trials our crowns we must win,
For here we contend 'gainst temptation and sin.
But one thing assures us, we cannot go wrong
If trusting our Saviour while marching along.
CHORUS.—Marching along, etc.

397

8 *lines* 10s.

Joyfully we move.

JOYFULLY, joyfully, onward we move,
Bound to the land of bright spirits above.
Jesus, our Saviour, in mercy says, come,
Joyfully, joyfully, haste to your home.
Soon will our pilgrimage end here below,
Soon to the presence of God we shall go;
Then, if to Jesus our hearts have been given,
Joyfully, joyfully, rest we in heaven,

2 Teachers and scholars have passed on before;
Waiting, they watch us approaching the shore,
Singing, to cheer us while passing along:
Joyfully, joyfully, haste to your home.
Sounds of sweet music there ravish the ear;
Harps of the blessed, your strains we shall hear,
Filling with harmony heaven's high dome:
Joyfully, joyfully, Jesus, we come.

3 Death with his arrow may soon lay us low;
Safe in our Saviour, we feel not the blow;
Jesus hath broken the bars of the tomb,
Joyfully, joyfully, will we go home.
Bright will the morn of eternity dawn;
Death shall be conquered, his scepter be gone;
Over the plains of sweet Canaan we'll roam,
Joyfully, joyfully, will we go home.

398 C. M.

Around the throne.

AROUND the throne of God in heaven
Thousands of children stand;
Children whose sins are all forgiven,
A holy, happy band.

CHORUS.

Singing glory, glory,
Glory be to God on high.

2 In flowing robes of spotless white,
See every one arrayed,
Dwelling in everlasting light,
And joys that never fade.
CHORUS.—Singing, etc.

3 What brought them to that world above,
That heaven so bright and fair,
Where all is peace and joy and love?
How came those children there?
CHORUS.—Singing, etc.

4 Because the Saviour shed his blood
To wash away their sin;
Bathed in that pure and precious flood,
Behold them white and clean!
CHORUS.—Singing, etc.

5 On earth they sought the Saviour's grace;
On earth they loved his name;
So now they see his blessed face
And stand before the Lamb,
CHORUS.—Singing, etc.

399 10s, 8s, & 11s.

Father in the promised land.

I HAVE a Father in the promised land;
My Father calls me, I must go
To meet him in the promised land.
I'll away, I'll away to the promised land.
My Father calls me, I must go
To meet him in the promised land.

2 I have a Saviour in the promised land;
My Saviour calls me, I must go
To meet him in the promised land.
I'll away, I'll away to the promised land;
My Saviour calls me, I must go
To meet him in the promised land.

3 I have a crown in the promised land;
When Jesus calls me, I must go
To wear it in the promised land.
I'll away, I'll away to the promised land;
When Jesus calls me, I must go
To wear it in the promised land.

4 I hope to meet you in the promised land:
At Jesus' feet a joyous band,
We'll praise him in the promised land.
We'll away, we'll away to the promised land·
At Jesus' feet, a joyous band,
We'll praise him in the promised land.

400 6s & 4s.

Temperance Hymn.

LET the still air rejoice,
Be every youthful voice
Blended in one.
While we renew our strain
To Him, with joy again,
Who sends the evening rain
And morning sun.

2 His hand in beauty gives
Each flower and plant that lives,
Each sunny rill;
Springs which our footsteps meet,
Fountains, our lips to greet,
Waters, whose taste is sweet,
On rock and hill.

3 So let each thoughtful child
Drink of this fountain mild
From early youth;

Then shall the song we raise
Be heard in future days;
Ours be the pleasant ways
Of peace and truth.

401 8s & 6s.

Not the drink for me.

THE drink that's in the drunkard's bowl
Is not the drink for me;
It kills his body and his soul:
How sad a sight is he!
But there's a drink that God has given,
Distilling in the showers of heaven
In measures large and free.
O that's the drink, that's the drink for me

2 The stream that many prize so high
Is not the stream for me;
For he who drinks it still is dry,
And so will ever be.
But there's a stream so cool and clear
The thirsty traveler lingers near;
Refreshed and glad is he.
O that's the drink, that's the drink for me.

3 The wine-cup that so many prize
Is not the cup for me;
The aching head, the bloated face,
In its sad train I see;
But there's a cup of water pure,
And he who drinks it may be sure
Of health and length of days.
O that's the cup, that's the cup for me.

402 S. M.

Temperance hymn.

MOURN for the thousands slain,
The youthful and the strong;
Mourn for the wine-cup's fatal reign,
And the deluded throng.

2 Mourn for the ruined soul;
Eternal life and light
Lost by the fiery, maddening bowl,
And turned to hopeless night.

3 Mourn for the lost; but call,
Call to the strong, the free;
Rouse them to shun that dreadful fall,
And to the refuge flee.

4 Mourn for the lost, but pray,
Pray to our God above
To break the fell destroyer's sway,
And show his saving love.

403 7s, 8s, & 6s.

The pearl for me.

THE pearl which worldlings covet
Is not the pearl for me:
Its beauty fades as quickly
As sunshine on the sea.
But there's a pearl sought by the wise,
'Tis called the pearl of greatest price,
Though few its value see.
O that's the pearl for me.

2 The crown that decks the monarch's brow
Is not the crown for me;
It dazzles but a moment,
Its brightness soon will flee.
But there's a crown, prepared above,
For all who walk in humble love,
Forever bright 'twill be.
O that's the crown for me.

3 The road that many travel
Is not the road for me;
It leads to death and sorrow,
In it I would not be.
But there's a road that leads to God,
'Tis marked by Christ's most precious blood;
The passage here is free.
O that's the road for me.

4 The hope that sinners cherish
Is not the hope for me;
Most surely will they perish,
Unless from sin made free;
But there's a hope which rests in God,
And leads the soul to keep his word,
And sinful pleasures flee.
O that's the hope for me.

404

9s & 7s.

Water for me.

SOME love to drink from the foamy brink,
Where the wine-drop's dance they see;
But the water bright, in its silver light,
And a crystal cup for me!

CHORUS.

O water, bright water, pure, precious, free!
Yes, 'tis water bright, in its silver light, and a crystal cup for me.

2 O a goodly thing is the cooling spring,
'Mong the rocks where the moss doth grow;
There's health in the tide, and there's music beside
In the brooklet's bounding flow.
CHORUS.—O water, etc.

3 As pure as heaven is the water given;
'Tis forever fresh and new;
Distilled from the sky it comes from on high
In the shower and the gentle dew.
CHORUS.—O water, etc.

405

Chant.

FROM the recesses of a lowly spirit
Our humble prayer ascends. O Father, hear it!
Borne on the trembling wings of fear and meekness
Forgive its weakness.

2 We know, we feel, how mean and how unworthy
The lowly sacrifice we pour before thee;
What can we offer thee, O thou most holy,
But sin and folly?

3 We see thy hand; it leads us, it supports us;
We hear thy voice; it counsels and it courts us:
And then we turn away; yet still thy kindness
Forgives our blindness!

4 Who can resist thy gentle call, appealing
To every generous thought and grateful feeling;
O who can hear the accents of thy mercy,
And never love thee!

5 Kind Benefactor! plant within this bosom
The seeds of holiness, and let them blossom
In fragrance and in beauty bright and vernal,
And spring eternal.

6 Then place them in those everlasting gardens,
Where angels walk, and seraphs are the wardens;
Where every flower, brought safe through death's dark portal,
Becomes immortal.

406 L. M.

Chant.

WITH tearful eyes I look around,
Life seems a dark and stormy sea;
Yet 'midst the gloom I hear a sound,
A heavenly whisper, "Come to me."

2 It tells me of a place of rest;
It tells me where my soul may flee,
O to the weary, faint, oppressed,
How sweet the bidding, "Come to me."

3 Come, for all else must fade and die;
Earth is no resting-place for thee;
Heavenward direct thy weeping eye,
I am thy portion, "Come to me."

4 O voice of mercy, voice of love!
In conflict, grief, and agony,
Support me, cheer me from above,
And gently whisper, "Come to me."

407

8s & 4.

"Thy will be done."

"THY will be done!" In devious way
The hurrying stream of life may run;
Yet still our grateful hearts shall say,
"Thy will be done."

2 "Thy will be done!" if o'er us shine
A gladd'ning and a prosp'rous sun,
This prayer will make it more divine:
"Thy will be done."

3 "Thy will be done!" though shrouded o'er
Our path with gloom, one comfort, one
Is ours: to breathe, while we adore,
"Thy will be done."

408

10s & 4s.

A chant.—Ministering angels.

ANGELS of light, spread your bright wings, and keep
Near me at morn;
Nor in the starry eve, nor midnight deep,
Leave me forlorn.

2 From all dark spirits of unholy power
Guard my weak heart;
Circle around me in each perilous hour,
And take my part.

3 From all foreboding thoughts and dangerous fears
Keep me secure;
Teach me to hope, and through the bitterest tears
Still to endure.

4 If lonely in the road so fair and wide
My feet should stray,
Then through a rougher, safer pathway guide
Me day by day.

5 Should my heart faint at its unequal strife,
O still be near;
Shadow the perilous sweetness of this life
With holy fear.

6 Then leave me not alone in this bleak world,
Where'er I roam;
And at the end, with your bright wings unfurled,
O take me home.

409

5s & 8s.

Life a race.

THIS life is a race,
And brief is the space
In which the great prize must be won;
Then do not delay,
For happy are they
Who early determine to run.

CHORUS.

Run in the race, run in the race,
Run in the race for glory.

2 At once then begin,
Cast off every sin
And weight that encumbers the soul;
And enter the track,
And never look back,
Till safely arrived at the goal.
CHORUS.—Run in the race, etc.

3 When faint and oppressed,
Some foe may suggest,
"'Twere better the race to give o'er;"
But do not sit down;
Just think of the crown,
And that will revive you once more.
CHORUS.—Run in the race, etc.

4 Yes, think of the crown,
And let the world frown,
'Tis better by far than its smile:
It shall not destroy;
And as for its joy,
It only allures to defile.
CHORUS.—Run in the race, etc.

5 Awake then, arise;
Contend for the prize,
What glories around it are flung:
O fly from the path
That leads down to wrath,
And run for the crown while you're young.
CHORUS.—Run in the race, etc.

410

8s & 7s

The good Shepherd.

ONCE I wandered on the mountain,
In the paths by sinners trod,
Heeded not the flowing fountain,
Trifled with atoning blood;
But the Shepherd kindly sought me,
Guilty, wretched, and unclean,
Pardoned all my sin, and brought me
To his pastures fresh and green.

2 In this vale of tears and sadness,
He's my Shepherd, ever near,
Turning all my grief to gladness,
When on him I cast my care.
Though a father may forsake me,
And a mother sink to rest,
Tender Shepherd, he will take me,
Pierced by sorrow, to his breast.

3 Strong temptations may beset me,
Snares my pathway may bestrew;
But he never will forget me,
He will guard and guide me too.
He observes each poor endeavor
To escape from sin's control,
And the sunshine of his favor
Cheers my fainting, struggling soul.

4 When the shades of death o'erspread me,
And the streams of life congeal,
Faithful Shepherd, do thou lead me
Safely through the silent vale:

When I lay aside the mortal,
  Immortality to prove,
Bear me through the heavenly portal,
  Place me in thy fold above.

411

7s, 8s, & 6s.

Little pilgrims.

THE way to heaven is narrow,
  And its blessed entrance straight;
But how safe the little pilgrims
  Who get within the gate!

CHORUS.

And we may join the pilgrim band
  That journeys toward the light;
For the golden gate of that happy land
  Stands open day or night.

2 The sunbeams of the morning
  Make the narrow pathway fair,
And these early little pilgrims
  Find dewy blessings there.
    CHORUS.—And we may join, etc.

3 They pass o'er rugged mountains,
  But they climb them with a song;
For these early little pilgrims
  Have sandals new and strong.
    CHORUS.—And we may join, etc.

4 They do not greatly tremble,
  When the shadows night foretell;
For these early little pilgrims
  Have tried the path full well.
    CHORUS.—And we may join, etc.

5 They know it leads to heaven,
  With its bright and open gates,
Where for happy little pilgrims
  A Saviour's welcome waits.
    CHORUS.—And we may join, etc.

412 6s & 4s.

Lord, is it I?

ONE night the Saviour said,
"My hours to live are few;
I soon shall be betrayed,
My friends, by one of you."
"Lord, is it I?"
They all do cry.

2 Beloved above the rest,
John leaned his gentle head
Upon the Saviour's breast
And softly whispering, said,
"Lord, tell me who
This thing shall do."

3 "One of this little band,"
The Saviour, answering, said,
"Will hither reach his hand,
And dip with me his bread.
Who dips with me,
The same is he."

4 Dear Lord, how could it be
That one who lived all day
And ate his bread with thee
Should thy dear life betray!
Ah! how could he
Thus deal with thee!

5 Not so would I reward
Thy tender love to me;
I would, my dearest Lord,
Thy faithful servant be.
For thou art he
Who died for me.

413 6s & 5s.

Of such is the kingdom.

ROUND the throne in glory
Happy children throng,
And redemption's story
Wakes the harp and song.

On the verdant mountain,
By the shining stream,
Or the living fountain,
Jesus is their theme.

CHORUS.

Glory to the Lamb,
Praise him and adore;
Glory to the Lamb
For evermore.

2 Robes of snowy whiteness,
Beautiful and rare;
Crowns of radiant brightness,
Such those children wear:
Safe from death's bereavement,
Sorrow and the grave,
Free from sin's enslavement
Victory's palm they wave.
CHORUS.—Glory to the Lamb, etc.

3 Now the skillful fingers
Sweep the golden lyre;
Not a harper lingers
In that ransomed choir;
Voices sweetly blending
With the tuneful string,
To the throne ascending,
Praise the heavenly King.
CHORUS.—Glory to the Lamb, etc

4 Children now sojourning
In a world of sin,
From your follies turning,
Strive to enter in:
Let your young affections
Round the Saviour twine;
And 'mid heaven's attractions
You shall sing and shine.
CHORUS.—Glory to the Lamb, etc.

414

12s & 9s.

Something to do in heaven.

THERE'LL be something in heaven for children to do;
None are idle in that blessed land;
There'll be loves for the heart, there'll be thoughts for the mind,
And employment for each little hand.

CHORUS.

There'll be something to do, there'll be something to do;
There'll be something for children to do:
On the bright shining shore, where there's joy evermore,
There'll be something for children to do.

2 There'll be lessons to learn of the wisdom of God
As they wander the green meadows o'er;
And they'll have for their teachers in that blest abode
All the good that have gone there before.
CHORUS.—There'll be something to do, etc.

3 There'll be errands of love from the mansions above
To the dear ones that linger below;
And it may be our Father the children will send
To be angels of mercy in woe.
CHORUS.—There'll be something to do, etc.

415

4 *lines* 11s.

Safe at home.

WHEN the battle is fought and the victory won,
Life's trials are ended, and life's duties done,
Then Jesus, our Saviour, will welcome us home;
No more in this desert of sin we shall roam.

CHORUS.—Safe, safe at home,
No more to roam.

2 The most youthful soldier will then have a share
In heavenly mansions prepared for us there;
The song of redemption from infants shall swell
As of Jesus, to wondering angels, they tell.
CHORUS.—Safe, safe at home, etc.

3 Though taken from earth in life's earliest morn,
The crown of our Saviour we'll ever adorn ;
More bright than the stars will thy ransomed ones shine,
For the radiance, dear Saviour, 's eternally thine.
CHORUS.—Safe, safe at home, etc.

4 O then will our hearts swell with rapture supreme,
For, Jesus, thy glories will over us beam;
Our minds with the riches of wisdom be stored,
For God will be known and forever adored.
CHORUS.—Safe, safe at home, etc.

416

11s & 9s.

When Jesus was on earth.

I THINK, when I read that sweet story of old,
When Jesus was here among men,
How he called little children as lambs to his fold,
I should like to have been with them then.

2 I wish that his hands had been placed on my head,
That his arm had been thrown around me,
And that I might have seen his kind look when he said,
"Let the little ones come unto me."

3 Yet still to his footstool in prayer I may go,
And ask for a share in his love;
And if I thus earnestly seek him below,
I shall see him and hear him above.

4 In that beautiful place he is gone to prepare,
For all who are washed and forgiven;
And many dear children are gathering there,
"For of such is the kingdom of heaven."

417

8s, 9s, & 12.

"What shall I do to be saved?"

O WHAT shall I do to be saved
From the sorrows that burden my soul?
Like the waves in the storm when the winds are at war
Chilling floods of distress o'er me roll.

CHORUS.

What shall I do? what shall I do?
O what shall I do to be saved?

2 O what shall I do to be saved
When the pleasures of youth are all fled,
And the friends I have loved from the earth are removed,
And I weep o'er the graves of the dead?
CHORUS.—What shall I do, etc.

3 O what shall I do to be saved
When sickness my strength shall subdue,
Or the world in a day like a cloud roll away,
And eternity opens to view?
CHORUS.—What shall I do, etc.

4 O Lord, look in mercy on me;
Come, O come, and speak peace to my soul;
Unto whom shall I flee, dearest Lord, but to thee;
Thou canst make my poor broken heart whole.
CHORUS.
That will I do, that will I do,
To Jesus I'll go and be saved.

418 8s & 7s.

Gently lead us.

GENTLY, Lord, O gently lead us
Through this lonely vale of tears,
Through the changes thou'st decreed us,
Till our last great change appears;
When temptation's darts assail us,
When in devious paths we stray,
Let thy goodness never fail us,
Lead us in thy perfect way.

2 In the hour of pain and anguish,
In the hour when death draws near,
Suffer not our hearts to languish,
Suffer not our souls to fear;
And when mortal life is ended,
Bid us on thy bosom rest,
Till, by angel bands attended,
We awake among the blest.

419 8s & 7s.

My days are gliding by.

MY days are gliding swiftly by,
And I, a pilgrim stranger,
Would not detain them as they fly,
Those hours of toil and danger.

CHORUS.

For O, we stand on Jordan's strand,
Our friends are passing over,
And, just before, the shining shore
We may almost discover.

2 We'll gird our loins, my brethren dear,
Our heavenly home discerning;
Our absent Lord has left us word,
Let every lamp be burning.
CHORUS.—For O, we stand, etc.

3 Should coming days be cold and dark,
We need not cease our singing;
That perfect rest naught can molest
Where golden harps are ringing.
CHORUS—For O, we stand, etc.

4 Let sorrow's rudest tempest blow,
Each cord on earth to sever:
Our King says, Come, and there's our home,
Forever, O, forever.
CHORUS—For O, we stand, etc.

420 7s & 6s.

Have courage to do right.

IF you would find salvation,
And taste its joys below,
Don't parley with temptation,
But promptly answer, No!

CHORUS.

Have courage to do right,
Have courage to do right;
The world may sneer, but never fear;
Have courage to do right.

2 If lured by sinful pleasure,
Look upward and resist;
For sorrow without measure
Shall rend the guilty breast.
CHORUS.—Have courage to do right, etc.

3 If sinners should revile you,
With patience bear the cross;
Their aim is to defile you,
And glory in your loss.
CHORUS.—Have courage to do right, etc

4 The world will strive to charm you,
And Satan hurl the dart;
But who or what can harm you
While Jesus guards the heart?
CHORUS.—Have courage to do right, etc.

5 Stand up, then, for the truthful,
Stand up, then, for the pure;
Let courage nerve the youthful
The conflict to endure.
CHORUS.—Have courage to do right, etc.

421 S. M.

Sing to me of heaven.

COME, sing to me of heaven
When I'm about to die;
Sing songs of holy ecstacy,
To waft my soul on high.

CHORUS.

There'll be no sorrow there,
There'll be no sorrow there;
In heaven above, where all is love,
There'll be no sorrow there.

2 When the last moment's come,
O, watch my dying face,
To catch the bright seraphic glow
Which in each feature plays.
CHORUS.—There'll be no sorrow, etc

3 Then to my raptured ear
Let one sweet song be given;
Let music charm me last on earth,
And greet me first in heaven.
CHORUS.—There'll be no sorrow, etc.

4 When round my senseless clay
Assemble those I love,
Then sing of heaven, delightful heaven,
My glorious home above.
CHORUS.—There'll be no sorrow, etc.

422 Peculiar.

Beautiful land of rest.

JERUSALEM, forever bright,
Beautiful land of rest!
No winter there nor chill of night,
Beautiful land of rest!
The dripping cloud is chased away,
The sun breaks forth in endless day.

CHORUS.

Jerusalem, Jerusalem, beautiful land of rest!
Beautiful land, beautiful land, beautiful land of rest

2 Jerusalem, forever free,
Beautiful land of rest!
The soul's sweet home of Liberty,
Beautiful land of rest!
The bonds of sin, the chains of woe,
The ransomed there will never know.
CHORUS.—Jerusalem, Jerusalem, etc.

3 Jerusalem, forever dear,
Beautiful land of rest!
Thy pearly gates almost appear,
Beautiful land of rest!
And when we tread thy lovely shore,
We'll sing the song we've sung before.
CHORUS.—Jerusalem, Jerusalem, etc.

DOXOLOGIES.

423 L. M.

PRAISE God, from whom all blessings flow;
Praise him, all creatures here below;
Praise him above, ye heavenly host,
Praise Father, Son, and Holy Ghost.

424 C. M.

TO Father, Son, and Holy Ghost,
One God, whom we adore,
Be glory as it was, is now,
And shall be evermore.

425 S. M.

THE Father and the Son
And Spirit we adore,
We praise, we bless, we worship thee
Both now and evermore.

426 4 *lines* 7s.

SING we to our God above
Praise eternal as his love;
Praise him, all ye heavenly host,
Father, Son, and Holy Ghost.

427 4 6s & 2 8s.

TO God the Father's throne
Your highest honors raise;
Glory to God the Son,
To God the Spirit praise.
Eternal King, with all our powers,
Thy name we sing, while faith adores.

INDEX:

THE FIGURES REFER TO THE PAGE.

THE END.

www.ingramcontent.com/pod-product-compliance
Lightning Source LLC
Chambersburg PA
CBHW021104270326
41929CB00009B/730

* 9 7 8 3 3 3 7 0 8 3 5 9 5 *